1/15

Blind
Curves

Blind
Curves

*A Woman, a Motorcycle,
and a Journey to
Reinvent Herself*

LINDA CRILL

Skyhorse Publishing

Skyhorse Publishing books may be purchased in bulk at special discounts for sales promotion, corporate gifts, fund-raising, or educational purposes. Special editions can also be created to specifications. For details, contact the Special Sales Department, Skyhorse Publishing, 307 West 36th Street, 11th Floor, New York, NY 10018 or info@skyhorsepublishing.com.

Skyhorse® and Skyhorse Publishing® are registered trademarks of Skyhorse Publishing, Inc.®, a Delaware corporation.

Visit our website at www.skyhorsepublishing.com.

10 9 8 7 6 5 4 3 2 1

Library of Congress Cataloging-in-Publication Data is available on file.

Cover design by Brian Peterson

Print ISBN: 978-1-62914-570-9
Ebook ISBN: 978-1-62914-877-9

Printed in the United States of America

To Bill,
Who taught me to cherish the
magic of words, love, and life

CONTENTS

1
Halston to Harley

After two difficult years I was tired of sympathetic voices, puppy-dog looks, and an environment filled with reminders to walk gently and pamper myself. Instead, I craved thundering noise, the thrill of speed. I wanted icy air whipping against my face, making me know I was alive. I wanted crescendo, vibrato, to drown my screams and tears behind the roar of a large powerful engine.

Opening the heavy glass door and stepping into the Harley dealership, I entered an unexplored world—hundreds of shiny motorcycles laden with chrome and leather, covered with colorful graphics and logos. I felt my courage falter. My light-hearted fantasy evaporated as the realities of my impulsive decision started to settle in.

Until a month ago I had never dreamed of riding a motorcycle. I didn't have a husband, family, or even friends who rode. At fifty-seven I was at the age when many of my friends were scaling down their physical activities as they edged toward retirement. There are many acceptable activities for a widow, but learning to ride a motorcycle wasn't on anyone's list—even at the very bottom, if such a list exists.

Motorcycles are designed to appear fast, flashy, and intimidating—and it was working. My normally rapid gait slowed and then faltered as I surveyed row after row of gleaming bodies clustered around the showroom floor. Viewed from inside my Dodge Caravan, motorcycles had always seemed more like overgrown bicycles or toys. Now, up close, they looked huge, expensive, and complicated. The one elevated in the center of the floor—painted neon yellow with orange flames flaring from front to back—was loaded with a multitude of switches, indicators, dials, gears, buttons, lights, pedals, knobs, and levers.

My stomach muscles tightened as a panicked voice inside cried: *How am I supposed to learn to ride this in just three days?*

Wanting to divert my attention away from this emotional outburst, I glanced at my watch reminding myself *class starts in three minutes, and I don't want to be late.*

I had barely convinced myself to continue walking forward when I passed the clothing section stacked with helmets, boots, shirts, gloves, and racks of black leather. Nothing here looked like the Fonz's simple leather jacket from the 1960s TV show. Nothing here remotely resembled anything I had hanging in my closets.

I stared at a black T-shirt with a metallic skull laughing down at me. Another displayed the profile of a busty woman that would have made a Barbie doll blush.

What was I thinking? I could never wear a shirt mocking death and certainly I wasn't ready to be a sex object. And what about all of my 1960s feminist protesting? *Am I supposed to violate all of my values for this?*

My attempts to slow down my racing heart were futile as I processed the sounds of engines revving, tools clanking, and hollering coming from the service shop in the back. All mixed with frenetic hard-rock music blaring from the speakers overhead. My heart pounded even louder wanting to be heard.

In two minutes, my rebellious plan—a delicious fantasy that I could use to shock others—shattered. Now I was the person being shocked.

❧

This motorcycle journey had been birthed a month ago during a routine Sunday evening phone call with my sister and brother-in-law. These weekly calls with Anita and Bruce were our way of staying in touch and their making sure I was moving forward with life. When we were ready to say goodbye, Bruce started into the ritual routine advice I had heard thousands of times. I called it "The Survivor's Trilogy" because, although there were different versions, the same three directives ended our conversations—eat well, exercise, get plenty of sleep. Up to this point I had always listened politely, but tonight I was too frustrated to remain silent any longer. I cut Bruce off.

"I've tried all of that. I'm eating, exercising, and sleeping better than anyone I know. I've over-achieved at following these recommendations. I keep waiting to feel better. It's not working . . . I'm . . . I'm miserable!"

I was surprised to hear myself say these words out loud because, up to this point, I had not even admitted them to myself. This standard, often-repeated advice for surviving a major loss wasn't working.

Now that I had started to express myself, months of pent-up frustration emboldened me as I defiantly searched for the most contrary behaviors to these directives that I could think of.

"My new plan is to go out and buy a jumbo-sized bag of lard-fried potato chips and eat them all in one sitting, and um . . ." I paused, struggling for something even more absurd and rebellious. Finally, I blurted out, ". . . and learn to ride a motorcycle!"

❧

Down a corridor off the showroom I found the classroom and surveyed its cramped interior. Sitting on folding chairs around two collapsible banquet tables were my fellow classmates, eleven in all. I had secured the last slot two days ago when I registered for their Rider's Edge program—a three-day motorcycling learn-to-ride course.

Two men stood at the front of the room. The one who was more than six feet tall with a ponytail, tattoos, and bulging muscles leaned against a chair as he talked to several seated classmates. "I'm retired from active duty now, but I've served in three wars. I used to train tank units for combat."

I flinched. *This guy is used to ordering soldiers around. What will he be like when I make mistakes?*

He looked up and spotted me still standing in the hallway. I had no choice. I took a deep breath, headed into the room, and slipped into the last empty seat.

Most of my classmates were dressed in well-worn blue jeans, scuffed boots, and over-sized, faded T-shirts with Harley logos splashed across them. I thought I had dressed down for the class but I must have looked big-city chic in my designer jeans, fitted T-shirt, and brand new running shoes. I made a note to revisit the clothing shop at lunch to buy at least one Harley T-shirt and heavy boots so I would fit in better tomorrow.

The towering man commanded our attention just by stepping to the center of the room.

"I'm Rocky and this here is Tom," he said, gesturing toward the man to his left. "We're your instructors for the next three days."

Tom was a short, thin man with a large handlebar mustache that took up almost half of his face. He reminded me of one of those scrappy kids on the playground from elementary school days whom everyone would leave alone, knowing that what he lacked in size he easily made up for in determination and feistiness.

"We're going to go around the room and introduce ourselves. Say a little about yourself, why you're here, and what's your experience with motorcycles."

Cathy, one of the two other women in the class, introduced herself. "I'm here just because my gung-ho husband wants me to learn to ride my own motorcycle instead of always sitting behind him. I'm not sure I can learn this stuff. Even if I pass, I don't know if I want to ride my own bike."

When Patti introduced herself, she parroted Cathy's statement. "I'm here to get my husband off my back. He's even bought me my own brand new motorcycle!"

Most of the men had ridden a motorcycle at some point in their lives, and some were simply there to pass the course's test to speed up getting their license. Two had even ridden their motorcycles to class without licenses. One was stationed at a military base nearby that required this training to ride a motorcycle on base. It was obvious he didn't need this beginners' class.

By the time it was my turn, I realized I was the only person new to both motorcycling and Harleys.

Following Rocky's instructions, I stood up, but before I could stop myself a torrent of unplanned words tumbled out.

"I don't know much about motorcycles, but life has been pretty rough lately. A year and a half ago I lost my husband to cancer, and I'm ready to do something new. There's a 2,500-mile motorcycle road trip down the Pacific Northwest Coast I can take in four weeks if I pass this course. I'm here to see if I can learn to ride a motorcycle well enough to go on that trip."

Surprised and embarrassed by what I had blurted out, I quickly sat down, wishing I could take it back. I wanted desperately to have an identity other than being a widow, but I had announced just that to this new group of strangers.

⸎

Just as driving a motorcycle wasn't something I'd ever thought I would do, likewise I'd never dreamed of taking a ten-day road trip on one. But often when I play with one possibility, like a magnet it attracts a series of reinforcing fragments, and this idea escalates into the only logical path to pursue.

And that is what happened with my original rebellious outburst about learning to ride a motorcycle.

The day after talking with Anita and Bruce, and before signing up for this class, I had lunch plans with my old college friend, Ron. We had dated for a while when we were both in our twenties, until our lives took us in different directions. For the past thirty years we had remained friends, getting together every so often to catch up, sharing stories about our marriages, watching our kids grow up, and tracking our careers and businesses.

When he heard about what had happened to my husband Bill, Ron told me he had lost a number of friends and never knew what to do or say to their families. He asked me if I'd share my journey and explain how one moves on with life after such a significant loss.

Walking into the restaurant out of the bright sunshine I could barely see in the dim light, but it was hard to miss Ron standing across the room waving. Over lunch, he asked me how I was doing. I told him about my phone call with Anita and Bruce.

"It's embarrassing. Now I'm taking out my frustrations on people who love me and have been incredibly good to me over the last two-and-a-half years. And where did I get that crazy idea about riding a motorcycle?"

"That's not crazy. I ride. A group of us take annual motorcycle road trips. We've been doing it for over twenty years."

"I didn't know you were a Hell's Angel."

"I'm not and neither are the others. My brother's a lawyer. Eva's an emergency room nurse, and her husband, Terry's a business owner. Jayk's a doctor. John and his wife run a touring business in Canada."

"Really?"

"Our trips usually take a week or two. We've been to Canada, Spain, Morocco, Germany, Mexico, and all over the US. In fact, we're planning another trip two months from now. We'll be starting in Vancouver, Canada, and riding down along the Pacific Coast through the redwoods to Mendocino, California, and then returning by an inland route through Crater Lake and the Washington Wenatchee apple country."

"I love the Pacific Northwest . . . especially the redwoods," I said.

"Why don't you come with us?"

"You've got to be kidding. I've never really wanted to learn to ride a motorcycle. I was just letting off steam and mocking traditional advice that doesn't work. Besides, I don't know how to ride, and there's not enough time to learn."

"Sure there is. You could do it. You're a great bicyclist and athlete. I've never known you to walk away from adventure—especially one laced with challenge. Remember what you did last winter with that MS ride?"

After Bill's death, when I needed a goal to get me out of bed in the mornings, I had signed up for the Multiple Sclerosis 150-mile fund-raising bicycle ride in Leesburg, Virginia. As a member of the local women's "Babes on Bikes" team, I biked the route in honor of Susanne Mershon, a former client.

"But I don't know anyone else going on the trip."

"It's a great bunch of people. We keep the group small—about four to eight riders. Everyone is someone we know and trust. You'd like them."

He continued explaining how when they were younger, they planned ambitious trips that had tested their endurance and character. But now they rode only 250 to 300 miles a day, so they could enjoy the countryside and the people they met along the way.

"On this upcoming trip, there were originally four of us, but now Eva's husband doesn't think he can leave his new business for ten days, so she can't go unless there's another woman to split the cost of hotel rooms with her. Without Eva, there's just my brother and me. It's always more fun with more people, so we're trying to find another woman rider fast. There's room. We need you. What do you say?"

I sat there, wondering what I had started with my ridiculous outburst.

After lunch Ron walked me to my car and urged me to at least think about it. I promised I would. And that is how the seed of taking this trip was planted.

Following our lunch, I vacillated for a month not doing anything—my indecision almost made the choice for me, proving what I have always told my corporate clients about change: *Indecision favors the status quo.* Without quick action, there wouldn't be enough time to learn.

Tired of waffling, I sat down at my computer and researched courses for learning to ride motorcycles. When I saw the local ones were filled, I was relieved and even entertained the idea that fate was protecting me—telling me this was too crazy. That thought was squelched when I stumbled across a Harley dealership near Richmond, Virginia, which had one remaining space in a class offered on the upcoming weekend.

Was this fate now telling me to go?

I filled out their online enrollment form and added my credit card information. But before clicking the enter button, my hand froze as my mind raced: *Is this really what I want to do?*

The more I thought, the more conflicted I became as my inner voices argued different preferences. Fed up, I silenced their chatter, shut my eyes, and journeyed deeper inward seeking clarity.

After sitting for a few minutes, relaxed and at peace, my right hand slowly reached up, took hold of the mouse, and clicked it. I sat there a few moments longer, surprised by my hand's independent action, but relieved to have taken any position. I lifted my head and stared at the screen message: *Registration Accepted.*

◈

A booming voice startled me. "Follow me! We're going on a tour." Rocky and Tom headed out of the classroom, and we trailed behind onto the showroom floor. As they explained the different styles of motorcycles and types of engines, my classmates chatted excitedly with each other, pointing out those they recognized and liked.

Everyone seemed comfortable using terms and numbers to describe these vehicles. I tried to feign interest in the type of motor, suspension, or exhaust system each had, but this information was too much, too fast.

By the time we reached the final stop in the tour, my eyes had glazed over and I had quit trying to understand all of the tour explanations.

We walked into the service and machine shop, the overpowering smell of exhaust and hot metal assaulting me, making me want to hold my breath until I could find less polluted air. To my surprise, a number of the men breathed in this pungent odor with deep inhalations, followed by slowly exhaled sighs, "Ahhh!" One even commented, "There's nothing quite like the smell of a machine shop." Several men around him grunted and nodded.

I was dumbfounded. They were reacting the way I would if I walked into a bakery with the aroma of cinnamon rolls wafting from ovens in the back. Never had I imagined that this machine-shop smell could be pleasurable.

I laughed silently as I thought about how many women fill their homes with lilac, rosemary, and apple blossom potpourri. They add scented sachets to their lingerie drawer and wear designer perfume from Paris and New York. There is definitely an untapped market for "eau de machine shop" to capture the attention of these men.

In the parking lot, Rocky's instructions were drowned out by ear-piercing sounds from a motorcycle in the last bay by the door. As the mechanic twisted the bike's throttle back and forth, explosive bursts roared out of its muffler. Everyone but me laughed, admiring its deafening roar; I just couldn't help but wonder how many people that motorcycle would disturb and frighten once it was on the road.

I was straddling two worlds. As a bicycle rider who pedals over a hundred miles a week, I was a proud member of a group called "tree huggers," or "greenies," by the rest of the world. It's easy to commune with nature and appreciate its beauty while quietly spinning on solitary bicycle trails. Daily I would notice new wildflowers, colorful birds, rodents, and sometimes even deer along the rail-to-trail Washington & Old Dominion bicycle path that runs for sixty miles from Washington, D.C., to Purcellville, Virginia.

However, while pedaling our bicycles in traffic, breathing hard, sweating, and eating gas fumes to get to the trail, it was hard not to look at passing cars and motorcycles with a bit of annoyance. Motorcycles with their loud roar, exhaust spewing out behind them, and leather-clad riders covered with tattoos were a sharp contrast to our spandex-covered bodies pedaling quietly on road bikes.

And now I was learning how to become one of those motorcyclists. Soon I'd be buying leathers so that I could join them roaring down the streets on one of these noisy machines.

How would I ever integrate these two opposing personas? Were they ever meant to belong to the same individual?

2
Learning Conundrum

Rocky told us to take a break, pointing out the vending machines if we wanted a snack. Instead of getting chips or candy, I headed to my van to get an individual packet of organic almonds. I slipped into the front seat and pulled the door shut behind me. I sighed, relishing its familiar surroundings, and collapsed against the leather seats. It was one element of my life that hadn't changed in the past eighteen months. I reached down on my left side for the automatic seat adjustment button and pressed it until the back was parallel to the floor.

Hidden from sight, I reviewed what had happened in the last several hours. I had gone from being thrilled about learning to ride a motorcycle to intimidated and wanting to flee the scene.

Should I drive away—admitting my mistake—or accept that I'm going to feel overwhelmed whenever I move outside my comfort zone? Wasn't it the desire for a radical departure from my normal life that had persuaded me to learn to ride a motorcycle and go on this road trip?

Crumpling the empty almond bag, I tossed it in the trash and opened the door. I still wasn't sure whether I was going to complete the training, but it was easier to finish this first day of class than execute a graceful exit. Besides, I had driven 125 miles to get here last night and checked into a local hotel for the next two days. I was already financially invested in the outcome of this class.

Back inside, Rocky outlined the three-day course. Today was classroom work—learning motorcycle operations, traffic rules, and driving risks. Tomorrow started with a written test (similar to the one given at the DMV), followed by learning to ride motorcycles on their outdoor range. Day three built on improving our riding skills but ended with the dreaded road test required for our motorcycle license.

Despite the dread, one prevailing force kept me in my chair—I had told everyone that I was going to learn to ride a motorcycle and take a road trip. After shocking them with my grand plan, I now played in my head the possible scenario of explaining how I had finally seen the folly of my actions and was returning to my safe, boring life with my tail between my legs—humbled by a Harley.

No! Staying and enduring, that's definitely the more desirable choice. Returning to my former routine would only produce more of the same mundane results. But neither option—going or staying—offered the immediate comfort I craved.

❧

That evening in my hotel room I flopped down on the perfectly made bed and let out an extended groan. This room looked like a thousand others I had stayed in over my thirty-year career traveling across the States and abroad, facilitating meetings and delivering a wide range of leadership programs for corporate leaders and their businesses.

I stared at the ceiling, thinking that at least I had ended this first day in a better place than where I had been at lunchtime. During the afternoon I had decided to tough it out, staying through to the end of the program—that is, if I managed to pass the written exam first thing tomorrow.

What a switch in roles. Now I was the student, worried by all that I needed to learn and remember for a test in the morning. My usual instructor's role would have been to prepare for what I needed to facilitate the next day.

Thinking about the courses I had taught over the years, I smiled and realized that today's experience would have made an excellent case study for my workshop on innovation and change. For that training I had developed a business model called "The Decision Pendulum" to illustrate the swing in attitude individuals experience as they implement new ideas.

Today I had followed that same classic mood rotation, starting this new adventure with excitement and confidence. Then, quickly the enthusiasm had faded into an "oh but" questioning stage as I entered the dealership and realized the complexity of learning to ride. Finally, after meeting my instructors and touring the dealership, confused by how to integrate my old persona with this new biker chick one, I had become ready to "forget it." Tonight I was swinging back across to "oh but," maybe I could do this after all.

I had not expected that learning to ride a motorcycle would be as hard as implementing a new business idea. And yet, it was—and even harder—since I was alone and there was no one else on my team to share this experience.

Bill had spent his career in new product development for technology companies. He had always said: "Ideas are cheap. It's their implementation that's difficult." He was right. It's easy to fantasize about embarking on an adventure vacation, riding down the Pacific coast through redwoods and vineyards and enjoying the camaraderie of like-minded souls seeking escape from conventional living.

More difficult was facing the reality that it took skill, knowledge, and hard work to learn to ride such a complex machine. My former rosy picture now had darker tones added to it. Grease, sweat, muscle, and practice were needed to make this motorcycle fantasy real.

The next morning we arrived carrying our coffee and books. Even the more experienced riders were shuffling through their notes and fidgeting. Rocky handed out the tests. I took mine, gulped, and began.

The late-night studying paid off. The broad smile on Rocky's face told the story as he strode back into the room waving our graded answer sheets above his head. "All of you passed. Now let's get out there onto the practice range and learn to ride." We bounded out of the classroom feeding on each other's excitement. We had passed—finished the bookwork. Now for the fun part!

We looked like dogs that had seen their owners pick up the leash to take them for a walk—our feet popping off the tarmac in leaps and bounces. As we rushed toward the course, I'm sure I even heard a few woofs barked into the air.

Around the corner of the dealership, reflecting in the sunlight, twelve gleaming Buelle motorcycles parked in two neat lines greeted us. "We get to ride!" I said, as I grabbed onto Cathy's arm.

She turned to me wobbling her head up and down like a bobble-head dashboard doll.

"Are you scared?" I asked.

"I don't know what I feel. Excited about learning to ride, but terrified that I'll wreck the motorcycle and get hurt."

"Me too. It's a weird combination."

Rocky, assuming his commander demeanor, stepped forward with his arms held out, halting our mad dash. Pointing at a line on the pavement he barked, "Line up there." Responding, we froze, shrank, and obeyed.

He assigned the first five Buelles to the more experienced riders. Tom had these men push their bikes to the far end of the course. "Linda, this is your bike," Rocky said, standing by the third bike in the line-up, and then heading to the next.

Excitement evaporated as my throat constricted. Heat flashed up my neck and flooded my face. My solar plexus throbbed with energy spinning in colliding circles. Staring down at the motorcycle's menacing black body, I crept forward, inching my leaden feet across the tarmac to stand next to it.

Wide-eyed and somber, we fixed our attention on Rocky as he demonstrated the proper way to get on a motorcycle, lift it off its side stand, start it up by following a specific series of steps, turn it off reversing the steps, replace it on its stand, and dismount it. I've never been good at memorizing precise movements, and there were so many to remember.

When it was finally my turn, I sat on the motorcycle and struggled to push it up off of its stand with my legs while tugging at it with my hands. The weight of this supposedly lightweight motorcycle was incredible. Upright, its five hundred pounds wavered precariously back and forth before I eventually held it centered. With my heart beating louder than any marching band base drum, I reassured myself: *You can do this*. At the same time I recognized how with one careless move this motorcycle could easily topple over, hurting it and me. I had forgotten that this unwieldy piece of machinery would need to be balanced. *How will I ever be able to lift my feet off the ground and place them on the foot pegs as I ride?* I felt five years old again and equally small—wanting the safety of training wheels to hold up this mammoth contraption.

Fortunately, the first drill was only walking our motorcycles forward. We sat on their seats, giving them just enough gas to move them across the width of the course, as we alternately stepped our legs forward on either side to balance them.

Following Rocky's instruction, I slowly eased out the clutch lever with my left hand while simultaneously turning the throttle grip toward me with my right. Filled with beginner's confusion and excitement, I couldn't believe how often I'd either let the clutch out too quickly, causing the motorcycle to jump forward, sputter, and die, or released it too slowly, revving the roaring engine as it barely moved forward. Glancing at my classmates, I was relieved to see them struggling with the same problems.

Rocky warned us, "The hardest part about riding a motorcycle is the slow ride. Anyone can balance a bike going down the highway at fifty miles per hour. Riding in parking lots with uneven surfaces and unexpected surprises is damn difficult. Every rider eventually drops their bike while barely moving, so we're going to practice lots of slow maneuver drills."

During the afternoon session we continued learning to shift up into second gear, make turns, ride through a plastic-cone obstacle course, and make tight U-turns. As we practiced progressive skills, it felt like the new pushed out what we had just been taught.

In motorcycling, each hand and foot has its own separate motion. The left hand holds onto the handlebar grip while its fingers reach behind to pull in the clutch lever when shifting. The right-hand grip is the throttle, and behind it is the hand-brake lever. With the right hand controlling both the throttle and front brake, beginners often become confused and make mistakes. The right foot rests on the right peg, but also reaches up to apply the rear brake pedal. The left foot rests on the left peg, and its toes are used to change gears by moving the shift bar up and down.

To make it more challenging, the gears are out of sequence. At the bottom is first gear. One click up is neutral. The next click up is second, followed by third, and then fourth.

Tom had explained that this out-of-sync lineup is necessary because when you're sitting on a motorcycle in neutral and suddenly need to move, stomping down is more instinctive than lifting up. Whatever the real reason, it confused me, like it does most new riders.

Typical of many motorcycles, ours had no indicator showing what gear the motorcycle was in. As I shifted, I tried to keep track of the gears in my overcrowded head.

Another factor in this coordination conundrum was remembering to manually flip the turn signal buttons on and off, because they didn't shut off automatically. Lastly, next to the turn signals were separate horn and lights buttons, so throughout the morning lights beamed, horns beeped, and signals blinked, all at unwanted times.

By late afternoon we had been introduced to a vast repertoire of skills to master. With furrowed foreheads, clenched teeth, and disgruntled complaints, we'd make the same mistakes over and over.

Just before the end of the session, Rocky yelled, "Are we having fun yet?"

We froze, shocked by his question as we tried to recall our reasons for learning to ride. So we unhunched our shoulders and roared back a resounding, "Yes!"

How fast the same activity, that moments before had been work, transformed back to being fun again. Instead of mentally berating ourselves for doing something wrong, we relaxed, remembering that riding was supposed to be pleasurable. With one sentence—"Are we having fun yet?"—we were kids again.

I beamed. I was actually riding my own motorcycle, making lots of VROOMing noises, passionately immersed in what I was doing as I steered my bike around the course. *Attitude is everything.*

Driving to my hotel after class, I realized that beyond the angst and hard work of learning to ride a motorcycle, I was happy tonight. I was grateful my parents had taught me to not give up when new activities got difficult.

Thinking about the influence of parental messages, I recalled one of Bill's father's favorite sayings: "You can never tell what twists and turns your life will take." A big twist in the road had happened two and a half years ago with Bill's unexpected terminal diagnosis. It instantly turned everything in our lives around. Too bad we don't get to choose these twists. Tonight, at least, I was learning a new way to navigate some of life's curves.

I was glad I had decided to stay and looked forward to the final class tomorrow, but I wished that it didn't include that dreaded road test. I decided to employ the power of visualization and mental practice used by many Olympic and professional sports professionals. I visualized myself operating my motorcycle with skill and confidence as I breezed through the exam and passed it.

The outcome of tomorrow's test strongly affected my rapidly approaching vacation plans. I didn't want anything—especially this necessary requirement—to derail them.

3
The Dreaded Road Test

We all wanted that coveted certificate stating that we had passed. Being tested by our familiar instructors along with supportive classmates was far preferable to taking the same exam administered by the DMV on a different test course. This paper was worth its weight in gold. With it we could go to the Virginia DMV and immediately get our licenses. There was even a commonly held belief that Virginia's DMV's road test was much harder to pass.

Rocky and Tom wanted to give us ample time to practice, but it seemed the more we prepared, the more mistakes we made. An often-repeated saying is, *Practice makes perfect,* but sometimes it just makes things worse as confidence erodes and overcorrection sets in.

"Ready?" Rocky asked.

"Yes," we groaned, wanting this test behind us.

Rocky motioned for the group to gather around him. "There are eight parts to the test. You accumulate points for not completing an exercise correctly. As long as your final score is twenty points or less, you pass. The only way to outright fail is to drop your motorcycle during any exercise. This is an automatic failure regardless of your score."

We looked at each other, but no one appeared concerned by his last comment. Several classmates had dropped their motorcycles earlier, but we were all more experienced now.

⟨∾⟩

As we approached the eighth and final section of the test, most of us were doing well. I was relieved that I had made no obvious errors. Rocky stepped in front of the group. "In this final exercise, one at a time you'll start from a stopped position, accelerate to a speed of at least thirty miles per hour while shifting up to third gear, then as your wheels pass over that painted line on the pavement, shift back down to first gear, use both your front and back brakes and stop your motorcycle in the shortest distance possible."

A large white line painted on the asphalt indicated where we needed to start applying our brakes. Behind this first line were smaller ones, marking off each successive yard. Rocky hadn't mentioned the exact stopping distance to avoid negative points, but we assumed shorter was better. Despite the complicated series of steps, they were familiar because we had practiced them in class.

Tom pointed to me. It was my turn. Pulling my motorcycle into position and wetting my lips, I reminded myself of the close call on an earlier emergency stop exercise when I wasn't aggressive enough in braking and almost over-ran the stopping zone.

Brake harder this time, I repeated to myself.

With concentrated determination and charged energy, I took off, shifting up through the gears. I hoped my speed was the required thirty miles per hour, but didn't have time to look at my speedometer because the front tire was already crossing the designated line.

I shifted down through the gears and applied both brakes hard. I was successful. My motorcycle came to a complete and abrupt halt by the second line. Excitedly I noted that it was a personal and perhaps even a class best!

Suddenly, I was flat on the asphalt, pinned down by the five-hundred-pound machine, which was crushing my right leg. Disoriented, I wondered where I was. Shock waves radiated up through my body.

I'd slammed down hard on the road's unyielding surface. My helmeted head, having bounced off the asphalt as I hit, pulsated with a high-pitched ringing sound.

I scanned my surroundings for something familiar, but I only saw swirling colors and fragments of unfamiliar objects. I tried to push my body up away from the ground to correct my confused perspective. After several fruitless attempts I collapsed against the hard road surface again, frustrated that I could not move the lower half of my body. I lay on my side, hopelessly defeated.

I had dropped my bike. I was stunned. Shocked.

As my vision slowly refocused, I saw my instructors and classmates standing there, mouths agape, no one moving. After what seemed like an extended pause, my seasoned coaches rushed over. Rocky positioned himself at the head of the fallen motorcycle and Tom at its back tire. Together they carefully lifted the heavy motorcycle off my body.

My big, burly instructor leaned over, supporting me under my arms as I tried like a newborn fawn to stand on uncooperative, wobbling legs that collapsed several times before finally holding me upright.

Quickly I brushed the dirt off my clothes, wanting everything to be normal as immediately as possible. If I could only get rid of this incriminating evidence, maybe I could turn back time.

"Linda . . ." Rocky paused, mouth open, no words coming out. "I have to . . ." Again he froze.

I realized this former tank-commander, veteran of three wars, was having trouble saying what needed to be said. Embarrassed that I had put him in such an untenable position, I wanted to rescue him.

"I know the rules. I've failed the test."

Rocky nodded, then put his arm around my shoulder as I limped off the practice range. I eased myself down onto the grass along the sidelines.

"Are you okay here?"

"Sure. I'll be all right. Go back and finish testing the others."

He cocked his head to the side and raised his eyebrows with his whole face asking: *Are you sure?*

I nodded, gesturing with the back of my hand that he should go. I needed him to leave while I still appeared to be holding it together. I had received enough sympathy for several lifetimes and didn't want any more, especially now.

After he turned and walked away to rejoin the group about thirty feet away, I let my shoulders fall and released a painful groan. Tom wheeled my damaged motorcycle off the course, its broken turn signal light dangling precariously on loose wires.

Alone, I eased my boot and sock off my throbbing right foot as I examined the damage. It was already swelling and sore. Since Rocky had indicated that they didn't have any ice in the area, I quickly put my boot back on, wanting to ignore this ancillary problem.

I tried to look up at the practice group, forcing a smile and telling myself that crying would have to wait until later, but the disappointment was too great. Tears streamed down my face in spite of my efforts to restrain them. I hoped everyone was too far away to see.

⁂

When the road test was finished, Cathy and Patti rushed over ahead of the others.

"Are you all right?" Patti said.

"Yes. Disappointed, with a bruised foot and ego, but otherwise okay."

"None of us could believe you dropped your bike. You were doing so good," Cathy said.

"Guess I tried too hard to get a higher score."

"We organized a protest on your behalf. We even threatened to walk off the course if Rocky and Tom didn't pass you. You're good enough. You deserved to pass."

"You did that for me?"

"Yes, and we meant it. Rocky agreed that you know how to ride, but said that if they passed you, it would put the whole program in jeopardy. So we finally called it off."

As we walked back to the classroom for the final graduation session, other members of the class came over to offer encouragement. I tried not to limp, but my foot was too sore, protesting each step.

It started to rain as I hopped up onto my van's seat after the closing ceremony. Ahead of me was more than a two-hour drive. I would need to use my aching right foot to press the gas pedal while driving.

Afraid of what it might look like now, I continued to keep my boots on. This injury could be serious and not just a temporary setback, but if I ignored the pain a little longer, I could delay having to deal with possibly more serious ramifications of the fall.

On the road and away from my classmates, it finally felt safe enough to release the emotions welling up inside me.

"Oh, Bill!" I wailed out loud. "What now?" I knew there wouldn't be an answer, but I still surprised myself by how often I called out his name when I felt overwhelmed.

Life wasn't fair. My tears flowed freely as I remembered I wouldn't even have my best friend to comfort me at the end of this day. How I craved Bill's warm embrace. He would have reassured me that everything would turn out all right. Cuddling with him at night had always dissolved the day's problems and fears. Pillows weren't the same.

Tears broke into sobs. I rarely cried out loud anymore. After all of my grieving the past eighteen months, tears no longer cleansed my emotions. Instead, they often just made me more miserable. But tonight's cry was like an overdue orgasm that had been building up slowly and backed off each time before being released. Now it exploded without restraint. My chest rose as I gasped multiple times with each new breath. I wondered if I should pull off the road and quit driving, but the speed of the car, the windshield wipers thumping wildly back and forth, and the flashes of random lights against the black scenery felt like the right accompaniment to my sobs. I kept driving.

My wailing eventually subsided. Wrung out, my body felt like a piece of unraveled rope with all of its fibers splayed out, but still reflecting the indentations of having been bound tight for so long.

When you have been a good person, followed all of the rules, taken care of others, done all of the right things and then the universe deals you a supreme blow by taking away the love of your life . . . you feel that the world owes you not just a break, but a very *big* break when you finally reach out to try something healing and new.

I was crushed. I believed I deserved compassion from wherever these tragic events were coming from. *Why this particular twist? Why now?*

During the rest of the drive home on Interstate 95, I wanted to quit feeling and thinking about what had happened that day, but there was little to distract me as I mechanically drove between the expressway's monotonous straight lines.

It felt like forever since things had been *normal*. In fact I could no longer remember what normal felt like. Whatever *normal* was, this wasn't it.

Wanting to feel better, I flipped frantically through my internal repertoire of life experiences and personal beliefs, hoping to find some way to put my failure and throbbing foot into perspective. I thought back to earlier times when I had facilitated business groups in initiating major changes. We always discussed how to handle the predictable setbacks that occur along the way. Yet, when this kind of *dark night of the soul* experience happens, most people are surprised and even embarrassed, feeling they've failed.

I had optimistically put together a tight schedule to prepare for this road trip, but I should have remembered the high probability that something could derail its success.

In large corporations when something goes wrong, a project's resources are often reduced, or worse yet, the whole undertaking is abandoned. We coached clients to seek "high cover" from a senior officer or group who could protect their project from this fate. But nowhere in my grand escape scheme had I arranged for assistance from others if something didn't go right. I was my sole resource. I had headed off to this training announcing to everyone that I would have my license by early next week. I had been the one to set the lofty expectations, now I was the one without support and cover.

Although frustration, humiliation, and anger can be tremendous sources of energy to be used or wasted, tonight was too soon to harness anything. I'd have to catch up with my anger before I could contain and redirect it. Right now it needed to run free, unbridled, unrestrained.

Reining in my rage by trying to hold my speed at sixty miles per hour was my greatest challenge. My spirit yearned to race through the night. A hundred miles per hour would have felt better.

At home I flicked on the front hall light with my elbow, released my luggage in a crashing heap inside the front door, and stepping over it, walked into the kitchen to drop off my coffee cup in the sink. The drive was behind me. At last I could face the consequences of the day by taking a closer look at my battered body.

Pulling off my shirt, I was surprised to find an abrasion running from my right elbow down to my hand. Removing my jeans revealed a scraped right knee with bruises. As I eased my right boot off my wounded foot, I braced myself, dreading what it might look like. I wasn't ready to head back out into the stormy evening to find an emergency room. My foot was swollen, turning red and blue in places. I knew from experience that by tomorrow morning, it would look even more dramatic.

Carefully, I pushed down on the tops of different foot bones, hoping there wouldn't be severe pain indicating a broken bone. I decided only my enlarged big toe might be broken, but with broken toes in the past, doctors had always said to just let them heal. There was no magic they could do.

My foot was tender, throbbing and ready for care. After gently wrapping it in a compression bandage and taking aspirins to decrease the swelling, I opened the freezer door, searching for an ice pack. Instead I just grabbed a bag of frozen peas sitting in plain sight.

As I passed the kitchen counter cluttered with multiple "to-do" lists, the rapid blinking light on the telephone answering machine caught my attention. I clearly had several messages, but I wasn't ready to talk to anyone yet. I had promised to call Ron and update him on the course, but what would I say? *Will his group even want me to join them once they hear what happened?* And what about my mother and my kids? If I told them I had dropped a motorcycle and gotten hurt, how would I ever justify going on this frivolous trip? I pushed these thoughts aside, too weary to deal with them. I'd wait until tomorrow to listen to my messages.

I felt defeated by my endless, ever-growing to-do lists—constant attempts to re-engage in life and create meaning—all the effort of doing . . . doing . . . doing. When activities failed to cheer me up, I'd try even harder, adding more tasks. For eleven months I had taken care of Bill—searching the Internet for treatments, working with doctors, experts, and friends to find ways to keep order in a world careening out of control.

Then after his death, again I was always on the move—traveling to see family and friends, repairing the house, working on estate issues, closing our family business, and learning to cook for one, to knit, to dance, to date, to ski. And now I was overwhelmed by all of this motorcycle and road trip planning. I had immersed myself in continual activity.

Tonight I was like a car—one moment speeding down the highway, the next suddenly shifting into reverse. All gears stripped, destroyed and burned, I could do no more.

Exhausted from processing these feelings, worn out by trying to silence the scared voices inside my head, I wanted desperately to curl up into a fetal position in my bed and burrow into a mountain of soft pillows under my down-feather comforter.

Limping along with slumped shoulders, I picked up the peas and headed for my bedroom on the second floor. As I started up the stairs, I led with my healthy foot, pausing on each successive riser for my hurt one to catch up. With each new step my mood grew darker, life felt more worthless, and the pauses between steps grew proportionately longer.

On the eighth step, I halted. *Why go any further? Why take another step?* The climb seemed pointless. *Where was I going after all?*

For the first time, there was no worthy goal in which to bury myself. No future destination held value or made sense. Tears streamed down my face as I felt the futility of life. I sank down onto the plush carpeted steps, dropping my forehead against one. Lying there I cried quietly, draining my body like an unplugged full bath of every sad feeling and heartbreaking experience. Swirling as different colors, they rushed down the drain. With one last burbling gulp, the remaining ones were gone. The emotional tub had been emptied. I at last rested—feeling only a huge vacuous space inside me.

For the first time in eighteen months, I had no plan for what to do next. The will to process the past with all of its connected stories or to control a future filled with new possibilities and hope had crumbled.

Internal struggles evaporated as I whispered into the carpet, *I give up.* I could do no more.

The endless chattering inside my head was silenced. Thinking ceased. Motionless, I lay there. Mind empty. Silence. Only silence. With no thought of the past or of the future, all other reference points gone—time stopped. Finally, there was only *surrender.* Unconditional surrender to the present moment. Everything was quiet. I waited, not moving, just remaining present, watching.

Slowly, I became aware of a wonderful peace blanketing my body and filling the space around me, inside and out. My body relaxed, merging with it. A beautiful, loving energy surrounded my heart, expanding both inward, deep inside me, and outward beyond me. It was everywhere.

As I felt my way into it, I became connected to everything but attached to nothing. I was both Linda and this expanded space at the same time. A weak voice from the old Linda asked: *What now?*

The larger space was flooded with warm compassion for this scared Linda, recognizing all she had been through. Every cell in my body softened, welcoming the unconditional love it had been seeking for so long.

As I greeted this magnificent energy, I realized it was more familiar than my own name.

Floating above Linda, as a part of this energy, I saw simultaneous flashing scenes from all the things she had so conscientiously done— for Bill, for family, for others, for Linda. There was such deep compassion for these efforts and for all she had been engaged in.

Surrounded by so much unconditional love, I instantly realized all of my effort was unnecessary. I didn't have to do anything to love myself or be loved by this energy. The love had always been there. I just had to create space for it to be felt.

I heard the words: *You don't have to do, just be*. I couldn't tell whether I had voiced these words inside my body or heard them as I floated in union with this expansive energy. It was such a simple message. A truth I immediately understood.

Still relishing the warm embrace of love that I was experiencing, I found myself back inside my body again still resting on the steps. Every cell inside me smiled, treasuring what I had been given. Almost as if I were being led, I stood up and glided up the stairs. I crawled into my bed, and fell instantly asleep—a restful sleep—one I had been wishing for, for a long time.

4
Unplanned Detour

wakened by sunlight streaming through my windows and hitting
my face, I lay there basking in the light, the warmth of my bed,
and my sleepy inner self. I whispered reflecting on what had happened
last night: "Don't do. Just be. . ."

A special treasure about my bedroom is that I can lie in bed and
watch the tops of pine trees swaying against the morning sky. It's a
wonderful way to awaken and expands my outlook on problems I may
have been trying to solve while sleeping. This view reminds me that I
am part of a larger universe and gives me a happy perspective from
which to start my day.

You've done it again, I laughed. At fifty-seven I knew myself well.
Still, it was surprising how often I repeated old patterns I believed I had
banished. For the past three days I had focused so intently on accomplishing a single goal that all other priorities had faded.

It has always been difficult for me to keep life balanced, because as
soon as I get excited about something new, I enjoy becoming immersed
in it. The only balance I have ever been able to maintain is what I call
serial obsessions. That's why my relationship with Bill worked. As I
threw myself into something, he'd either join me or simply step aside,
realizing that when I resurfaced, I'd be ready to concentrate just as hard
on him and our relationship.

In the past two years I had rummaged through volumes of spiritual teachings in my hunger to re-assess life's purpose and understand why suffering is such an integral part of human experience. Many Eastern teachers point to the role our expectations play in creating pain. When we set strong expectations about what is supposed to happen, we open ourselves to disappointment if the results don't measure up. Instead of seeing the beauty in whatever has happened, we notice only its perceived shortcomings. Since observing this pattern, I had watched how what I labeled *bad* at one moment—because it didn't meet my expectations—became *good* in the next.

I wasn't sure how I would ever see yesterday's dropped motorcycle, failed test, and injured foot as good, but looking back at my life, it often happened that initial failures later turned into blessings, as well as the reverse.

Last night I had been miserable and hurt, but life is full of the unexpected, and this morning I was through resisting it. In contrast to what I had been through these past several years, yesterday's fall was a minor—I searched for the right word—"event" was too significant; perhaps "blip" was a better choice, because with the passage of time its significance would diminish to a mere speck.

Lying in bed reviewing my options, I told myself that my reaction to what had happened at the Harley course was my choice. My family and friends would follow my lead. If I treated the fall as a failure and emphasized my injured foot, everyone would give me sympathy and advise me to stop. If I emphasized how much I had learned and still needed to accomplish, they would offer support and encouragement for that effort.

What do I want?

I began crafting my message.

The course was great. I learned a lot but still need more practice before going on the trip. I am waiting to see how much I improve in the next few weeks before deciding whether I'll ride the route on a motorcycle or drive it in a convertible. That felt right.

My next challenge was to find a motorcycle to use in practicing for the DMV test and the road trip. Rentals were out since most places require a rider to have had a motorcycle license for at least a year. Few motorcyclists will lend their motorcycles to an experienced rider, let alone a beginner. Ron was my only hope.

Walking into my kitchen to make coffee and breakfast, I looked at the blinking message light and pressed the playback button.

"Hi, it's Mom. Just wondering how it went. Call when you've got time to catch up."

My eighty-five-year-old mother and I had both had husbands in hospice at the same time. My stepfather died just two months after Bill. We called each other often to offer support. I hadn't known what to say to her about my learning to ride a motorcycle and the pending road trip because I didn't want to worry her. On the other hand we've always had an honest relationship, so I had told her my plans. I was sure she had the date I'd be returning from my road trip circled on her calendar as a day she could breathe more easily again. I decided to wait until after breakfast to call her and punched the button for the next message.

"Hey Mom, just calling to say that everything's on schedule. My plane arrives tomorrow at Dulles. I'll call you when I land."

It was my twenty-year-old daughter Lindsey. She went to college in Texas and was coming home for the summer. We got along well, and it was always nice to have her home again. Now the house wouldn't feel so empty.

Hitting the play button a final time, I heard: "How'd it go? Did you get any medals for being top student? We've got to get you out practicing. Call me."

I recognized Ron's cheerful voice. I pushed the call-return button to talk about the next steps.

Later that afternoon Ron pulled his motorcycle into the empty parking space in front of my town home. I was happy to see him but gasped as I stared at the size of his motorcycle. It was huge compared to the Buelles we had ridden at the Harley training.

Walking out to greet him, I realized my neighbors would have something new to gossip about with the arrival of this two-wheeled visitor. They were already shaking their heads as I headed out on daily bicycle rides. If they thought year-round bicycling was extreme for a woman of my age, imagine their response to this new venture. Without a garage, there was no way to hide his vehicle. On my quiet dead-end street, its noise would bring people to their windows. I guessed from now on there would be fewer sympathetic looks but I had wanted change, and this achieved it. I walked out to meet him.

"Wow, it's huge."

"It may look big to you, but this is only a medium-sized one," Ron said, laughing as he turned off the engine and dismounted.

After reviewing where everything was located on the bike, I invited Ron in for a visit before driving him back to his home.

"You look frazzled. What's up?" I said.

"Things are so busy at work that I haven't had time to reserve our trip lodging and it's getting awfully close."

"Let me do it. I have the time."

Sitting at the kitchen counter studying a map of the trip, Ron explained how John was the group's West Coast contact and would be renting us his motorcycles. On previous trips John and his wife had ridden with the group, but they couldn't come this time. He had emailed Ron a list of recommended routes, things to see, and suggested lodging for each day.

"I'll email you John's list tonight. Most can be booked online."

As I drove Ron back to his home he reminded me that in addition to getting a valid motorcycle driver's license, I needed more riding experience. He suggested I aim for at least five hundred miles of practice on his motorcycle with some of it done on major highways going sixty miles an hour. If I was not proficient by the time the trip started, I could still rent a car to drive along with the group. I was determined to use this contingency only as an insurance plan and not as a reason to be less motivated in learning to ride my own motorcycle.

"What do I need to take on a trip like this?"

"You know how guys are. We just grab a stack of T-shirts, some jeans, socks, underwear, throw in a shaving kit and we're done. Talk to Eva, she'll know what to suggest. She likes to dress up sometimes at night, so you'll need her to tell you what she's planning. Give her a call."

"But we haven't met."

"We're going to get together early next week for drinks and more planning. Ask her then. I'll let you know when and where."

As I pulled up in front of Ron's house, he reminded me to contact John with my credit card information so he would reserve a motorcycle for me. "We pay for our motorcycle rentals, hotel reservations, and flights in advance. Most are non-refundable so there's no backing out now," he warned as he got out of my car.

As I watched Ron walking up the sidewalk to his home, I noted how with each successive step I was investing more time and money, further committing myself to this trip. No longer could I back out without substantial consequences. My first decision had cascaded into an avalanche of others that now barricaded earlier quick escape routes.

This decision also altered my daily life—all of my former routines were disrupted. I hadn't had time for my daily workouts, hadn't slept well, and was grabbing whatever food I could without considering its nutritional value.

Old habits crumbled. New priorities set in. The butterflies in my stomach were back as I realized I still hadn't completed the first requirement—my license.

⌒⌒⌒

The nearest DMV with motorcycle testing was in Leesburg, Virginia, and that was twenty miles away. To get there, I would need to negotiate four-lane roads cluttered with stop signs and traffic lights. Riding in suburban Washington, D.C., traffic, crowded with impatient commuters, would require more proficiency than I currently had. All of our riding at the Harley training had been on their football-field-sized practice range. We had never ridden on public roads, shifted beyond third gear, or gone faster than thirty miles per hour. My plan was to practice riding in one of the local corporate parking lots in the evenings when it would be empty.

There were many low-traffic streets near my home where I could practice, but without a motorcycle license, I was supposed to have another licensed motorcyclist riding with me. This was a hurdle I couldn't meet. I decided the best I could do was have another driver in a car. With Lindsey home for the summer, I'd recruit her to drive our PT Cruiser behind me as I rode the eight or so blocks on community streets to get to the corporate parking lots. This way if I had any problems, there would be two of us. Also, with Lindsey driving behind me, my backside would be covered by a sympathetic driver.

It was a real twist to have my daughter supporting me as I learned to ride while making typical new rider mistakes. I was grateful for every time I had bitten my tongue and searched for ways to remain calm five years earlier as Lindsey learned to drive. I had never expected the tables to be turned so soon in this unusual way.

Walking into the house after the first evening practice, Lindsey couldn't contain her laughter. She was enjoying this role reversal and my less-than-stellar performance, especially since I've always been known to drive cars assertively and fast.

"Mom, for a beginner you're not doing too badly, but you're only doing twenty-five in a forty-mile speed zone. So it's a good thing I'm driving behind you. You're a turtle!"

"You've got to be kidding! I felt like I was flying."

"No, Mom. I even checked my speedometer twice to make sure. For the first time ever, you've got to drive faster. Bet no one ever told you that before."

No one at the DMV, including the examiners, could believe I was going to take the road test riding a large motorcycle. Weaving in and out of the closely placed cones on the obstacle course and turning a motorcycle within the tightly confined spaces painted on the test course is easiest on a little scooter, not a large motorcycle. Most people borrowed something small to use in taking the test, but I had no other option.

The rumor that the Virginia DMV road test would be more difficult than the one I had taken a few days earlier at the training class appeared true. The driving range looked more compact—a quarter of the size of the area at the course—allowing less room for error. The cones appeared to be less than six feet apart, not twelve. The sharp corner turns appeared more squared-off with a narrower inside riding lane.

The weather was also going to be a challenge. At nine o'clock in the morning it was already over ninety degrees and humid. I had borrowed a heavy-leather riding suit to wear. With no shade on the course, it was going to be like practicing in a cast-iron skillet. The ambient heat waves rising in visibly shaky patterns off the black surface made that frying pan image even more realistic as my bike's hot tires sizzled across the asphalt.

On my first day of practice at the DMV's course, I worked nonstop for three grueling hours. In the end, I didn't even try to take their test. I was humbled and defeated by the course, large motorcycle, and humorless DMV officials who didn't want to leave their air-conditioned building to go outside to conduct a road test in the heat.

Thank goodness no one yelled, "Are we having fun yet?" My answer would have been disappointing.

On the second day, after three more hours of unrewarding practice, I gathered the courage at least to take the test, figuring I had nothing to lose by trying. When I went inside the DMV to sign up, I was asked for my driver's license. There wasn't a place to stash my purse on Ron's motorcycle so I had stuffed everything I thought I would need into my jacket pockets, and I had left my automobile driver's license at home since I wasn't driving a car. But without a driver's license, I wasn't permitted to take the test.

Practice day three arrived. Again I practiced for several hours on the hot asphalt. Even though I knew I wouldn't pass the test, I decided to take it for experience. After an hour's wait in line, I headed back out into the heat. Halfway through the exercise, the clipboard-carrying officer, eager to get away from the searing sun, halted the testing, explaining that I had too many penalty points to pass.

On the fourth day, after more hours of sweaty practice and still making too many mistakes, I was convinced I'd never pass this test riding a large motorcycle, so I concocted a two-part plan.

First, I strategized how I would sacrifice points to make some impossible tasks easier. Normally, when I tried to weave in and out of the tightly placed cones after the first or second one, I would veer so far off course that I ended up missing the rest of them. If I sacrificed every other cone, I might be able to stay on course and only accrue ten points for each missed one. Since the most penalty points I was allowed to accrue was twenty, I still might pass the exam. My immediate goal was to get the motorcycle "M" on my regular driver's license and escape this joyless course. More practice I could and would do on my own.

The second part of my strategy was based on perseverance and odds. Since I was convinced it would take a miracle to pass this test, my plan was to create the maximum opportunities for that to happen by showing up at the DMV every day for the next two weeks and attempting the exam daily. Eventually, I had to get lucky. Either that or the examiners would pass me just to get rid of me, since nothing limited the number of successive days an adult could take this test.

With my new strategy in place, I headed inside.

A man in his mid-forties with bandages on his arms and face stood in front of me in line. He turned and smiled.

"Was that you out there practicing on that motorcycle?"

"Yes," I admitted, embarrassed that anyone had seen me.

"So, ready for the big test?"

"No, not at all."

After signing the appointment register, we sat down on folding chairs next to each other, while waiting for our names to be called.

"What brings you here?" I said.

"That's me and my truck," he said as he handed me a copy of the *Washington Times* newspaper and pointed to its lead article and photograph.

"I was driving my oil tanker last night on I-295. Came up over the top of a hill, in front of me was a truck jack-knifed across all lanes. I knew I couldn't stop in time, and so I did my best to keep my tanker from rolling over. I succeeded, but as I was afraid, when we hit my cab burst into flames. I got out okay but my wallet, CDs, and everything else I own burned up in the blaze. I'm here to get a replacement driver's license."

"I'm sorry. That's quite a story—a front-page one at that."

"Spent all night in the emergency room getting fixed up. Can you believe the police showed up at the hospital this morning to give me a ticket for reckless driving? Now I won't be allowed to drive hazardous material anymore, and without that extra cash, my income is severely cut. How am I expected to pay for these hospital bills now?"

"That's unfair. You should be congratulated for your skill, not punished. Can't you at least go to court and explain that you had no alternative?"

"No, it's D.C. courts, and they don't like truckers."

I shook my head sympathetically, wishing there was something I could say or do to help.

"I used to ride Harleys. I'm impressed at how hard you were practicing. And in this heat! You're going to ace that road test."

"No way. I keep making the same mistakes over and over. The bike's just too heavy to maneuver in that confined area. And the course is even on a slight downgrade. I failed it yesterday and will probably do the same today."

"No, you're going to make it, and I'll be on the sidelines cheering you on. No way you're not going to pass. You're plenty good."

I heard my name called over the loudspeaker and walked toward the officer heading out the side door toward the course. I started up my motorcycle, pushed it backwards out of the parking space, and drove it thirty feet to the start box at the beginning of the test course. I thought about how today not only would I fail again, letting myself down, but now I'd have a disappointed fan as well.

My new ally stood back by the DMV building. He lifted his hand high in the air, giving me a thumbs-up hand signal. Looking at him, I decided to go for it. I completed the sharp ninety-degree left turn perfectly, keeping my tires well inside the narrow lines, and stopped with my front tire generously inside the designated box. With one successful part behind me, I moved on and completed the tight U-turn, surprising myself when I used less than two-thirds of the boxed-in space. Next was the emergency stop—the exact exercise where I dropped my motorcycle during the Harley test. I had replayed this exercise over so often in my head that I probably could have done it blindfolded. This time I was careful not to over-brake, and my bike remained standing at the end.

As I faced the final exercise—the impossible cone weave—I felt encouraged. So far the officer hadn't stopped the test. As I lined my bike up behind the starting line, I remembered the words from the stair steps: *Don't do, just be.* I'd let the bike do the work this time. Both the front and back tires curved in and out of every cone perfectly as I focused on the next ones. Never had that happened on this course, I had no penalty points. I had been given a reprieve and miraculously passed the test in a long overdue break in life's twists and turns . . . and with a perfect score!

The testing officer must have not comprehended the miracle that had just taken place because she would not have blandly said, "Okay, you passed. Go inside and get in line for your license."

I sat motionless on my bike, still halted in the middle of the test course. I had passed the test that I deemed un-passable. It felt as if I had just won an Olympic medal. The silly piece of plastic with an "M" signifying that I was allowed to drive a motorcycle had become the prize I had to obtain at any cost.

On the sidelines my loyal fan raised his hands with palms upward in the air giving me the universal body signal for "what happened?" I shook my head hard as if to make sure I was awake and not dreaming, rushed to park my cycle, and bounded over to him.

Even though we barely knew each other, I threw my arms around him and gave him a huge hug. It was gratifying to have someone to share this moment with. His whole face lit up as he grinned down at me.

"So you passed it just like I told you!"

"Boy, did I ever! And with a perfect score. If you're this kind of good-luck charm, the way my life has been going, I need to keep you around."

Inside the DMV building another official directed me to get in line to have my picture taken for a new driver's license. I stepped back, shocked by the news.

A driver's license is used for all sorts of occasions, and a person with a bad driver's license photo is open to endless teasing. I had been out in humid, ninety-degree weather wearing a full leather outfit and a padded helmet that covered my whole head. My hair was matted, my makeup was destroyed, and my face was red and dripping.

I started to take off my leather jacket, wanting to look more present-able, but my new ally shook his head emphatically, "No!"

"Be proud of your new, well-deserved image. You're now a real biker."

I pulled my jacket back on, realizing my carefully guarded public reputation was forever being altered. This ten-day road trip was no longer a secret private event that would be tucked away and forgotten after the vacation was over. Something substantial was happening. My tight, old, protective cocoon was being shed and left behind—my fragile widow image crumbled away. Space for something new was being created.

Deliberately I replaced my endless internal chatter with a quieter, more deeply centered voice. *What matters most is that I am happy. After all, how many people have a photograph of themselves exhibiting this much joy?* I straightened my leather jacket, stood up tall, combed my fingers through my hair, and had my photo taken—red face, wild hair, and all.

Ironically, it's one of my favorite photos to date. That kind of beaming look can't be produced by someone behind a camera simply commanding: "Smile." I was radiating a smile that came from deep inside—no prompting necessary.

Walking outside the DMV, I was thrilled. This was such a well-earned moment of celebration that I wanted to extend it. I sat on my bike holding my license with my eyes shut, savoring the triumphant joy I was feeling. I hadn't felt this solid in two and a half years.

For me joy is such a different feeling from happiness. I have always heard and felt vibrational tones and pitches and am surprised to find others don't process life this way. Happiness is a higher-pitched feeling often floating in my upper body, especially around my head. It's accompanied by a lot of internal excited jabbering. But joy is a deeper vibration with lower, richer tones. I feel it radiating inside my body around my heart and solar plexus area. With joy, there are no chattering voices, just an inner feeling of connectedness—the external world uniting with an internal sense of "I am."

This type of wondrous feeling didn't come from acquiring a physical object—my motorcycle license. Instead, it originated from the tremendous energy I had funneled into accomplishing what I believed was an almost insurmountable goal, continuing despite unanticipated obstacles and finally succeeding.

As a result of this achievement, I had a new self-trust. *I can count on me again. I don't need all of my former protection and pampering to shelter myself from the real world. I can once again tackle a difficult goal and work hard to make it happen.*

I pulled out of the DMV parking lot and entered the highway fully licensed and legal. Playfully I pulled back on the throttle several times, eliciting a wonderful revving VRR-OOM-VROOM-VROOM roar and laughed.

This loud commotion was only a fraction of the VROOOM-like rumble that was vibrating inside me.

As I roared off down the road with my beaming smile that was echoed in every cell of my body, I was already planning whom to call and in what order. *Mom's first. Although she's concerned about me riding, she'll be thrilled to hear me sounding like my spunky old self again. Then Lindsey and I will go out for a celebratory evening. She's earned it for being a loyal cheering section.*

5
Getting Directions

The doorbell rang. Opening the door I was pleased to find my dear friend standing there. Yvonne and I had been friends for many years. She was born in Scotland, and I've always enjoyed her quick wit and fiery spirit.

"I was in the neighborhood and thought I'd drop by and see how you're doing. Got time for a quick visit?"

As I made a pot of tea and searched through my cupboards for something for us to nibble on, we caught up on recent news. Finally seated at the dining room table she asked, "So how's your motorcycling? Excited about your upcoming trip?"

"Excited. Overwhelmed. I'm a lot of things, especially indecisive. I keep asking myself if I've taken on too much and whether I can handle such an ambitious road trip."

"I thought you'd already decided to go," Yvonne said as she reached toward the plate of oatmeal-raisin cookies.

"Not completely," I said, pushing the dish closer to her. "Sure, I took classes, borrowed a motorcycle to practice on, purchased plane tickets and all. But I kept thinking, I can back down at the last minute if it doesn't feel right. I've been mulling over go/no-go scenarios all along."

"What did your Harley instructors think about your taking this trip?"

"They talked about the fun I'd have, but they've been riding for years. Can they even remember what it's like to be a beginner?"

"Well, how about your classmates?"

"They said go for it. But whenever I talk to friends and neighbors, they insist on telling stories about people they know who have gotten hurt, or worse yet, been killed motorcycling. Some have even told me that they used to ride, and they'd never go on an ambitious trip like this."

"So you're worried you'll get hurt?"

"Sure. And what about my kids and family? Haven't they been through enough?"

Yvonne smiled, lifting an eyebrow. "So you want this decision to be easy—with all opinions pointing to one answer."

I sighed and began meticulously folding my napkin into smaller neat squares as I sorted through possible responses. Finally I looked up. "I just wish I had a magic globe to look into the future and see if I survive in one piece."

"Maybe you're wanting the kind of clarity you had with Bill during the last year of his life. Then you eliminated superfluous things and focused on what mattered—keeping him alive and happy. Life rarely offers that kind of singular mission and clear-cut priorities."

"I never thought about it like that," I answered as I looked up at her and nodded. "You're right. Nothing feels important, and I can't replicate that same feeling of certainty."

"So the real question is—what do *you* . . . want to do?"

"I don't know. But I need to end this inner debate. I've even tried to use the decision-making tools I taught in business, but they don't work on this."

Yvonne smiled, her green eyes twinkling as she leaned forward, put her hand on my forearm, and whispered, "I don't think you're going to get an answer to this one by using your head. Deep inside, you already know your answer." Pointing to my heart she added, "Your answer's here."

⁂

Walking into a restaurant in downtown D.C., I saw Ron sitting with a man and a woman. As I reached their booth, the woman said, "Hello,

I'm Eva. Come sit here." She patted the bench next to her as she scooted over, pushing her purse and coat into the far corner.

Not waiting for anyone to introduce him, the deeply-tanned man sitting across from me said, "Hi, I'm Alberto." He rose from his seat and extended his hand to shake mine. I relaxed, appreciating his friendly but slightly formal manner.

"We're finally together," Ron said, beaming as he looked at the three of us who would be joining him on the upcoming road trip.

Sitting quietly, I nodded and smiled at appropriate moments as I observed their conversation. Ron had told me that Alberto was a lawyer. His raw silk jacket and contrasting dark shirt reflected his upscale international clientele. Alberto sat back, letting Ron and Eva do most of the talking until he felt strongly about something. Then he'd jump in and present his case with vigor.

Eva, on the other hand, had to have been a former cheerleader. She was attractive, animated, and bubbling with enthusiasm, suggesting ideas on every subject that came up. Ron's earlier quick profile of her had included the fact that she was from Germany. When she discovered I had lived in Germany for a couple of years, she seemed delighted. After exchanging a few trial sentences in German, we laughed, realizing the freedom our dual languages would offer. Ron and Alberto sat across from us looking puzzled, neither of them understanding our quick exchange. I expected Eva would bring a lot of fun to everything we did on the trip.

Eva, Ron, and Alberto's families often socialized and vacationed together, so there was a lot to share about their spouses, kids, and mutual friends. They seemed to get along well even though each one appeared to be a natural leader used to being in charge. Riding as a group, we would be dependent on one another. From having facilitated team building with business groups for so many years, I wondered how four such assertive personalities would manage spending so much time together.

It was Eva who finally turned the conversation to the upcoming road trip.

"You guys have convinced this woman that she can ride a motorcycle on the trip with only a few weeks of riding experience." She leveled a solemn gaze at Ron and Alberto. "Just think about it for a moment. If anything happens to her, we're all responsible."

"She'll be fine. She's taken classes, gotten her license, and she's out practicing every day," Ron said.

"Eva, you're being too protective. She looks like she can handle it," Alberto said.

"It's hard riding a motorcycle all day," Eva insisted. "It gets tiring. One of us should go out on a two-hundred-mile trip with her so she can get a feel for a longer ride. She needs strenuous back-road and interstate experience too."

"What do you think about riding several hundred miles a day for ten days in a row?" Alberto asked me.

"When I moved from California to Pennsylvania, I drove my car solo across the United States in five days, putting in a couple of six-hundred-plus-mile days. On my bicycle I've ridden a hundred miles in one day, and that's riding on skinny tires and sitting on a seat not much bigger than a baseball cap. The distance, roads, and long hours in the saddle aren't my concern, I just don't know how to judge what it's like to do all of that on a motorcycle."

All three stated they were impressed with how far I had come in such a short time; however, they wanted to be certain I recognized the dangers of such a trip for others and myself. I knew from riding my bicycle in groups that one bad move by any cyclist could ricochet through the pack, taking down innocent others. I felt they were generous in inviting me to join them as I compounded the risk of the trip.

"Look, I'll talk to John about renting her a motorcycle similar to mine. That way she won't have to get used to having things located in different places on another motorcycle," Ron said.

"We could also rent her a less powerful model than ours. The down-side will be she'll have to work harder to keep up and her ride will be less comfortable. But it will be easier for her to control," Alberto said.

We kept open the option of my driving a sag car—a vehicle used to carry equipment and luggage—or riding behind one of the other members on their motorcycle. The initial decision would be left to me. On the trip, if it looked as if I weren't doing well or couldn't keep up, the group would step in and insist on one of these backup alternatives. We all agreed the ultimate goal was to have a safe, fun vacation.

"I have only one strong concern. Are we going to be doing any off-road riding? Riding over rough terrain or on gravel is beyond me at this point," I said.

"Don't worry. When I join these guys on a road trip, we have agreed-upon rules: no gravel or off-road riding," Eva said, as Ron and Alberto reluctantly nodded.

I appreciated Eva's concerns about my safety. Still, her earlier remarks about the trip's challenges for a new rider were unsettling and left me struggling with my next decision.

As the guys drifted into a conversation about last night's Washington Caps hockey game in which a last-minute penalty had given the team a much-needed edge to score the winning goal against the Flyers, Eva and I talked about motorcycle clothing. She suggested I look on the Internet for used leathers, since it was an expensive investment for just one trip. But time was running out, and I've never been successful in buying clothes without first trying them on. I was surprised by the amount she planned to take on the trip. In addition to Ron's items, she was bringing a skirt, sweater, hoodie, bathing suit, sandals, raingear, make-up, hair dryer, jewelry, iPod, cell phone, camera, books to read on the plane, and the list went on.

How would I fit all of that onto a single motorcycle?

Eva assured me that she always had carried this much on past trips, in a large and small duffel bag tied down on top of the passenger seat behind her and in the two side saddlebags.

⚮

As I drove home from the meeting, I continued to sort through all of the advice I had received to date. People's opinions resembled a Rorschach test with their recommendations reflecting their own personal fears, limitations, preferences, and experiences. If they'd recently had a scary or good motorcycle incident, this was mirrored in their advice. Likewise, if they wanted to go or not go on a vacation similar to this road trip, that choice affected their position. People with high-risk tolerances said yes. Those with low ones thought I was crazy.

Listening to people's varied reactions, I wondered if they ever considered my own personal strengths and weaknesses. In business when I led groups in decision-making, I had noticed a common phenomenon. When research didn't point to one clear answer, some asked for more information, believing more input would increase clarity. But a critical point arrives when more study only creates more data, not certainty. The eventual result is too many conflicting facts, which causes a *decision freeze*. Eyes glaze over, minds freeze, and decision-making paralysis sets in.

I knew it was time to stop soliciting advice. I had enough data. It was my inner debate that needed resolution. I remembered Yvonne's advice and headed upstairs to my bedroom and my red leather armchair where I read and meditated. It was time to shut out external influences and journey inward.

I'm not an accomplished sitting meditator. Most of my spiritual insights and moments of clarity are reached while exercising, out in nature, or after taking a shower when my conscious thinking naturally rests, allowing my inner voice to be heard. Sitting still in a meditation pose and observing my breath while trying to remain in the current moment was something I managed for only brief periods. I also knew that expecting to find an exact answer to a specific question while sitting in meditation was even more improbable. But the experience I'd had on the stairs two weeks ago encouraged me that the effort and practice of focusing inward were worth it.

I lit a candle, kicked off my shoes, and sat in my chair, enjoying the leather's soothing caress against my skin. I rested my hands in my lap and shut my eyes. Following my breaths, I turned the edges of my mouth upwards, imagining my internal organs and every cell smiling.

It's time to rest my mind and be present, I repeated to myself.

Focusing on the current moment, I heard birds chirping in the trees outside my bedroom. The candle's gentle pine scent wafted through the air. A subtle breeze from the ceiling fan stirred the air around me. I watched my body breathe—in and then out. At first my breathing felt forced and awkward. Then, as I relaxed, it became more natural. Gently I pulled my thoughts back from things that needed to be done when I finished, as well as away from processing what had happened in today's road trip meeting.

I no longer fought myself when I trailed off on these mini brain excursions. Meditating with my active mind was a bit like walking a spirited dog on a leash. I kept having to repeat: *Heel. Don't race off into the future. Don't chase after something that's passed by.* Softly I would add: *Stay. Be present. Walk with me. There is no place you need to go that's better than here and now.*

My racing thoughts slowed, then faded. An inner awareness began to spread throughout my body and expand into the immediate space around me. I opened my eyes, enjoying the peace that accompanies feeling more integrated.

From the first time Ron had mentioned this road trip, an energy inside me was urging me to go, telling me that it was the right thing to do. It kept saying this trip holds discoveries I need for recreating myself as a single woman. But my head kept shouting warnings that the trip was too dangerous, questioning whether my motivation for ignoring the inherent risks was a desire to run away and escape my real life still filled with loss and empty spaces.

Sitting in silence that night, I recalled an exercise I had learned many years earlier and decided to use it to test these opposing viewpoints. I positioned a "don't go" answer above my head in the air to my upper left and a "go" answer above and to my right.

Looking straight ahead I asked the question: *Should I go on this road trip and ride my own motorcycle?*

I shut my eyes, looked upward to my left at the "don't-go" choice and waited for my reaction. Sadness and disappointment flooded my entire body. Their weight pressed against my shoulders and chest as my body buckled inward and downward. Thoughts inside cried out: *Oh no, not more of the same!* Not wanting to remain there any longer, I retreated to the neutral position.

I stated my original question a second time. *Should I go on this road trip and ride my own motorcycle?*

Eyes shut, I turned my head and looked upward to my right in the direction of the "go" choice. Instantly I smiled, feeling as excited as a small child going out for ice cream on a hot summer night. The air around me expanded and felt light and cooling. My chest lifted, shoulders dropped, and my breathing slowed and deepened. Freedom and excitement raced through and around me as I enjoyed this pleasurable space filled with both known and unfamiliar possibilities.

Moving back to center and opening my eyes, I shook my head and laughed. I had used this exercise on various occasions, but never had I experienced such divergent reactions to the opposing options. I had wanted to gain clarity by accessing my inner voice, and I had been given a compelling display. I sat there stunned by the results.

One of the problems for many people my age is how to keep passion in their lives. After decades of following the pack, raising children, volunteering, doing community service, and pouring hearts and minds into jobs, satisfying clients, colleagues, and bosses, we suddenly find ourselves needing new mountains to climb with fresh challenges and surprising vistas. Many of our old behaviors, which have served us well, no longer make sense.

"What now?" we ask when it's time for something different. "What can I do now that has meaning and fills me with excitement again?" Ready to act, we look around with energy to move forward, but no new direction feels quite right.

Since Bill's death, I had longed for a way to express myself—to find a way to make my heart sing again and my spirit soar. It was time to rise up and discover what else there was to fill the new empty space inside me. My inner voice was saying: *Go! It's time to play again. Time to explore what you don't know. Erase your self-drawn boundaries and old rules. What have you got to lose?* But heading into the unknown was like driving a car at sixty miles per hour into a blind curve with my hands clenching the steering wheel. My foot would hit the brake and I'd get ready to accelerate halfway around the bend to pull me out and steady the vehicle, hoping that whatever might be around the other side would be better than what I was facing now.

Heading into a blind curve was a risk. A huge risk; I could spin out of control, run off the road, find greater chaos, or even encounter more of the bland sameness that was draining my soul.

I've learned to trust this internal direction that I have given up naming. Sometimes I've called it my soul, internal knowings, spiritual guidance, inner consciousness, or the God found within every person. In business, I have often used a more masculine term to describe it:

"gut feeling." Many women and some men relate more to the term "intuition."

Never have I regretted following this inner guidance when it is strong. More importantly, I have often regretted ignoring it.

Tonight I decided to listen to this inner direction and end my debate. My research was complete, analysis finished, and decision reached.

I was going on the trip and at least begin the journey riding my own motorcycle.

6
Buying Leathers

Since I knew that buying a leather jacket and pants would be an expensive investment, I had put off making this final purchase until I was sure of my commitment to ride a motorcycle on the road trip.

For the past three weeks I had been scrutinizing passing motorcyclists and was surprised by the variety in their clothing. It ranged from simple jeans with sleeveless T-shirts to flashy one-piece designer riding suits.

Safety was the first priority of my group, with comfort and fashion secondary. When I met with Ron, Eva, and Alberto, everyone insisted that I ride wearing full protection—a leather or microfiber jacket and pants with interior metal or plastic reinforcements, a full helmet with full clear face mask, protective gloves, and sturdy motorcycle boots.

All of this gear would be costly for just one motorcycle trip since I couldn't envision myself ever going on a second one. But having dropped my motorcycle during the training course, I already knew how bruised and scraped up a person could get from a simple fall on a stopped motorcycle, so I understood their protection requirements.

Many serious bikers wear a heavyweight motorcycling outfit for colder weather and a lightweight mesh one for warmer days. On this trip I would need heavier clothing for the fifty-degree weather expected along the coast in the mornings (wind chill could make it feel an additional twenty degrees colder) and lightweight clothing for the expected ninety-plus-degree days riding in central California. But I wouldn't have room for two outfits and certainly didn't want to spend more money than necessary. My plan for today was to find the best single compromise. I picked up my car keys and directions to four motor-cycle dealerships and headed out the door.

Walking into the first, I felt like Alice just after she had fallen down the rabbit's hole and nothing made sense. I ran my hands over the leather jackets hanging on a rack but had no idea how to figure out what was best. I looked around and was grateful when a young woman in her early twenties approached.

"Hi, I'm Penny. Can I help?"

"I'm a new rider, and I'm headed out west next week on a road trip, so I need to buy a leather jacket and pants, but I have no idea what I'm looking at. Could you help me?"

"The women's jackets are over here," Penny said, pointing at a rack on my left. "Do you see anything you like?"

"I definitely know that I'm not interested in the pale pink jackets or any of these with fringes and fuchsia embroidery spelling out 'Hot Babe.' I was told to get a jacket with internal protection."

"If you want a jacket with armor, we only have two women's styles."

She handed me one to look at, but when I took it from her, my arm dropped six inches.

"It's heavy!"

"Surprising isn't it? Here, let me show you how much armor is inside," she said, taking the jacket and opening it up on a nearby counter.

Penny pointed out the extra pieces under the lining located at the tops of both shoulders, behind the elbows, and in the middle of the lower back. She explained the large back panel protected the kidneys. Noting my confused look, she added that puncturing a kidney could kill you instantly. I nodded, not wanting further explanation about a subject I was trying hard to avoid.

"Some pants have extra protection," she said, pointing out the ribbed layers over the knees on one pair. "Let's take these jackets and several pants for you to try on in our dressing room."

As I examined the leather, it was considerably heavier than the softer, pliable version I was used to in casual clothing. I pulled on a pair of pants and a jacket and headed back out into the showroom.

"Wow, you look hot!" she said.

As I peered into the full-length mirror propped on top of several cardboard boxes in the corner, I gasped. The heavier leather and inner armor added bulk to my body. I resembled a football player in full gear. I didn't feel very sexy, so I was surprised by the oohs and ahhs I got from several men in the dealership. My definition of "attractive" started to change as I quit staring at my bulky knees, shoulders, and elbows caused by the extra padding.

Just as I had learned how many men like the smell of a machine shop, I was experiencing how a woman dressed in full leather also commands attention. I noticed the inches added to my figure, but these men saw something different.

As I moved in the outfit and stretched out my arms, the sleeves felt too short—pulling at the shoulders—and the pant waist was too big, bulging out in the back. Other jackets and pants had different problems. I even tried on men's jackets to solve the arm-length problem, but then everything else was too big. Penny was emphatic: while riding a bike all day, the rider needed to be comfortable and the outfit had to fit properly.

I was surprised to discover that finding a well-constructed leather jacket and pants that fit was as hard as buying a bathing suit. I tugged at the leather, trying to get it to cover places it wasn't, while pushing it back from other areas where it draped and shouldn't. For a woman I have the long arms, large shoulders, and a small waist that make me a formidable swimmer, but always leave me with few choices when buying women's jackets and blouses.

By the time I arrived at the fourth dealership I was exhausted. All of the places had considerably less women's inventory than men's and much of the women's clothing focused more on fashion and being sexy or cute than protection and comfort. I finally purchased a leather jacket with an outer leather layer that could be unzipped and removed, leaving behind a lightweight mesh inner jacket. I also bought long leather pants with a zipper running up the outside of each leg that could be unzipped to the top of each thigh when I got off the bike on hot days. This seemed the best compromise solution for one outfit to use in all kinds of weather.

⬟

The last evening before leaving on the trip I finally packed my suitcases and set them next to the front door. It had taken the whole day to organize, stow everything in as little luggage as possible and tie up loose ends.

Ten days felt like a long time to be away from home. Starting the next day I'd be surrounded by other people throughout the trip, and that concerned me. My solitary, self-contained life was about to be interrupted. I set my alarm clock for five o'clock in the morning.

Climbing into bed I wondered what my father-in-law would think of this twist in the road that I had created. In this blind curve would I discover a jack-knifed semi, like my DMV friend had encountered, more of the same confusion, or triumphant joy like I felt when I finally earned my license?

7
Ready, Set, Roll

As my flight prepared for takeoff from Washington-Dulles International Airport, I felt small and insignificant sitting inside the jet's powerful shell. The plane's engines roared and its body rattled as it made its awkward metamorphosis from top-heavy bus to soaring falcon. During this transition, my spirit similarly ascended and my body quivered, mimicking the drama of the plane. As part of me reveled in beginning this adventure to one of my favorite regions of North America, another recoiled, intimidated by the impending bold challenge and wondering why I had insisted on erasing my life's old boundaries and expanding its former familiar circumference.

Studying the plane's interior, I realized that despite its familiar setting, life still felt surreal. Little in the past year and a half had felt real. *How could I ever have agreed to do something I previously thought so unattractive? I was a bicyclist, not a motorcyclist. I was a greenie and not a noise polluter.*

One of my favorite sayings is, "The only rule is that there are no rules." It amazes me how whenever I announce that I definitely won't do something, a new situation crops up requiring me to do just that.

Pushing my seat back as I tried to get more comfortable in the cramped quarters, I remembered a moment from my life immediately after college. I had started my career working with non-profits and vehemently announced that I would never work for a large corporation. But twelve years later, I initiated a job search with a multinational corporation and readily accepted a management position with Citigroup at their headquarters.

Having gone through junior and senior high school in the small town of Elizabethtown, Pennsylvania, I said I could never live in New York City. Compared to the serenity of Lancaster County's Dutch Country, the thought of living in a giant, impersonal city was too foreign. But at age thirty-four I found myself moving to midtown Manhattan to secure the right career experience.

Six years later when I headed to San Diego, California, to start my own business, I said I'd never live in a cold climate again. Five years later I moved back to the East Coast to be closer to my aging father in Harrisburg, Pennsylvania.

As a former sixties protesting hippie, I couldn't imagine I'd ever marry someone who had worked for the FBI. Yep, did that one too, when I married Bill.

At this stage in life I had quit making never-pronouncements or forming absolute rules, because I knew it was a sure *guarantee* that the next life situation would demand I do exactly that. I looked for wood to knock on if I even silently thought an "I would never do . . ." judgment statement.

Often I have witnessed how significant change is easiest to imagine when things are going poorly and there's little to lose by trying something new. I knew from my previous corporate work that the greater the discomfort and dysfunction, the more willing individuals are to initiate and accept change.

Once I was invited to facilitate a major business reorganization throughout a service company while they were experiencing an impressive twelve-percent annual growth in revenues. The proposed new processes were strongly resisted by employees, who pointed to the company's current success as a reason to continue doing more of the same. Years later the growth halted and it was too late.

Another company facing imminent bankruptcy was a different story. There I facilitated the work of five executives in developing forty radical initiatives to be completed in the next three months. They rapidly implemented the plan and saved the company.

I didn't expect riding a motorcycle to resolve my ennui and unhappiness. I just needed to try something new. The allure of this adventure and the chance to be with a group who didn't know what I had just been through was enticing. I was ready for drama of my own creation.

What do I have to lose?

As I thought about the group I would be riding with, I found it interesting that all were married but no one was taking their spouse on the trip. Eva's husband rode, but he was building a new business and didn't want to be away from it for ten days. Ron and Alberto's wives not only didn't ride their own motorcycles, they didn't even enjoy sitting behind their husbands. I remembered how Bill and I used to have different hobbies and interests too. On his birthday, I'd go to his regular yoga class, and on my birthday he'd go on a long bicycle ride with me, but the rest of the year we were happy to support each other in these activities from the sidelines.

While I was learning to ride a motorcycle, I had asked Lindsey what she thought Bill would have said about my new activity, but neither of us could predict his probable response. He had shared my go-get-em spirit for trying new things, but the risk associated with motorcycling would have made him uncomfortable. It was an answer we would never know.

⤺⤻

Five hours later, the plane landed in Vancouver, Canada. Since the four of us were on different flights, we had planned to meet at baggage claim. We breathed a collective sigh of relief when everyone showed up on time, and all of our luggage arrived with us. We had pulled off one miracle. I wondered how many more I would experience in the next ten days.

Somehow Eva and I ended up retrieving all of the baggage, while Ron and Alberto headed off to figure out how to get a taxi to take us to our rental motorcycles. As Eva and I struggled, lifting the bulky pieces off the carousel and onto two luggage carts that rolled away as soon as we tried to scoot anything onto them, we looked at each other, wondering how we ended up with this job. But this wasn't exactly the type of trip that would allow us to worry about preserving a manicure or avoiding physical effort. I had already given up the idea of being eye candy while riding behind a guy on his motorcycle when I persisted in learning to ride my own bike. It was too late to feign helplessness.

Pushing our precariously over-laden carts outside the terminal, we spotted Ron and Alberto standing next to a cab waving. They looked as proud as two men who had run down and captured a lion barehanded in the jungle. They greeted us with the appreciative question: "What took you so long?"

Without responding, Eva and I jumped into the waiting van, letting Ron and Alberto figure out how to load it. For the moment, we had done our share.

The Vancouver airport is located on Sea Island in Richmond, British Columbia, about ten miles from downtown Vancouver. Our plan was to take a taxi from the airport to a nearby hotel where we'd pick up our motorcycles from John and T. J., our Canadian contacts.

As soon as we arrived at the hotel, Ron, Alberto, and Eva bounded from the taxi to greet two men standing thirty feet away beside several motorcycles in the side parking lot. I made sure the taxi was unpacked and then shyly walked over to join the celebratory reunion.

Both men were in their late fifties, and unlike us, they looked like serious motorcyclists—long hair pulled back into neck-length pony-tails, well-worn motorcycle clothes, scarves tied around their foreheads. Their skin was tanned and weathered, but the heavy lines on their faces were friendly ones. I immediately liked them.

"Come meet John and T. J.," Ron said.

"So you're the new one. I wondered how smart you'd be since you're riding with these guys. Don't believe a thing they've told yah, cause they don't know nothin'. They're just a bunch of Rubbies!" John said.

"You're right. We don't know nothin'," Ron said.

"What's a Rubbie?" I asked.

"They're <u>R</u>ich <u>U</u>rban <u>B</u>ikers. They only ride a couple of times a year, yet they think they're real bikers. We think they're really pretty stupid, but they can be a lot of fun."

"We call their bikes *parts*, cause they rarely ride them. Everything's still brand new—just like they've come straight out of a box," T. J. added.

"Go get changed. We've got to get you guys packed up and on the road if you're going to make that three-thirty ferry." With that John tossed a hotel room key to Ron and handed another one to Eva.

John owned three of the motorcycles being used by our group. He had rented mine from another supplier so that I could ride a model similar to the one I had been practicing on in Virginia.

"Come over here," John said, waving his arm, signaling me to join him. He was standing next to a shiny new motorcycle. "This one's brand new. She's only got a thousand on her."

Looking at the motorcycle I would ride for the next ten days, I was relieved to see that all of the switches, indicators, brake levers, and pedals were in the same places as on Ron's motorcycle. The most notable differences were that it was newer, bigger, heavier, and equipped with side saddlebags. This would be the most powerful motorcycle I had ridden so far. Its size would make it easier to keep up with the group but would also add more power behind any mistake I might make.

I threw my leg over the bike and sat on its seat, wanting to get a better sense of it. I lifted it off its stand and sat balancing it between my legs.

"How's she feel?" John asked.

"Great," I said. But inside I recoiled in panic. I felt like a student who has pulled an all-nighter studying for a final exam and as soon as the test is passed out, her mind goes blank.

I was relieved when Alberto called John over to ask something about his motorcycle. Sitting there I retreated into my own internal world, while Ron, Eva, and Alberto continued to laugh and exchange stories about previous trips with John and T. J.

Although John was excited to see his old riding buddies again, I sensed he was assessing me not only for my ability to ride, but also for how great a liability I'd be to the group and myself. The basic rule of all motorcycle renters is that riders must have their licenses at least a year before renting. My three-week history fell sorely short of this standard. John was a small operator, renting only a few motorcycles, as well as a close friend of the group, so he had made a huge exception for me. I knew I needed to ride my best today. Yet, my best might not be good enough to convince him that his concession had been wise.

We began packing the side bags and tying our soft luggage onto the back passenger seat using bungee cords. It was important for the luggage to be balanced and tied down securely. Luckily, I had taken the pre-trip advice that it's impossible to have too many bungee cords and had brought plenty. It was a pleasant surprise to discover how much could be packed into the side bags and on top of my motorcycle. The downside was that each evening I would be unpacking everything, taking it inside my hotel room, and then repacking it the next morning. As a frequent traveler, I knew the wisdom of leaving extra room at the beginning of a trip for things accumulated along the way. Assessing my fully loaded motorcycle, I decided photographs would have to be my primary mementos. I had no real idea what I would actually need, and so I was playing it safe by taking too much.

Bikes finally packed, our plan was to ride them to the ferry that would take us from Vancouver to Victoria Island, the major island between Vancouver and the Pacific Ocean. The word "island" can create a misleading impression, given Victoria Island's significant size. It's nearly double the area of Newfoundland.

We would only be staying overnight in the city of Victoria, located at the southern end of the island. Exploring the rest of Victoria Island would have to wait for another trip. Tonight there was a big reunion planned at our hotel with John, T. J., and other members from previous western motorcycle trips.

Huddled around Ron's motorcycle, we listened as John went over the route to our ferry. He also handed Ron a map of Vancouver in case we needed it. The rest of us didn't need directions or maps—just follow the leader was the plan. I was grateful for the cell phone inside my upper jacket pocket with programmed numbers of everyone in the group. Keeping the four of us together would be like rounding up humming birds. There didn't seem to be one follower in the group. Everyone was competent; everyone was a leader. It would not be a boring ten days.

Sitting on my bike, I repeated everything I had learned about how to start a motorcycle. I carried out this memorized sequence and sighed in relief when my motorcycle turned over and started on my first try. However, I was the only one of the group who was impressed by my accomplishment. They were all immersed in their own motorcycles and the fun ahead. It was obvious to me that I was expected to rise to the group's level and join in. I sat biting my lower lip, waiting any second for the group to "roll" out of the parking lot and onto the pulsing city streets.

The moment of truth had arrived.

Without warning, Ron turned his bike over and roared out of the parking lot onto Vancouver's streets. A shiver rose through my body. The anticipated moment had arrived—the ride had begun. I knew Ron expected others to jump in close behind, but I couldn't react that fast.

8

Vancouver: Life on the Edge

In contrast to Ron's smooth exit into Vancouver traffic, I began my robotic process of repeating each memorized step: I brought my motorcycle upright and pushed back its sidestand; I lifted my left foot and shifted into first; I eased out the clutch lever with my left hand while giving it gas with my right. I held my breath while walking my bike forward with my feet until there was enough forward momentum for it to remain balanced on its own. Finally, I placed my feet on the bike's foot pegs.

I stopped at the edge of the parking lot and looked left, then right, clenching my teeth and frowning as I calculated the exact moment to ease my bike into the streaming traffic racing past me in four lanes. I decided to go *Now*, and gave the bike gas as it leaped forward and my body reeled backward. *Wow, this motorcycle reacts powerfully to the slightest twist of the throttle. I need to be cautious with how fast I twist its throttle.*

I beamed, thrilled to have made it onto the city streets, but there was no time for a victory celebration. Leaning forward, my heart pounding louder than the roar of my motorcycle's engine, I focused on Ron's motorcycle's taillights several blocks away. I caught up with him and fell into line, thinking that if I ever had a heart attack, it wouldn't be while I was in bed sleeping, but rather in a moment like this. My personal weight trainer would be disappointed to hear that the last minutes were more strenuous than any gym workout I'd ever done.

Behind me the sounds of other motorcycles roared, and I reasoned it must be Alberto and Eva. I wondered how we would ever find each other without a back-up plan or maps, if we got separated. I cut this thought short. My current focus had to be how to stay connected with Ron, the present leader. I had to break this habit of continual concern for everyone else. It was time to let go and trust others' competence and problem-solving abilities.

It was hard to believe I was riding in a strange city of a half-million people on the far side of the continent. One part of me was in awe of what I was accomplishing, while another asked how I had willfully done this to myself. I pried my attention away from my emotional thinking and redirected it to my riding, doing my best to remember all I had been taught, but there were so many details.

The new motorcycle that rumbled beneath me was only the third I'd ever ridden. Even though this was the most powerful to date, its smoother responses as I clutched, shifted, braked, and accelerated made it exhilarating to ride. In the midst of my current confusion about controlling it, I anticipated the fun ahead.

As I rode, so many factors required my simultaneous attention. My eyes jerked from one demanding scene to the next and never remained on one view for more than a few seconds. For three seconds I scanned the road's surface in front of me for potholes, cracks, gravel, liquid, or manhole covers. Then for two cursory seconds I glanced at my left side mirror to see what traffic was doing behind me, followed by fleeting peeks—over my right and left shoulders—to check out traffic in neighboring lanes. Next, for four seconds I surveyed the traffic ahead, sorting through the lights for Ron's bike's blinkers to see if he was signaling a lane change or potential turn.

Then, remembering to look upward, I scanned the higher horizon for traffic lights and noticed the next one changing from yellow to red with all traffic around me slowing and halting. After shifting down, braking and stopping, I had ninety precious seconds during which I could stop riding and remind myself to breathe.

But instead of resting, I played with my motorcycle's clutch lever in my left hand and throttle in my right, trying to get a feel for the exact place where the motorcycle began to engage, giving power to the wheels and moving the motorcycle slightly forward. When this happened, I quickly pulled in the clutch lever to cut off the movement, and the motorcycle rocked backwards slightly, staying essentially in the same place.

I repeated this exercise, rocking forward and backward, learning to identify this motorcycle's particular "friction zone" as they had referred to it in class. When the light changed, I surged forward with the traffic, shifting up through several gears.

I remember sometimes seeing flashes of water off to my right or left but never taking the time to notice whether it was a lake, river, bay, or ocean. There was no time to think anything beyond: *There's water.*

As I concentrated on the road ahead, edges of my vision flooded with colors flashing by out of focus. My eyes jumped so quickly between scenes, I felt as if I were at target practice in a fair booth, objects suddenly popping up from out of nowhere: *Where'd that truck come from? Oops, there's a caution light blinking yellow. Watch out for that pothole! Which direction is that siren coming from?*

I noticed an inordinate number of Asian characters on buildings and vehicles and noted that this was strange. In a saner moment I would have remembered the important connection between Asia and Vancouver, but at a time when the brain was already crowded with so much riding commentary, there was no room for being a tourist or processing non-essential information.

I know there must have been many sounds around me in such a busy city, but the only ones I heard were the screaming inside my head, my roaring motorcycle, and the pounding inside my chest. Since so much concentration was being forced into each second, I have no idea whether we drove ten, twenty, or forty minutes to reach the ferry, but suddenly we were slowing down and making a right turn.

Arriving at the British Columbia Ferries Terminal in Tsawwassen— about ten miles south of the airport—I felt like a crewmember on one of Columbus's ships, which had just sighted land after being lost at sea for months. I was ready to get off my motorcycle and kiss the parking lot asphalt. We had arrived safely at the loading dock for traveling to Swartz Bay on Victoria Island.

A parking attendant directed us to ride into one of the three motorcycle lanes filled with thirty or so other motorcyclists. To our left were twenty more lanes filled with cars. As we parked our cycles, we watched a ferry pulling up in front of us with SPIRIT OF VANCOUVER ISLAND painted on its side. The pilot expertly maneuvered it into the dock and hands onshore rushed to catch the large ropes and tie the ferry to the pier. Its big iron ramp slowly lowered and hit the shore with a loud kerplunk that reverberated through the lot. My heart clenched as I gasped, noticing that the ramp's driving surface was a metal grate with a steep grade. I had never ridden up a grate before but knew it could be difficult to keep a motorcycle balanced as its tires fought to grip the irregular open-spaced surfaces.

Watching as first the motorcycles and then cars descended the ramp, I realized that when it was our turn to board, the motorcyclists would go first. If I made any mistakes on the ramp, I'd have a large audience. I started my bike while watching the motorcyclists around me as we eased forward in single file, and I copied the others' speed and distance between bikes.

Despite the frightening distraction of riding in the middle of thirty other roaring motorcycles, I was still able to control my motorcycle as it took off up the ramp. However, my body was less cooperative as my heart throbbed, and I over-clenched my fingers around the handle grips. Surprisingly, the uneven traction of the bike's tires against the grated surface didn't cause the motorcycle's wheels to wobble much. In less than five seconds, the dreaded grate ordeal was behind me—a true anticlimax after so much trepidation.

Inside we parked our bikes perpendicular to the side of the ferry. We were told that the biggest motion on a large ferry is side-to-side swaying. By parking our motorcycles facing the sides of the ferry and placing large blocks in front and behind our tires, we could keep them from rolling or toppling over when it rocked. The twenty-three-mile trip to Victoria Island would take about ninety minutes, so we headed for the stairs leading to the upper decks to enjoy the coastal views.

This ferry had two passenger levels. The first contained a large windowed interior room with buffet food service and rows of tables and benches. Encircling this was an outer open deck that ran around the circumference of the level. It also had extra viewing areas in the front and back. We headed to the unenclosed, less crowded, top deck lined with benches and what we imagined would be a more scenic view of our surroundings. Even though it was the middle of June, it was still chilly—the temperature only in the sixties—and the sky was overcast.

As soon as we sat down on the benches, Eva pulled her lipstick, compact, and hairbrush out of her bag. She was an attractive woman who enjoyed looking her best. With lipstick refreshed, she snapped her mirror shut, looked at me and said, "Well, let me get a better look at you in your new motorcycle clothes."

"What do you think?" I awkwardly turned and posed for her.

She squinted her eyes, a discerning frown crossing her forehead as she scanned slowly from my head to my boots. I felt like a second grader being inspected by a parent before heading off to school. As a child I often failed these inspections. I was never allowed to put on my "good clothes" until just before we were ready to depart because I had a knack for getting dirty.

"I like your leather jacket and pants. Unzip your jacket, I want to see what you're wearing underneath."

I complied, opening my jacket to reveal a purple T-shirt with the Harley logo and name of the Homestead, Virginia, dealership on it in metallic silver.

"Something's not quite right. I'll be right back."

She headed downstairs in the direction of our bikes. A few minutes later she returned carrying a handful of colorful railroad handkerchiefs.

"You need one of these," she said, waving the scarves in front of me. After tying several different ones around my neck, she decided that the well-worn black one was best.

"Now at least you're wearing something that doesn't look so new," she said, satisfied with her final touches.

"What about us?" asked Ron.

Alberto nodded. "Yeah, no playing favorites."

Eva walked over and tied handkerchiefs around their necks as well.

Aside from being a fashion statement, I learned that this scarf would serve other functions. On hot days it could be doused in water and tied around my neck to keep me cool as the wind from riding blew across it. Also, leather against skin on a hot day could be uncomfortable and sticky. The cotton handkerchief would provide a welcome buffer. On chilly days, it would make a tighter seal against cold air entering between my neck and jacket collar. But the real reason I was wearing it today was that it completed my outfit. I hoped future corrections would be this easy.

"Now, picture time," Eva announced as Alberto and Ron shook their heads while exchanging knowing glances. We had all brought our own small digital cameras, which meant posing long enough so that each of us could get the same group shot using our own camera. The process seemed endless. Eva always wanted to see how she looked. If the photo didn't suit her—which was the case more than half the time—she'd insist it be erased and retaken.

After we pulled away from the dock, the shoreline disappeared and there wasn't much to see from our upper deck other than open water horizon to horizon. We hadn't had lunch so we headed down one level to the buffet.

The food was unmemorable, but our full stomachs on top of a long day helped us to realize that the best way to enjoy the rest of this ferry trip was to fall into the gentle rhythm of the rocking ship and snooze on the benches. The gray water and hazy sky reinforced our lazy mood, compensating for the uncomfortable contortions necessary to sleep on the unpadded seating intended only for sitting.

As with many vacations, most of us had spent several hectic days before this trip and had gotten less sleep than normal the previous night. The constant low droning of the ship's engine was the final instrument of this soothing lullaby. We were lulled off to sleep, rocking gently on our journey.

Approaching the ferry's Schwartz Bay Landing, we raced downstairs, renewed and ready to ride again. I was more relaxed as we disembarked, leaving the ferry and turning south onto Highway 17. We rode through farmlands and several communities on our eighteen-mile jaunt to the southern end of Victoria Island.

Since Alberto led, followed by Eva, all I had to do was fall in behind her. I realized this was going to be a routine I could enjoy. On this trip all I'd need to do was follow. What a relief. This role reversal from leader to follower felt long overdue.

In less than a half hour, we entered the province's capital. Our hotel was easy to find as it sat directly on the bay in Victoria. I was grateful when we reached the parking lot behind the hotel—it had been a long day, starting with an early morning flight.

"You did it," Eva said as she hopped off her bike and started unpacking her luggage. "I knew you'd be okay. Let's check into our room."

I was glad Eva was on this trip. She readily offered encouragement and was protective of me.

That evening other motorcyclists from previous trips joined us at the hotel for a reunion and impromptu party. As I walked into the hotel bar to join the crew, I was ready for a victory toast to the day. We had ridden only twenty-eight miles in both Vancouver and on our way to Victoria, but so far I'd made it in one piece to our destination. That met my criteria for a successful day—survival and no mishaps.

As we sat at the bar, stories flowed along with beer and shots. While talking and enjoying generous hors d'oeuvres, our conversations were interrupted by a loud rumbling noise, accompanied by explosive popping sounds coming from outside. Even inside the bar the noise felt deafening as it got closer. Everyone laughed.

John announced, mostly for my benefit, "Smokey's just arrived. You can hear him all over the island. His sound is so distinctive and ear piercing he can never cheat on his wife. Everyone always knows exactly where he's at."

Smokey was a small-framed man—only about five feet, four inches tall and maybe around one hundred twenty-five pounds—but he had decorated his body with the appropriate tattoos, was dressed like a seasoned biker, and walked with attitude. Somehow I had envisioned a huge man to match the sound. Napoleon or not, Smokey was a fun guy and everyone was excited to see him.

As with most groups, the stories that survived over time were ones about mistakes, misfortunes, and difficulties people had shared. Each dramatic retelling made me further question my decision to embark on this trip. First there was the one about Ron and Alberto losing each other in Romania without a plan for how they'd meet up again since neither had a cell phone. Miraculously, they did find each other and everyone laughed about what could have happened instead.

This account was followed by another about motorcycling in the Alps where, in the middle of a sharp hairpin curve during a steep climb up the mountain, all six riders in the group—one after the other— dropped their motorcycles. With traffic backed up behind them, they had taken turns helping to lift up each other's heavy bikes and then remounted them to try again.

There was a narrative about another friend, Jayk, who had hit a ditch deer that had unexpectedly jumped out of a ravine and onto the road in front of him in Montana during the last western trip. He broke several bones and missed the rest of the trip but was back riding again.

Ron, Eva, and Alberto told more stories, laughing and joking with the group. My attempts to fit in and smile at their recollections was a cover-up for my inner butterflies. Certainly on this ten-day trip we would create some of our own memorable stories. I both wondered and dreaded what they might be.

A number of the people in this extended riding group had nicknames like King, Dog Whistle, and Mom that were only used on motorcycle road trips and gatherings. They wouldn't tell me the origins of the names, saying I'd eventually figure them out. Mom was easy because she was John's wife and was already taking care of everyone. King, I figured, got his name because he would only ride on Harley Road King motorcycles. But I could only guess that Dog Whistle had to be able to hear sounds others couldn't. Either that or he attracted dogs everyplace he went.

I asked why some people had nicknames while others didn't and was told that you only got one when the group decided a name had been justly earned. No one got to pick their own. Not every nickname was complimentary, but all were terms of endearment.

The party began winding down as the three-hour time zone change was starting to catch up with us. We agreed to meet at 8:30 for breakfast the next morning. That would allow us adequate time to check out, pack our bikes, and make the 10:30 morning ferry from Victoria to Washington State.

Our plan for the next day was to land in Port Angeles, Washington, and take Highway 101, first heading west across the state to the Pacific Ocean where 101 turns and continues southward along the coast. Tomorrow night, we'd stay in Aberdeen, Washington, where we had reservations at a bed and breakfast. It would be an easy riding day of about two hundred miles. But even this so-called easy day would be the farthest I had ever ridden on one ride and the most miles in one day.

Although Eva was going to be a fun person to room with on this trip, I knew I'd never be able to keep up her pace when it came to being the life of the party. She had boundless energy and kept the group both lively and in line. Tonight I learned that her nickname was "Miss Nightcap." I surmised with that nickname she would probably be one of the last to call it a night. I quietly excused myself and headed up to our hotel room ahead of her, not ready to challenge that reputation.

Having been surrounded by people the entire day, I was glad for a few minutes alone to think. I felt relieved to have managed flying across the United States, riding a new motorcycle on city streets and onto the ferry, and finally meeting the veteran members of the previous group. Everyone seemed friendly and enthusiastic about motorcycling.

Although I felt content tonight, I also noted an undertone of fear entrenched in the background behind my satisfied mood. I wondered how long this unwelcome companion would stalk me and asked why I continuously sought new challenges and chose to push life to its limits.

Several months earlier I had posed a similar question in a conversation with Ron. I had told him I felt as if I were living delicately balanced on the edge of a sharpened knife blade. Outwardly I appeared fine, but inside I was wobbly and recognized how volatile I really was. One wavering misstep—right or left—could mean a disastrous fall down the slick sides of my knife into a valley of awaiting doom. He surprised me by saying I wasn't alone, and that most people feel that way.

The sharp edges I had experienced when I talked with Ron were ones I hadn't chosen. They had come with trying to figure out how to be single again, survive the significant loss of love and partnership, and create meaning in a life without Bill. But tonight's sharp edges came from an activity I had deliberately chosen. *Had these edges always been in my life? Would they always be with me?*

These questions reminded me of a vacation I had taken four years earlier with Bill and Lindsey to Zion National Park in southern Utah. We loved the jagged, colorful, treeless mountains and couldn't wait to get up to the top of several of them. After hiking for three hours, we reached the pinnacle of one mountain.

From this elevated perch, we could view both sides of the mountain range and appreciate its exposed history as we surveyed the polished sandstone and textured sides. A narrow trail ran across the upper ridge, connecting several peaks. At one area for about thirty feet, the path was only a couple of feet wide with dramatic drops off both sides. One misstep could result in a person plummeting down either steep side of the mountain. Walking this course gave true meaning to the phrase "living on the edge."

Fortunately, park rangers had attached a rope anchored firmly with metal cleats hammered deep into the stones so hikers would have something to hold onto for extra support. As I grasped this rope, I knew I was capable of walking along the narrow path and that my hand holding firmly onto the line just added back-up security.

Noting the steep thousand-foot drops on each side of the summit, my brain refused to factor in the additional safety the rope contributed to my situation. My legs trembled as I crept along, clenching the line in a tight hand-over-hand motion. As I moved, a calm voice inside my solar plexus repeated: *I am okay.* It battled against the terrified protest inside my head: *It's too dangerous. You could die!*

I have always had an exaggerated fear of heights, even in safe situations, and often wished I could overcome this. I'd watch my father and brother walk to the edge of a canyon and gaze at the valley below as I scooted cautiously forward, sitting on my rear, afraid to stand too close to the edge. They'd stride across a fallen tree over a ravine, while I'd linger behind, waiting for the added safety of a hand, a tree branch, anything to grasp and bolster my safe passage.

Thinking about my anxiety tonight, I had an insight about why heights and taking even calculated risks provoke such strong fear in me. While concentrating on the top edge of my knife, its shiny sides reflect all the dangers lurking around me. In these mirrored images, even the smallest details of life become prominent as each is reflected on the knife's blades from the more hidden valley below.

In such volatile moments I retreat from thoughts of the past or future and become focused on the immediate present. Every heartbeat is heard. Every breath is felt. Every hair is raised. In this extreme state of alertness, I evaluate my center—my goals, values, thoughts, character, and especially which voices inside me to tune in or out.

In most of life, I take living for granted and assume I have plenty of time to accomplish anything I want to do. Since time seems so bountiful, it's easy to waste it doing nothing. How often have I spent a whole evening in front of boring television, eating unsatisfying junk food, feeling sluggish and dull? In moments like these, life is cheap and its exquisite value unappreciated. But at times when I am pushing life to its limits, there is recognition of the volatility of life. In these moments life is priceless. The present moment, all moments, become sacred. Full attention is paid to each second—to each detail. Nothing is missed or unexamined.

At the top of that mountain in Zion and on this evening in Vancouver, I recognized the preciousness of life and how much I want to honor, live, and preserve it. The risks and challenges I have chosen in life have been carefully assessed and calculated, and not carelessly assumed. They are an attempt to live life to its fullest and add value to each day.

But now as I crawled into bed, it was time to quit thinking. I had a lot to prove tomorrow on my first full day of riding. After having dropped my motorcycle at the Harley school, I no longer believed that pure will was enough to sustain me. It would take more than determination and good intentions to survive tomorrow.

9
White-Knuckled Imposter

As I woke up the next morning, the German saying, *Aller Anfang ist schwer*, or *All beginnings are difficult* surfaced. This advice was repeated to me often as an eighteen-year-old exchange student living in Germany, struggling to learn their language and culture while living with my host family, the Standaus.

This morning as I crawled out of bed and dressed for breakfast, I thought about the challenge of motorcycling a couple hundred more miles today. Since we really hadn't done much riding yesterday, today would be my first real test of whether I could keep up with the group and be competent enough to continue riding my own motorcycle during the next nine days.

From experience I knew that as the trip progressed, these hard starts would give way to easier and easier days. Rocky's message—"Riding should be fun!"—reminded me to enjoy today's journey.

After breakfast we rode across the street to board the ferry from Victoria Island to Port Angeles, Washington. We lined up so early that we were the first motorcycles to board. As we rode onto it, our group was split in half. A crewmember directed Ron and me to ride along the left side of the ferry to the front and Eva and Alberto on the right.

Signs on the walls instructed us to park our motorcycles parallel to the outside walls—the opposite of yesterday's instructions. There were no blocks to immobilize our tires. Instead, ropes tied them to the ferry's sides. Standing back and evaluating our tethered bikes, we decided they appeared vulnerable, but we were still novices at motorcycle ferry travel, so we reluctantly complied with the posted instructions and headed upstairs.

On the deck above, we were excited by our excellent view of the port's activity. A small airport ran alongside our ferry's wharf. Planes with pontoons took off and landed next to us in the water. I counted at least eight small water taxis nearby that carried about twenty people each. There was bustling energy everywhere and we enjoyed being a part of it.

An hour after leaving the dock, as our ferry moved out of the protected waters of the bay and headed across stronger opposing cross-currents coming down the strait from the Pacific Ocean in the west, our ferry rocked severely from side to side, and everyone had to grab onto something to avoid falling.

Alberto and Ron looked at each other, nodded, and ran downstairs to check our motorcycles. When they returned, they were shaking their heads. Both Alberto and Eva's motorcycles, parked on the right front of the ferry, had fallen over. Neither had been badly damaged as both had engine guard bars that had kept their sides from hitting the floor, but there were still several minor scuffs on each.

Ron told me that, luckily, our motorcycles, parked along the opposite wall, were still standing. He mentioned that my new rental motorcycle had no engine guards on it. If my motorcycle ever fell over, minimally a turn signal light and possibly more would break. I gulped and nodded. My immediate thought was that if I ever bought my own motorcycle, engine guards would be the first accessories I'd purchase.

Ron suggested that as soon as we disembarked in the States we should find a gas station and fill up, since not all of our bikes had full tanks—some had been trailered to the hotel where we started, and others ridden.

As with many motorcycles, our bikes didn't have gas gauges. Several had reserve tanks. All had a red warning light on the speedometer face that should come on when a tank was almost empty. The word *should* is a deliberate choice, since everyone knew of circumstances when their bike was suddenly gulping for gas without the warning light being lit.

With many reserve tanks, riders can simply reach down and flip a switch to engage their backup. This can be done while still riding at normal speeds, but I wasn't excited by the prospect of having one more new thing to execute while riding. I already felt I needed two more sets of hands. Controlling a motorcycle that is riding roughly because it needs more gas, while fumbling to locate a switch somewhere on the side of my bike, was an exercise I suspected would be beyond my capabilities—especially in traffic.

The two common methods for estimating the level of fuel in your gas tank are using mileage, or when you really know your bike, noting that it's heavier when full and lighter when empty. I decided to use the mileage calculations since subtleties like the varying weight of my motorcycle were too hard to notice. Motorcycles always felt heavy to me.

After leaving the ferry in Port Angeles, Ron signaled and turned into a gas station. I pulled up to an available pump, uncertain what to do next. Although some people fill their motorcycles without getting off them, I decided that it would be easier for me to first dismount instead of trying to keep my bike perfectly balanced with my legs as I reached over to press buttons on the pump and lift the gas nozzle. Besides, I needed to remember where I had stashed my credit card.

As I started to get off my motorcycle, while holding my gloves in one hand and keys in the other, it leaned heavily against my left leg. As the bike tilted still further to the left, I realized that I must have forgotten to put down its kickstand. It continued falling over as I tried to bring it back upright by pulling on the handlebars and pushing against its body with my left thigh, but I wasn't strong enough. The teetering motorcycle fell over with a heart-breaking kerrish sound as its side hit the cement, followed by a loud pop and clinkering noise as the left turn signal bulb split and shattered, fulfilling Ron's earlier prediction.

I had made another beginner's mistake. I called out to Ron and Alberto for assistance, and they helped me lift my motorcycle back to a standing position. It was undamaged except for the broken left yellow turn signal. The bulb looked pathetic dangling by its wiring. I had remained standing, so this time I wasn't crushed under my motorcycle's weight—at least I had learned that much.

I could feel the heat rising in my cheeks and knew my embarrassment must be showing in my red face. Eva cheerfully tried to put a positive spin on the situation. "Don't worry. Riding without a front turn signal light isn't a big deal, especially since you'll be traveling in the middle of our group." She walked over, slung her arm around my shoulder, and gave me a quick shoulder hug, determined to bolster my spirits.

"Got any duct tape?" Ron asked.

I pulled it from my bag and patched the light into place, but its yellow cover was too far gone. Duct tape and bungee cords are fast solutions for many biking problems. Unfortunately, neither works on bruised pride.

Why is learning the hard way always such a powerful teacher?

Sitting on my bike waiting for the rest of the group to reappear from inside the station, I started to think about macho behavior. My understanding of the term "macho" was male behavior emphasizing strength, determination, and aggression to achieve a desired result. I had recently heard a new term "macha" used to describe the female equivalent. I wondered whether I had just experienced the negative side of this macha behavior.

A few moments earlier when I realized my motorcycle was starting to fall over, if I had acted quickly, I could have called on Ron or Eva who were standing less than a few feet away to help me out. Instead, I chose to attempt the undoable myself. I pride myself in being a strong woman and enjoy the well-earned exhaustion that comes after hard physical work and play. I also love learning and accomplishing things without unnecessarily relying on others. This behavior, often an asset since I live and work alone, had today become a liability.

On the road again I thought about how I could take this road trip, leaving a lot of my personal history behind, but still I couldn't escape who I was. I have often felt that life is like a masquerade party. Life's lessons keep reappearing disguised in different costumes and playing out in new venues. Hadn't I just recognized yesterday how nice it was not to have to do everything while surrounded by such competence?

It was time to take a vacation from this persistent independent streak I had been forced to master these past eighteen months. No longer could self-sufficiency be the extent of my repertoire; it was too limiting. Leading a balanced life would mean choosing to be either independent or assisted, based on what made sense, not on what had become habitual.

Over the next several hours, as we drove across the northern end of Washington State on Highway 101, the chattering inside my head drowned out the noise of both my motorcycle and the wind. On this first full day of riding, I was awash with emotions and self-talk. As feelings of fear and insecurity rose inside me, I'd quickly talk myself clear of them, excusing them, returning my full attention to riding. Processing and giving fear a voice while riding was a needless distraction.

Since little about motorcycling was routine, I constantly recited what I needed to do each moment, every second. I was grateful that I had memorized the sequences of starting, stopping, shifting, and braking during the motorcycle classes. Then the acronyms and phrases seemed silly, but now these verbal tools were my most trusted companions.

We rode through many small and medium-sized towns peppered with stop signs and traffic lights, giving me plenty of shifting, stopping, and starting experiences. As we approached each light, I'd smile if the light remained green or suddenly turned to green so that I wouldn't have to shift all the way down, come to a complete stop, then shift up through the gears again as I started back up. Stacked in these routine sequences were too many opportunities to mistime, misjudge, or just plain forget a step.

Since my motorcycle had no instrument showing what gear I was in, as I shifted through the gears, I'd say each one out loud to remind myself where I was in the series. Later I knew I'd be able to do this from the motorcycle's performance, vibrations, and sounds, but for now this was the only way to know what gear I was in.

Although I was tense riding a different motorcycle, it was also a lot of fun. I have always loved learning, and that day, what I was learning was obvious and visible. Each time I did something new or made it through a series of challenging turns, I'd grin.

Riding in our group I felt protected. Ron and Alberto were strong, seasoned riders. They divided themselves, one always riding up front in the lead position with the other bringing up the rear of the group. Eva was a strong rider too, but she readily admitted that Ron and Alberto were more experienced. It had also been over a year since she had last ridden; she had sold her BMW the previous year. So Eva and I rode cocooned in the middle, occasionally changing positions with each other, and I watched her constantly for cues about what to do next. It felt good to always have members of our group between me and other vehicles.

We usually traveled in a scattered formation in the same traffic lane. The lead motorcyclist rode on the left or right side of a single lane. Then each rider alternated (right and left in the same lane) so that we were always in a zigzag formation. This served a couple of purposes: by claiming the whole width of a lane, it kept cars from trying to share part of our lane as they passed us, and the alternation allowed each biker more room to brake safely if we needed to stop suddenly. When we pulled up to stoplights, we formed a tight pack lining up in two-by-two formation.

Our routes were chosen for their scenery, riding fun, and being as far away from mainstream traffic as possible. The more twists, turns, ascents, and descents a road had the more excitement for a motorcyclist and anyone who preferred enjoying the ride over reaching a destination. Even though I had some riding practice on Virginia country roads before this trip, this was a new experience. I'd never taken curves at any real speed, in heavy succession, or over long distances.

At midday, heading south on Route 101, the highway became a challenging four-lane curving road. Through every twist and turn in the road, I practiced what I had learned in Harley school—decrease a curve's bend by going from the outside edge of my lane before the curve to the inside edge in the middle of the curve and then back to the outside of my lane at the end. Doing this while traveling fifty to sixty miles per hour, with cars streaming by in three lanes around me, was frightening. I leaned forward, gripped my handlebars, and held my breath through the S-curves.

Remembering the story from the previous evening about how Ron and Alberto had gotten separated in Romania, I gritted my teeth as I regulated my speed, determined to remain solidly in the middle of the pack behind Eva.

With the curves coming toward me faster, one after another in rapid succession, I wondered if it was time to give up this too-fast pace and slow down. Or could I hold on just a little bit longer and hope the road would straighten or the traffic would thin out? I couldn't imagine nine more days of such intense challenge.

Just as I was ready to unfurl my white surrender flag, I noticed Eva deliberately slowing down and allowing an ever-increasing gap between herself and Alberto, who was leading the pack. Letting out a heavy sigh, I copied her pace, silently praising her as I decreased my speed and unhunched my shoulder muscles.

Ron, who had been riding behind me in the last position, passed Eva and me waving, but Eva continued to hold her slower pace. Now for the first time we were the last riders. The four of us no longer traveled as a single compact motorcycle pack. Instead we rode in two groups—the men ahead and women behind—separated by at least a half-mile.

At the onset of the trip, we had agreed that we would ride as a group. *But whose responsibility was it to keep us together? Should the faster riders decrease their speed or the slower ones speed up?*

On the outskirts of the next town, we saw Ron and Alberto parked on the side of the road next to a restaurant. As we approached, they signaled us to join them. Eva and I pulled over, parked our bikes, and hung our helmets with gloves inside them from our handlebars.

"Those guys are crazy," Eva said to me.

"Hurry up, you slowpokes, we're thirsty," Ron called out as he held the restaurant door open for us.

"You guys are taking too many risks. You're going too fast," Eva said as she stomped by him.

"Aw, come on. It's just that you haven't ridden in a year. You're out of practice," Alberto said.

"You've ridden that fast on previous trips. Sometimes you've even gone faster than all of us," Ron said.

"You can ride any speed you want, but I'm not going any faster than what I feel is safe. And what about Linda? We'll just travel in two groups if you want to race like that."

I was grateful for Eva's strong stance and decided that I didn't need to say anything. It was obvious that I was pushing myself at any speed—even her slower one. Instead, I watched, curious to see how the group would work out its differences.

"We weren't going over the speed limit," Ron said.

"I don't care about the speed limit. That was too fast through all those curves with heavy traffic!"

After picking up our sodas and seating ourselves around a nearby table, Ron said, "Okay, you win. Look, staying together is important. So the slower riders will influence our pace."

"I agree," Alberto said, "and if any of us wants to charge ahead through a series of fun curves, we'll go ahead of the group, then pull off afterward on the side of the road. When the group passes, we can jump back in line at the end."

"That works for me," Eva said as Alberto and I nodded in agreement.

"One more thing," Ron said. "Anytime the front of the group can't see the back in their mirrors for more than five minutes, they'll pull over and wait. If the rear doesn't catch up in a reasonable amount of time, the front runners will turn around and go back to look for the missing members."

This sounded like a good practice since it would be easy for the group to get separated on curving roads where we didn't want to ride bunched up or when passing other vehicles on two-lane roads. It would also help when stoplights changed after the first riders had already passed through them. And there was always the possibility that a motorcycle or rider might break down, so this additional agreement made sense.

I was amazed at how easily Ron, Alberto, and Eva had resolved this issue. I knew from my corporate work in managing conflict that the clear initial goals set by Ron before the trip, combined with all of the trips they had taken together in the past, made what could have been a difficult resolution in other groups easy for this one. I was impressed. As a new member, I was enjoying watching and learning.

❧

It took creativity to be able to communicate during our rides. Occasionally, when we stopped for a long traffic light we'd yell to each other, but with insulated helmets covering our ears and multiple motorcycle engines roaring beneath us, it was difficult to hear each other.

The primary way was with hand signals. Some were common ones used by all bikers: A hand with the pointer finger held high over the head by the leader meant single file. A left arm and hand held straight down at seven o'clock indicated slowing or stopping. Whenever anyone spotted danger in the road—gravel, glass, oil, pothole—they would point at it with a shaking hand or foot motion as they approached the area.

Most groups create some of their own gestures and we were no exception. Our signals also became a great way to joke around and play. One favorite that always caused everyone to laugh was, rather than flipping someone the bird with a single middle finger, we'd simply hold the whole hand high in the air, wiggling all fingers back and forth. Somehow this gesture of five fingers flying had more impact than merely one finger. These flying fingers were used as a way to laugh, relieve tension, or indicate a minor victory in response to a challenge from one another.

However, one hand signal confused me. Alberto and then Eva held their left fists at helmet level, opening and closing their fingers as they passed. Perplexed, I returned the gesture, hoping that was the correct response.

On many motorcycles, turn signals have to be manually turned on and off after each turn. Since little about riding was automatic, I had not yet developed the automatic response of doing this and often forgot. With the roar of the engine, it was impossible to hear the subtle clicking of a turn signal that we hear in our cars. After receiving the opening and closing fist signal several times, I tried to figure out what it might mean. *Was it something about my glove? Did we need to talk at the next break?*

Finally, I noticed my right turn signal blinking on the front of my bike when my last turn had been over five miles ago. *That's what my fellow riders were trying to tell me: Turn off your turn signal.*

As we pulled up and halted at a light in the late afternoon, I realized I had barely noticed the scenery all day. I could recall only the most basic logistics of our ride. After arriving in Port Angeles, Washington, we had navigated local streets leading through an industrial part of town and turned west onto Route 101. I vaguely remembered that our route had passed through the edge of the Olympic National Forest, but other than the park signs announcing it, I couldn't recall a single image of these spectacular forests. At some point in the day we had seen the Pacific Ocean a few times, but I had only been able to afford fleeting glances in its direction.

At this point the adventure of the trip didn't involve observing beautiful scenery; instead my attention was consumed by my bike, the immediate highway, traffic surrounding me, and keeping track of where I was in relation to others in our group. I could have been in Kansas, Florida, or Vermont and not noticed the difference. Disappointed to be missing so much, I hoped I'd be able to notice more tomorrow.

Around 6:30 in the evening, at the end of what seemed like a very long day of riding, we were on the outskirts of Aberdeen, Washington, where our bed and breakfast was located. Since I had reserved our rooms for the trip, it was my job to direct the group to our lodging at the end of each day. To make this task easier, I had made a spreadsheet of information I had taken off the websites as I booked each place. Additionally, I had printed off a couple of pages about each town.

According to my research, Aberdeen is a small town of roughly 16,500 people on the east side of Gray Harbor. If we had wanted to drive our motorcycles twenty minutes west, the website for our B&B claimed we would be on the Pacific Ocean. It also boasted "breath-taking views of the Wishkah River, the Chehalis River, Gray Harbor, the port and activity-filled city of Aberdeen."

Finally, pulling into the driveway of the Harbor View Bed and Breakfast, I smiled as I parked my motorcycle. What was enticing was not the promised "breath-taking view" that was currently blocked by trees and other buildings as we stood in their courtyard, rather it was that I could exhale and breathe normally again. Leading the group up that last steep hill with four or five successive stop signs had meant stopping and then starting again on an incline—managing clutch, throttle, and brakes—while trying to read street signs and decide where to turn. I had held my breath enough. What I needed were *breath-giving* views, not *breath-taking* ones.

Our bed and breakfast was a cozy four-story, colonial revival house perched high on the hill overlooking the town. We were greeted by the owners and shown to our rooms furnished with Victorian antiques and lace accessories. The fragile rooms stood in sharp contrast to our heavy boots, leathers, canvas luggage, and grimy bodies.

As we were hungry and ready to relax, we hurriedly changed out of our biking leathers, showered, and put on jeans. We were refreshed and ready to walk into town for dinner.

Walking down Eleventh Street from Broadway Hill into the town below, I was more thirsty than hungry. The town's website had stated that in its earlier days Aberdeen was the roughest town west of the Mississippi, due to its prostitution, gambling, drug use, and violence. Well, at 7:30 on a Sunday evening in June, we could have sat down in the middle of many of the streets and played an undisturbed game of cards.

None of us was particular about where we ate this evening, which was a good thing since most restaurants were closed. After walking several blocks, we found a Chinese restaurant that was open and still serving dinner.

Inside we quickly ordered and began exchanging stories about the day. Everyone was excited by the scenery and to be on a road trip again.

"Here's to our newest rider. Linda, you did an awesome job today," Eva said as she lifted her glass in a toast.

Ron and Alberto joined her by nodding, lifting their glasses, and clinking mine.

"I can't believe you. Look how well you did today. And you've only been riding for four weeks! I truly didn't believe you could do it," Eva said.

"You were great," Ron said.

Alberto smiled and nodded.

"Your praise is way too generous. You guys took care of me all day. You put me in the middle, protecting me. What about dropping my motorcycle this morning and all the mistakes I've made all day, stalling my engine at lights and driving with my turn signal on for miles?"

"Very few people could have done what you did. You're incredibly brave," Eva said, reaching over and patting me twice on the hand.

When Eva decided on something, it was useless to argue. In the short period of time I had known her, I had already learned if I resisted, she'd simply dig in deeper. But her word *brave* to describe me was too much. I was many things—bold, terrified, determined, adventure-some, focused, confused, frightened—but *not brave*.

I couldn't remember a day when I'd ever been so continuously scared, berating myself for tackling such a hard goal, sure I might get injured at any moment. I had redefined the term *white knuckles*. Thank goodness for riding gloves to hide them and a vibrating bike as cover for my own shaking body.

"You guys have no idea how scared I've been all day. I'm anything but brave. I might have had a smile on my face, but that was only masking my true inner fears. You can't call me brave."

"Heck, I was scared today. I hadn't ridden a motorcycle in over a year," Eva said.

"Me too," Ron admitted. "I was on a different motorcycle. We were on new roads traveling through some complex curves. Around some of those corners you never knew what you were going to find."

"On a trip like this it always takes a few days to get back into the rhythm of riding again. Sure, I was scared too at times," Alberto said.

"It always takes a while for a group to relax and fall into comfort-able patterns. You're doing great," Ron said.

I had thought I was the only one masking my fears, but now I was finding out that my feelings had been a normal response and typical reaction to the first day of a road trip.

I had felt like an imposter all day, trying to act the part of a brave motorcyclist so I would be accepted. No one had shown fear on their faces, no one had talked about being afraid, but sitting at the table that evening, I was shocked that it was an easy topic for them to discuss. No one was embarrassed to admit feeling fear. In fact they laughed and accepted it as routine as they talked about it.

⁂

As we walked back to the bed and breakfast after dinner, we were quiet. The last quarter mile was uphill and although it wasn't a strenuous climb, we started to string out, no longer walking clustered together. None of us was used to continuously being a part of a larger interde-pendent group. This was our first opportunity all day to find our own space off our motorcycles.

Walking alone I thought about the discussion at the restaurant about fear and feeling like an imposter. Back in the mid-1980s when I had been in Citigroup's Private Banking group, female vice presidents were still outnumbered ten to one by men. Another woman in my business, also named Linda, and I decided to hold a cocktail party for the other women in our division. Twenty crowded into my Upper Eastside studio apartment, and it was hard to circulate.

The other Linda, who would have loved to have hosted her own TV talk-show, suggested that we go around the room introducing ourselves by answering the question: "What career did you aspire to and how did you get to where you are today in Citigroup?"

As woman after woman introduced herself, we were amazed by their impressive former experiences—a *National Geographic* photographer, a Peace Corps volunteer in Central America, a teacher of autistic children, small business owners, PhDs with impressive research. Everyone had a fascinating story.

Despite the striking array of skills and experiences, the consistent message was—*I'm not a legitimate banker, I didn't study finance or accounting, or if others truly knew my background, I'd never have gotten where I am today.* All implied they were imposters. Yet these women were leaders with impressive financial performances and achievements. Pat was a leading bonds trader who regularly outperformed her male peers in the market, Linda a top trust officer, and Jane a high-ranking relationship manager with an impressive and easily recognizable list of famous clients.

We sat there, mouths agape, as we listened to impressive histories coupled with confessed embarrassment. *How could such a vibrant group of intelligent women feel they were illegitimate frauds?*

When I went into work the next day, different men inquired about what had happened at the all-woman party. I shared our shocked discovery. Then I uncovered something equally amazing as man after man individually confided that he didn't feel legitimate either. One had graduated from a Class B school not in the Ivy League. Another studied humanities and not finance. All of these people possessed amazing qualities and were known as accomplished professionals, but when I pointed out these current accomplishments, they attributed their successes to luck, timing, professional contacts, or significant contributions by others.

What was different tonight from my corporate business experience was this road trip group of equally strong personalities readily admitted to feeling fear. I wondered, *Why this discrepancy?*

I noted that when I skied, people would talk about feeling fear before they headed down a difficult slope that challenged their abilities. In running, when we lined up at the start of a large 10K run or half-marathon, everyone spoke about not feeling up to the run, mentioning some injury or shortcoming in their preparation. Before they get on a scary amusement ride people often will boast about how frightening the ride is going to be and even make fun of their fear. Before and after making a speech, people willingly talk about stage fright.

I concluded: *Imposter fear comes from believing we've fooled others with our performance and now others will expect us to continue to perform above our ability.*

I didn't want Eva, Ron, and Alberto to believe that I was a better rider than I actually was because I felt I had ridden beyond my true level of competence today. It was scary to think that having seen me survive this day's challenges, they'd expect an even higher level of performance tomorrow.

I felt like a non-swimmer immersed in water, standing on her tiptoes, just barely keeping her nose above the surface. I didn't want to have to venture into deeper water tomorrow and drown. But I had learned today by watching Eva that all I would have to do is pull back if I felt the ride was getting too hard or dangerous. It was good to be with fellow riders who could talk freely about competence and fear, each of us taking responsibility for our own ride and safety.

I smiled, realizing what a special group I had been invited to join. At the end of the first day of riding I felt deeply satisfied. At least today's hard beginning was behind me. Even though I no longer felt as worried about being an imposter, tomorrow we would be riding a two-hundred-sixty-mile stretch along the coast of Oregon, and I wondered if I could repeat today's beginner's success.

10

Ménage à Trois
in Oregon

Be-be-be-beep, be-be-be-beeep, interrupted my deep sleep. As I reached over to hit the snooze button on my alarm clock, I felt disoriented and struggled to remember why I was sleeping in an iron-framed bed covered by a patchwork quilt like my grandmother would have made. Outside the window an unfamiliar sound of *kee-ow*, *kee-ow*, *kee-ow* pierced the morning air as a seagull flying overhead joined in a duet with my alarm clock when it went off a second time. Both were high-pitched sounds—one staccato, the other more glissando. In concert they roused me enough to remember that I was at a bed and breakfast in Washington beginning the third day of my motorcycle trip.

Lying in bed enjoying the precious silence before the alarm's next assault, I realized I was not alone. Two other noisy companions had joined me, delivering simultaneous monologues. These dichotomous partners—fear and excitement—had boarded the plane with me two days earlier and were still accompanying me.

Excitement chattered on enthusiastically about seeing the Pacific Ocean today and riding into scenic Oregon this afternoon. "Be proud, you're doing great," she encouraged. She raced on, praising me for how much I had learned yesterday and how great this whole adventure was.

Fear's stern voice roared that yesterday's performance was just beginner's luck. She forewarned that today would be even more challenging with the potential for failure looming everywhere.

The alarm interrupted again, playing its final trump card. Looking at the time, I realized I had ten minutes before I was supposed to be joining Eva, Alberto, and Ron at the breakfast table. Fortunately, hair styling and makeup weren't important on a trip like this. I'd soon be pulling on a helmet and hiding my face behind its shield for most of the day. I threw water on my face, ran a brush through my hair, pulled on my clothes, and raced downstairs. I'd finish packing after we ate.

As we pulled out of the parking lot and onto the city streets, I noticed how relaxed and natural Eva, Ron, and Alberto looked as they rode their motorcycles. They were familiar with which sounds and vibrations were noteworthy and which could be filtered out as normal. As an inexperienced rider it was all new to me—every significant and inconsequential sound and bike response caught my attention almost equally.

Back home while driving my car following a familiar route, I was often surprised by how little I remembered about the actual trip once I arrived at my destination because I had been so absorbed in thinking about other things. I quickly learned that on a motorcycle this behavior was dangerous, especially for a new rider like me.

Just as in any kind of intense sport or activity—whether it's motorcycling, tennis, a video game, or even operating a table saw—rapid actions and constant changes force participants to remain in the present, noting and responding to all new variables. Losing focus for even a moment can result in significant consequences.

I was already used to riding my bicycle on city and country roads so I was familiar with some of their hazards, but on a motorcycle, moving at faster speeds, things happened more quickly, escalating the price of inattention.

Yesterday I had been managing so many thoughts that I found myself reacting to what was happening to my motorcycle instead of studying what was around me and moving my bike across the safest areas of the road. Concentrating on the highway's surface ahead of my motorcycle, I realized that the road was like a never-ending conveyor belt continuously moving toward us. Our job as riders was to survey the belt ahead for dangers: cracks in the asphalt, gravel strewn across its surface, holes, bumps, manhole covers, sewer grates, pieces of tire tread, sand, leaves, painted lines, or mirror-like liquids (oil, power-steering fluid, air-conditioning condensation) pooled into slippery drips and puddles. Staying between the repetitious yellow and white ribbons to our left and right, our work was to find and steer across the road's best surface.

At times when all areas of the road appeared equally safe this became a mind-numbing chore, and the conveyor's monotonous voice lulled us into a land of no thinking, just repetitious riding. Without warning the belt could become a breath-stealing construction zone offering no sliver of safe driving surface. Gripping our handlebars, we'd bump across its gnarled surfaces, lifting our rear ends off the bucking motorcycles below us, trying to smooth out our ride. Leaning towards our windshields, we hoped the few inches of gained sight would give us an extra edge in making difficult choices.

From lullaby to hard rock we'd ride this continuous loop, never knowing what song would serenade us next—around the blind curve, over the hill's crest, or beyond the vehicle in front of us. It was an adventure we all enjoyed.

As the morning progressed I realized that motorcycling was a bit like dancing or listening to good music—the fun was in the moment-to-moment activity without anticipation of completion. A favorite saying among motorcyclists is: "It's all about the ride." I was amazed by how relaxing this present-tense focus was becoming. My mind felt less encumbered as it expanded with more silent spaces. My inner voices were mute.

I smiled and realized that I was doing the kind of mindfulness meditation on my motorcycle that I had been trying to learn to do on a cushion—staying present without letting my thoughts drift into ones about the past or future. Just remaining centered in the present moment without resistance. For me bicycling, skiing, dancing, and now motorcycling are my meditations of choice.

At midday, we saw the Astoria-Megler Bridge ahead of us. Its span reaches four miles across the mouth of the Columbia River from Point Ellice, Washington, to Astoria, Oregon. As we approached the bridge, I encountered another challenge of riding a motorcycle. Noticing the toll barriers ahead, I realized I would need money to pay the fee. But riding fully occupied my hands, and there was no way to get it out in advance. I tried to recall where I had stashed my wallet. Groaning I realized it had to be in my purse, stuffed inside one of the saddlebags, but which one?

I began plotting my course of action. When we arrived at the tollbooth, I'd have to stop my bike, put it on its side stand, hop off and open the side pockets to retrieve the necessary cash. I imagined a long line of irritated drivers as I rehearsed this scenario in my head.

As we approached the tollbooth, Alberto signaled that he was paying for all of us. I sighed in relief, again I was being taken care of by this group as I learned the ropes. Keeping a small change purse handy in a jacket pocket with money and credit cards for gas and tolls would become part of my ever-evolving motorcycle routine.

It was both scary and exhilarating to ride across this four-mile bridge with its arched, green body towering mightily above the Columbia River. Unlike in a car, where the automobile's body blocks much of the outside surroundings and muffles sounds, our motorcycles treated us to unobstructed panoramic views through the bridge's open, metal-body frame: water below—Columbia River to our left, bay connecting to the Pacific Ocean to the right—clouds above, Oregon straight ahead, and reflected in my two side mirrors, Washington growing smaller behind us.

I wanted to enjoy the experience as we rode across this structure, but the exposed views, flashing from all directions, revealed how high we were climbing into the sky. My battle to manage my aversion to extreme heights returned.

My furrowed brow and clenched hands reminded me of when I was a teen and learning to drive our fin-tipped 1962 Mercury Monterey across a long span over the Susquehanna River. I had been desperate to reach the other side, afraid that I would sideswipe either an approaching car or the cement side of the bridge. On the other hand, I wanted the thrill of staring at the spectacular river view. I ended up concentrating on keeping the hood ornament lined up with the white side road line and missed the scenery. But I had avoided my imagined catastrophe.

Again I was caught battling my dual partners—fear and excitement—pulling me in opposite directions. I wanted to lose the fear persona but wondered if his dismissal would wipe away excitement as well. Again every sense was heightened by my fear. Sounds of tires vibrating against the bridge's surface reverberated in my ears. Flashing metal of the bridge's structure consumed my sight. My alerted body was ready for flight, every muscle was tensed and ready to react to impending disaster.

My inner voice of reason stepped forward. Sitting rigidly on my motorcycle was dangerous, especially when riding on an uneven surface. Gently I did an inventory of my posture, reminding myself to straighten up, unhunch my shoulders, loosen my grip, drop my wrists, align my elbows, lift my head, and relax my jaw and stomach muscles.

Enjoy this wonder, I told myself as I gazed upward at the fluffy clouds approaching us, and then smiled as I gazed down at the dot-sized ships below in the sea on my right. The edges of my knife could also be used to intensify the beauty of this moment.

On the other side of the bridge we pulled into a sandwich shop parking lot to stop for lunch. I set my tray down on the table and scooted into the seat across from Eva.

"How about riding across that bridge?" she asked.

"It reminded me of getting on a rollercoaster as a kid. As my car crept up that first hill, I'd berate myself for going. After the first exhilarating descent, I'd continue the ride yelling, 'Hooray,' then 'Oh no,' followed by, 'Whoopee!'"

"It's like that for me too, scary but lots of fun."

As Alberto and Ron joined us, I asked them, "Have you noticed how fear and excitement come together as two sides of the same coin?"

After riding across that bridge, battling those two emotions, I thought about how every major change in my life has included simultaneous feelings of fear and excitement: graduation, marriage, starting a new job, and becoming a mother.

"What about skiing?" Alberto said. "Every time I stand at the top of a challenging descent, feelings of excitement mix with fear. But that's what makes it so much fun. Without the challenge and accompanying fear, there's only bland skiing."

"Admit it, you felt pretty good once you made it across that bridge," Ron added.

"I'm learning I can do a lot more than I thought. I love the adrenalin rush and satisfaction that follows doing something difficult. It makes me feel freer and lighter to discover there is one less thing to fear in life. On this trip alone, I feel as if I've already shed twenty pounds I'd been carrying around."

"It's funny how we avoid fear, protecting ourselves from it so we can enjoy life," Ron said. "But it's facing the fears and overcoming them that gives us the freedom to experience life."

Another light bulb had just lit up for me. This was probably one of the reasons Ron and I had stayed friends for so many years. We made each other think differently about life.

Motorcycling and skiing were teaching me to deal with my emotional partners and not run from them. I was learning that I was stronger than I'd ever thought. I enjoyed the aftermath of overcoming challenges, but wasn't ready for a life filled only with difficult hills and scary obstacles. I might be willing to drive over another high bridge tomorrow, but I was glad for what I hoped would be easier routes ahead of me today.

For most of the ride along the Washington coast on Highway 101, we were just far enough inland to have only a few glimpses of the Pacific Ocean, but once we rode into Oregon, the highway hugged the coast through most of the state, giving us great panoramic views of the ocean.

While riding, I could hear waves crashing, taste sea salt on my lips, and feel moist ocean breezes. Life so exposed was rich. I caught fleeting glances of the spectacular ocean scenery, then dutifully returned guilty eyes to the dull road ahead. At last, Ron signaled and pulled over into a roadside overlook area. We lined our motorcycles up next to his and dismounted.

"Look at this view," Ron exclaimed, raising his arms in the air as the four of us stood peering between tree limbs at an obstructed vista of ocean waves and sandy beach below.

"This isn't good enough," Eva said as she scaled the guardrail and began climbing down the headland's steep sixty-foot slope to the beach below. The three of us scrambled after her, unwilling to be left behind.

Most of my trip preparation had gone into learning to ride a motorcycle, none had been spent learning about the natural beauty and geography of the Pacific Northwest. As a result I was open to innocent discovery and unprejudiced by guidebook descriptions or geological explanations of the natural phenomena surrounding me.

Standing on the vast beach—at least one hundred yards deep and stretching for miles to the north and south—we were amazed. To our right, majestically rising out of the ocean close to shore was a rocky monolith. In front and to its left stood several smaller ones. They aroused my curiosity as I surveyed the area around me, trying to conjecture how they had been created.

"They're sea stacks, formed by the surf pounding against those cliffs and eroding the shoreline until only those pillars remained," Ron explained as he laughed, pleased at having accurately read the confused look on my face.

From a distance the tallest chocolate-colored stack appeared speckled with ivory sugar dots. We walked toward them, wanting to inspect them. Approaching the tallest one that stood several hundred feet high, Eva called out, "Look! Those spots are birds."

Hundreds of large white birds were nesting on its craggy surface and swarming in the air above and around it. When several birds landed close to us on the beach, they looked like seagulls with their light bodies, black heads, webbed feet, and long bills. I overheard a father nearby telling his young son that they were called terns.

As we continued walking north along the shoreline, we saw groups of people huddled around large tidal pools protected from the pounding ocean by clusters of rocky boulders. Peering into several we were amazed by the collection of pastel colors and variety of sea life—miniature sea urchins, sea anemones, kelp, and even a few small starfish and crabs.

Walking closer to other smaller rocks near the water, we discovered they were densely covered with clusters of small bivalve shells, barnacles, and rust-colored algae. As interior decorators and artists know, assembling common objects in a large collection often makes them more fascinating. If I had seen a single dark-colored shell growing on a rock, it would have been mildly interesting, but a colony of hundreds jammed tightly together created a spectacular texture.

Now I was ready for the science lecture and slide show I would have yawned at in high school. I wanted to know: *What's the relationship between these bivalves and the rocks they're cemented to? How long do they live? Why do they collect here and not somewhere else?*

Gazing at this captivating collection with childlike wonder, I wanted to reach out and touch it—first, to guarantee it was really there, and secondly, to learn more about how it reacted to being poked. Fortunately, there were signs cautioning visitors not to disturb these delicate ecosystems. I switched back into my adult persona and complied.

Even though it was early summer, the breeze was cool and our leather jackets were welcome, so we weren't tempted to take a quick dip in the ocean. But these beaches were still delightful, without swimming or wading.

From the road we had no way of knowing that the beach would be so alive and entertaining. There is much to be said for adventure following its own schedule. We had serendipitously stumbled onto an unannounced treasure. Thank goodness for Ron's impulsive stop and Eva's desire to get closer.

In the afternoon as I assessed the traffic around us, I felt dwarfed on my bike by SUVs, RVs, and pick-ups dragging campers or boats. Riding a motorcycle in this vacation-laden traffic was like being a small child in a crowd of giant adults, waiting for a track announcement in New York's Penn Station where the track numbers for departing trains are posted only when a train is ready to be boarded. Once the impatiently awaited track announcement comes crackling over the loudspeaker, everyone rushes madly in that direction, dragging their heavy suitcases behind them, trying their best to outmaneuver others in securing the most coveted seats on the non-reserved train.

As they rush towards the trains, most are not thinking about the possibility of a small child being hidden in the crowd—their sole focus is on their personal gain and destination. The shorter child may be able to outmaneuver and squeeze through smaller spaces to get to the front of the line, but there are also the hazards of being run over by suitcases, hit by elbows, or squeezed between larger merging bodies.

It's much the same on motorcycles. We could maneuver through traffic more easily than cars, taking advantage of narrower spaces, but our risks were greater. We were outweighed by several tons by most other vehicles on the road. And hazards were everywhere. Uneven pavement, or anything lying in the roadway, could throw our two-wheeled vehicles off balance, and we were invisible to the majority of drivers who only checked for similar-sized vehicles, if they even looked at all. Making a mistake in a car may mean only a crushed fender, but on motorcycles, we're the part that gets crushed.

Simple routines were settling in as we grew more comfortable riding together. We had formed a functioning pack armed with enough procedures, signals, and flow to be able to relax with each other as we rode.

Occasionally we'd see something unusual or noteworthy, such as a field full of llamas, a license plate that said "FRGTABTIT" that made us laugh, or a van with a pull-down TV screen playing Road Runner cartoons for the kids in the back seats. Using our well-developed sign language, we'd point out these humorous scenes to each other, nod, and laugh.

At rest stops we compared notes about anything memorable we had encountered and thought might interest the group. One such story involved an RV that drove fifteen miles under the speed limit for thirty miles, weaving back and forth across the centerline and making it hard for us to pass safely. We had all encountered it, but we each had our own version about what happened when we tried to go around it. So a simple incident grew into a complex anecdote as we shared and embellished it while sipping our cold drinks. It made me appreciate how tall tales such as those about Paul Bunyan might have gotten started. We were becoming animated storytellers.

These refreshment breaks and occasional stretches of easy roads offered times for restoring our energy. Ready to roar again, we'd head off on a side trip, looking for greater challenges, most often found on less well-marked back roads. We welcomed these byways as opportunities to tackle unknown canvases. Adrenaline pumped, energetic play erupted, and our spirits soared as we enjoyed the road and each other.

It had been a long time since I'd laughed, hollered, or belted out songs, but this was another advantage of riding on top of a roaring machine. It was like singing in the shower. The motorcycle's noise gave the illusion of privacy and covered up flaws in my singing and gleeful outbursts.

VRR-OOM became one of my favorite sounds to make. It vibrated up from my lungs and exploded through my lips. It's impossible to say vroooooooom without smiling and laughing. It's even better with the added animation of holding onto handlebars and pulling back on the right throttle as you elicit the noise.

As kids we had enjoyed making these machine sounds accompanied by matching gestures. Most kids pushing a toy vehicle on the floor will make engine noises. I guess it took becoming a kid again for me to fall back into that kind of fun.

Riding was now becoming more automatic. As I approached a stop, I'd shift my motorcycle and brake without verbally reciting the sequences out loud. I no longer popped the clutch by releasing it too fast. I drove more defensively, anticipating problems and making necessary early adjustments.

People say horses can sense a rider's fear and act out by balking, ignoring instructions, or running away. Although motorcycles are inanimate objects, I still believe that they sense the fear and ineptness of their riders and respond accordingly.

My motorcycle and I were becoming friends. It would be harder to say goodbye to it tonight. Now I understood why some motorcyclists furiously protect their bikes and would probably take them into their houses at night if they could. We were becoming symbiotic extensions of each other.

I have always enjoyed learning, but the real fun came when I made it past the beginner stage where mistakes and poor skills can abruptly interrupt the enjoyment. My learning curve had been steep these past five weeks, and I was still climbing with every additional hour on the motorcycle.

We had just pulled over for a late afternoon break after a challenging stint on a heavily traveled four-lane expressway when Alberto motioned me aside. He walked me away from Ron and Eva who were headed into the diner. At the edge of the parking lot he began:

"Linda, you're riding well for a beginner. I'm impressed. But I want to let you know that you made a serious error when you passed that black Jeep Cherokee a while back. You pulled back into her lane too soon, cutting her off. If the driver hadn't braked hard, you could have been killed. You have got to use your side mirrors and allow more space when changing lanes." As he awaited my response, the wrinkles on Alberto's forehead faded and his eyes softened.

A cold chill blasted through my body starting at my head and descending downward to my feet in a rippling wave. My body had been put on alert by his words: "You could have been killed." The sentence echoed, reverberating through me, permeating every cell. My earlier concern about too many places to look had been validated. The internal voice cautioning me that this road trip was too ambitious, that I wasn't ready for such a challenge, gained volume and roared. Another fearful warning about becoming too confident joined it. Reacting to this frightening chorus of fear-driven messages made a part of me want to give up and coil into a ball.

Instead, I tuned into the part of me that was more seasoned and rational. The one that had successfully led me through many more difficult minefields than this—the one that knew how to build strength, learn, and continue to flourish. I rested a moment in this center. I had felt so sure that I had been using my side mirrors well and allowing enough space before reentering lanes, but apparently I needed to be more vigilant and allow for a wider margin before pulling into any lane.

There was no use in trying to defend my performance. Instead, I looked directly at Alberto and said, "Wow, that's not good. Thanks for telling me. I'll be more careful and check my mirrors more often. Please let me know if I don't improve. I want to be safe."

He nodded, smiled, and appeared satisfied with my response. We turned and walked back toward the restaurant to rejoin the group.

Although we both jumped into Eva and Ron's conversation as if nothing had transpired, this wake-up call still resonated through me. Alberto's words kept repeating inside my head: *You could have been killed.* This was not a message to be forgotten.

One of the many things I appreciated about being older and traveling with others in my age group was that, in general, we were more skilled in being gentler with each other and with ourselves than when we were younger. Alberto had pulled me away from the others to tell me privately what he wanted to say. He started his feedback with praise about my overall riding performance and delivered his message succinctly. Then he remained silent, ready to listen to what I had to say.

I was able to accept his coaching without explaining or defending my actions. When we rejoined Ron and Eva, they felt no need to ask about what had transpired or to add to Alberto's message. It was managed and dropped.

Our society and the media often glamorize youth, but performances like the one I had just taken part in more often happen with maturity and experience. I sat silently eating, grateful for the miles we all had ridden in life and appreciating the skills we had developed.

I often find myself interpreting things that happen to me as good or bad. I've invested a lot of effort seeking out experiences I label as *good* while minimizing and avoiding those I consider *bad*. But how should I label Alberto's warning? Was it good, or was it bad? Similarly, what about dropping my motorcycle during the Harley training class—was that experience good or bad? Looking back in time at that fall, I believe it made me a better rider and prepared me for this trip, so now I view it as *good*. Four weeks ago when it happened, I was devastated and defeated. I even called it a "dark night of the soul" experience. But I learned a lot of important things from dropping it, such as how easy it is to underestimate the power and weight of even a small motorcycle. And it takes more than determination and intent to ride one well.

That accident forced me to practice many important skills to pass the DMV's difficult road test. I now knew that without that fall during the test, I probably would have opted to spend the majority of my pre-trip practice time having fun riding on highways, and spent only a small token of it practicing the more important, though boring, slow driving control and maneuvering in parking lots.

Now that I was facing the challenges of motorcycling on this trip, I was grateful for all I had learned from every riding mistake I'd made. I viewed the fall as *good* and an important experience that helped get me to the point where I could ride a motorcycle well enough to enjoy this trip. The dropped motorcycle in class might have even *saved* my life!

As a child I looked forward to adulthood when, I believed, I would finally know all of life's answers. But now I realized that life continues with its ever-evolving lessons. Maybe what I needed to do was change my habit of labeling things as *good* and *bad*, since these valuations continually changed.

I kept falling, brushing myself off, and promising to learn from my mistakes so they wouldn't be repeated. Maybe the key was simply to embrace life's adventures and relax, knowing that all perspectives change with time. Perhaps I needed to quit giving my life and performance a daily report card. I was learning that my grading system was faulty. It was finally time to *just be*—moving forward by accepting life's twists and turns, constantly changing routes, and the uncertainty of blind curves.

11
Set On Cruise Control

At the end of each riding day our alternatives for what to do in the evenings were restricted to the immediate vicinity around the small towns where we stayed. We tried to take life as it happened and not resist it, so some memorable times evolved naturally out of the minimal opportunities at hand.

On the third evening of our trip we concluded our day's ride near the small town of Yachats (pronounced YA-hots), boasting a population around 675 people. Despite its size, Yachats was the biggest town within twenty-five miles. A website listed the community's slogan: "We're all here because we're not all there." The corollary slogan was, "Everybody has to be somewhere."

Yachats was the closest town on the map that met our two-hundred-fifty-mile daily riding average. John had recommended we stay at our hotel for this evening because he said it sat less than a hundred feet from the Pacific Ocean. Several weeks earlier when I'd booked this place for the group, I hadn't fully appreciated its true value from the inch-and-a-half photo posted on a travel website.

Pulling into the parking lot, we nodded at each other and gave a thumbs-up sign of approval. The website was correct, we were directly on the ocean, close enough to hear waves crashing as we parked our motorcycles, and we walked in the direction of the office. *We'll hear this lovely sound all night,* I thought, smiling.

Remembering my goal not to do everything, I hung back and continued listening to the surf, letting Eva register for us. I shut my eyes, allowing the ocean's sounds to lead me to a relaxed place.

"Look! We got one on the second floor, facing the ocean," Eva announced waving the motel's room map in her right hand as she ran toward me. "We'll have a great view."

Unable to match her energy, I smiled appreciatively and nodded. *Where does she get all of that bounce?* I wondered blearily, while trying to focus on the moving map she held several inches from my eyes.

My head and chest were tired from the constant beating they'd received all day, blasted by the self-created wind of traveling on a motorcycle. My brain was awash with the daylong repetition of the road's surface of monotonous dreary colors—grays, blacks, slates, beiges, taupes, browns, ivories, whites. I was worn out from studying the subtleties of cement, blacktop, tar, sand, gravel, dirt, painted lines, and liquids on the road. My body longed to be free of its protective armored shell—helmet, jacket, pants, gloves, and boots—as my skin needed to touch the world around me.

Laden with motorcycle gear and multiple pieces of hanging luggage, I stumbled across the parking lot toward our motel room. I imagined collapsing on the awaiting bed, shutting my eyes and savoring a moment of rest and no outside stimulation.

Instead, as I jammed the key card into our hotel room lock and pushed the door open, I was bombarded by brilliant oranges, reds, and yellows streaming across the room toward me from the picture window and balcony at the far end of the room.

Dropping my gear on a bed as I passed it, I raced out onto the porch and breathed in colors with the gasping inhalations of a scuba diver who has just resurfaced after running out of air. The vivid sunset quenched a thirst that moments earlier I hadn't recognized. But now, staring at the vibrant colors, I wanted to dart outside and dance, engulfed by them.

Turning toward Eva, I was once again her energy equal. "Come on. Let's change and go down to the ocean before the sunset fades." Without waiting for her response, I quickly changed into jeans and sweater and dashed out the door with Eva running close behind, trying to catch up.

Moments later we were at the water's edge, hopping from rock to large rock along the shore, trying to get as close as we could to the surf without slipping or getting soaked by the crashing waves. After a day of breathing diesel and unleaded exhaust, I welcomed the natural beach smells of fish, kelp, salt water, and wet sand. Gentle sea spray blew across my face, carried by soft breezes that swirled around me as though unsure which direction to dance off to next. I inhaled deeply, shutting my eyes, still seeing the sunset's brilliant colors on the insides of my lids.

Everything wonderful becomes enough at some point, I thought. Although I enjoyed the motorcycling, this gentler energy tonight felt like a luxurious correction.

I was awakened from my brief meditation with a shout. "Hey, over here!" It was Ron waving at us with Alberto standing on the rocks nearby. Eva and I looked at each other, nodded, and jogged over to join them.

The Pacific Ocean often pounds its shores with more force than the Atlantic, and I love its drama. All along the beach were large rocks, many piled together, forming lines that jutted out into the ocean. The tide was coming in, making the ocean's actions more intense. As successive waves rolled in, building in volume and strength, every fifth, sixth, or seventh one hit the rocks and sent a geyser-like eruption of water shooting upwards into the air fifteen to thirty feet. After this great crescendo that included a series of several repetitive bursts, the size of the waves would wane again until the ocean became gentle, almost calm and whispering, before repeating the same scenario. It was a beautiful display against the sunset's fiery backdrop.

Finding seats among the rocks, we counted successive waves, calculating when the next big wave would crash and onto which rocks. But too soon the light show faded, leaving our stage black, while the ocean continued its symphony without visual accompaniment. We stared longingly at the horizon, wishing for an encore but knowing it was over for the evening. Reluctantly we headed back to our rooms, making plans as we walked for when and where to meet for dinner.

Although I have always enjoyed being a woman, I have deliberately rewritten her stereotypical behavioral boundaries to include a more androgynous mix of feminine and masculine traits. It was fun riding a macho vehicle, wearing male-influenced, durable clothing, and pushing myself both mentally and physically to control a powerful machine. But now another part of my personality was surfacing. It was more subtle, but equally powerful.

After three days of wearing heavy leather jackets and pants, T-shirts, and railroad handkerchiefs, Eva and I were ready to dress up and feed our frillier, softer, feminine sides. We dug to the bottom of our road bags for the high-heeled sandals and skirts we had packed for such a moment. Forty-five minutes later—having showered, applied makeup, curled our hair, dressed in our sexy outfits, and added some fun jewelry—we had transformed ourselves.

"Not bad," Eva said as we examined ourselves in the same mirror.

While we were getting ready, the men had scoped out a gourmet restaurant in the small town nearby and arranged for the local taxi to pick us up. It was our routine to take taxis at night, parking our bikes, so that we could enjoy good wines with dinner. As we stepped toward the taxi, I found Alberto opening the door for me. I looked up and smiled sweetly. It was good to be treated like a lady again—there was no need to fit into a male world tonight and we were all enjoying the change.

We were hungry and our excitement built as we huddled around the gourmet menu posted on the restaurant's window. However, when Alberto tried to open the door, despite his strength it didn't budge. Confused, he pulled on the door handle several more times, but all it did was rattle louder without opening; it was definitely locked.

"Look," Eva said, pointing to a sign listing the restaurant's hours. "Isn't tonight Monday? That's the only night of the week they're closed."

We looked around disappointed that our taxi had left. We'd need to find another place to eat within walking distance, but downtown appeared to be only a few blocks long, running directly along the main highway. Most of the neighboring two-story buildings appeared deserted and there weren't any people around. Searching the area for someone local to help us out, Eva spotted a man locking his office door.

"Are there any good places to eat within walking distance?" she asked.

"Well, with shoes like those, you have few options. Most local businesses close by 7:30 on weeknights. Too bad this spot's closed," he said pointing to the restaurant behind us. "It's a nice place."

"Are there restaurants outside of Yachats we could try?" Ron asked.

"Well, there's a number of good places north on 101 in Newport. Or you could go south and try Florence, but that's more of a retirement community, so they probably closed up early. Both are about a twenty-five minute drive."

It was already 8:30. By the time we made it back to the hotel, changed into motorcycle clothes, and rode to either town, we knew there would be little chance of finding any restaurant open. Asking a few more questions, we learned our only choice, other than vending machines, was a bar a few blocks away. It had a restaurant next door that would be closed, but our helpful guide was certain the bar itself would have some food.

Convinced this was our only choice, we decided to make it into our next adventure. Eva and I we were overdressed for a local bar, but we were past the age when fitting in was always important. We'd still have a good evening, just a different one than imagined.

The bar was at the far end of a long building sitting directly on the highway. From the outside at night it didn't look very interesting, and as I walked in the front door, my heart sank. The entry room was dimly lit and felt gloomy. In sharp contrast to the fresh ocean breezes we had inhaled at sunset, this air was filled with stale cigarette smoke. Every sensory organ in my body shouted, "No!"

The place was almost empty except for a few people sitting at the small bar just inside the front door. Across the floor next to darkened windows were a few small tables with mismatched chairs and a dance floor the size of a postage stamp. There was a large game room to the left with four full-sized pool tables. We pushed two tables together, pulling up chairs after rejecting several that wobbled.

A young blond girl, close to the age of my youngest daughter, hesitantly approached us, holding a small tablet in her hand. She stood in front of us, gazing down at the floor, not saying anything.

"Could we see menus? We'd like to order dinner as well as drinks," Alberto said.

"I'm sorry, the kitchen is closed," the waitress said.

"We were told you had a bar menu. Could we order some bar food?" Eva asked.

"I'm not allowed in the restaurant kitchen, so I don't have any way to cook anything. The best I can do is cold ham and cheese sandwiches."

Rather than grumble, we began talking with her. Amidst our laughter and joking, she began to want to help us with our hungry plight.

"Could you just look the other way and we'll sneak into the kitchen and heat up something ourselves?" Ron asked.

We all played along, leaning in to show her our most desperate wide-eyed faces.

"If you'd like, I could use the microwave and warm up some clam chowder to go with the sandwiches."

When we didn't respond, she rushed to add, "No, really, it's great chowder. It's homemade."

Then bending in closer toward our group, looking cautiously over her shoulder to her right and then to her left, she continued in a low voice while we played along, leaning forward to hear her whisper, "I shouldn't say this, but it's even better than my grandmother's chowder, and hers has a reputation for being the best."

"Then I'll have a sandwich and your prized clam chowder," Ron said.

"I'll have the same," Alberto added.

"Since you already have ham, cheese, lettuce, and tomatoes, instead of a sandwich, do you think you could make mine a large salad?" I asked.

"Me too?" Eva said.

"Sure," she said, pleased with her ever-expanding menu. She finished by taking our drink orders.

We cheered her on as she disappeared to prepare our simple dinner.

I was surprised by the attitude of our group. This was so opposite from the gourmet dinner we had envisioned at the beginning of the evening, but everyone simply accepted it, ready to enjoy whatever came along.

Concert posters covered the poolroom walls and the jukebox was filled with classic oldies. Alberto collected quarters from everyone and loaded the box with his choices. He had exquisite taste. It's amazing how fast the atmosphere of a place transforms with the right music. Soon we were singing along to the familiar 50s and 60s oldies, laughing because we all knew most of the lyrics to the same old favorites.

It's impossible to hear The Five Saints' popular song, "In the Still of the Night," and not join in on the "Shoo-Bee-Do" backup singers' part, or to hear the chorus of "Gloria" sung by Them and not join in spelling out her name G-L-O-R-I-A in the chorus. And when songs like "Good Lovin" or "Good Golly Miss Molly" are played, it's hard not to dance in your seats or better yet, on that postage stamp of a dance floor.

Many of these oldies' lyrics were ones we had taken so seriously when we were teenagers. But now, many years later, they made us laugh.

Times were easier when Fats Domino sang, "I want to walk you home," the Beatles recorded, "I want to hold your hand," and The Big Bopper belted out, "Chantilly Lace." Our greatest romantic concerns were being walked home from school or holding hands with a boy. Sex appeal, as described by the Bopper, was having a swishing ponytail and wearing lace. These songs dated us, but they also connected us because we shared a love for them. They were a backdrop for our lives in the 1950s and '60s.

Dinner arrived and the chowder was as our waitress had described—it would easily win first prize at any state fair. Our salads were delicious. She had become so inspired that each plate was filled with many extras—croutons, hard-boiled eggs, peppers, onions, olives—the works.

To our left were empty pool tables with no players. I am never good at games that require exacting calculations and precision moves, so I was hoping no one would suggest we play, but that wish wasn't granted.

Eva jumped up saying, "Let's play!" Meandering toward the tables, I reluctantly picked out a cue stick and chalked it. I reminded myself that this trip was about breaking out of my comfort zone and erasing old boundaries. Besides, saying no to this group about something fun wasn't possible.

Tuning into his competitive side and ready for a quick victory, Alberto called out, "It's men against the women." Not having played in twenty years, I was sure we women would give the men the quick victory they hoped for. But life can be unpredictable.

No one took the game too seriously. We laughed when balls that were perfectly lined up, and should have gone in, bounced off the sides of the pockets. Other shots that shouldn't even have been close teetered on the lip of the pocket and then fell in.

The score wasn't as important as the joy of playing and the unending script it gave us to find something new and amusing to joke about. It's hard to tell if it was the Long Island Iced Teas Eva kept ordering and then insisting that the men finish, our inappropriately distracting clothing that was not suitable for leaning over a pool table on long shots, just wild luck, or the magic of a road trip—but we managed to come from behind and win the best two out of three games.

"You thought you had us, didn't you?" Eva chastised Alberto and Ron. "Never underestimate the power of two biker chicks." She grabbed my hand and raised it high above our heads in a victory pose. "Well, where are the cameras? I want this moment preserved for history. By tomorrow, you'll be claiming it never happened."

We were so entertaining several people from the bar finally wandered over to meet us. As locals often do when strangers invade their home-town haunts, they had been guessing our history all night. Now, no longer able to contain themselves, they wanted to find out who was right. Their bar tab was riding on our answers.

The only hypothesis they had right was that none of us was married to another in the group. They had ruled that out, they laughingly explained, because we all got along too well together. They were fasci-nated to learn that we were on a motorcycle trip. This possibility had eluded them. We were too dressed up. Since Eva and I had occasionally spoken German to each other as we plotted our team's strategy at pool, they had decided we were Europeans on holiday.

Walking out of the roadhouse, I realized my original impression again had done a 180-degree reversal. This was a place I'd gladly revisit. Also the local Yachatians in the bar were people I wished we had engaged earlier in the evening. I should have figured that one out by the sweetness and resourcefulness of our young waitress. She stopped our spirits' downward spiral and set our evening spinning in an upward trajectory. It was amazing what a good time we found in this little town and the Landmark Bar.

Those of us used to living in large metropolitan areas have literally hundreds of options to fill our social time: whom to spend time with, what restaurant to go to, and what activity we would like to do on any particular night of the week. There are so many choices that a lot of energy and time can go into discussing, choosing, and arranging the best plan. But even with this wealth of possibilities, at the end of any evening we are often left wondering whether a different restaurant or another pastime might have been a better choice. Remorse amongst riches is not uncommon.

Rural communities are much different. I know from growing up in a small town that although they may offer limited choices, residents become expert in crafting celebrations out of ordinary events. A snowstorm becomes a sledding party or neighborhood pancake breakfast. A hot night in August turns into a reason to have a picnic and sprinkler party. A purportedly important visitor may bring out the whole town.

Our road trip was a bit like living in a small town where the people are the primary source of entertainment. Whatever was offered each day—the sunset, ocean, chowder, jukebox, pool tables, or local people at a bar—became the source of great amusement and a stage for the group's escapades. Accepting the area's limitations without resistance allowed our group to funnel our energy into playing with what was available.

If we'd had twenty restaurants to choose from that night, it would have been more difficult to plan. Instead, our only choice was to embrace our one limited option, discover its possibilities, and create from whatever was present. From limitations came wealth. Our palette had been minimal, but we had created a masterpiece of a good time and memories to talk about on this and future road trips.

12
Guard Rails

Sipping from my water bottle during our first break of the morning, I leaned against a guardrail overlooking scenic Coos Bay in Oregon. I admired the impromptu fashion show created by motorcyclists as they pulled off to view the panoramic ocean scene below. Turning to Eva I confided, "Isn't this great? I've never been around so many bikers before. Some are fairly comical, but others are worth a second look."

"After this trip, you'll be changed forever. Men in leather can be so hot," said Eva.

"I love people-watching. This reminds me of an Easter Parade—like in old movies where New Yorkers dressed in their finest, strolling down Fifth Avenue just to be seen."

"What are you girls talking about so seriously?" Alberto interrupted as he and Ron joined us.

"Oh, we're just discussing how no one rides a motorcycle to be ignored," Eva said.

Just then, on the highway behind us, a pack of twenty bikers roared past. When we could finally hear each other again, I asked, "Why are motorcycles so loud? Can't they be made quieter like cars so they don't disturb everyone else's peace?"

"Motorcyclists will tell you, *loud pipes save lives,*" Alberto said. "Every biker has personal stories about nearly being run over by cars and trucks changing lanes or pulling out in traffic. If they won't look for us, at least we want to be heard."

"Oh, I thought it was all about rebellion, sounding tough and being different," I said. "Our bikes aren't that noisy, are they?"

They nodded and laughed.

"We're all loud. You just don't notice it when you're wearing a padded helmet and your sound is roaring behind you," Ron said.

"Linda's got a point," Alberto said. "Many motorcyclists spend a lot of effort fine-tuning their sound to be distinctive and unlike others. It's their own personal signature as well as a way to make a lot of noise. That's what we guys like to do—make noise and blow things up."

As I walked back to my bike, I thought about how motorcyclists with their noise, customized bikes, and distinctive dress, make statements and rebel against mainstream lists of "proper" behaviors. Paradoxically, as with all alternative groups, in their break from the norm they've created an even more stringent list of acceptable "ins," or in this case, "outs."

As we got back on our bikes and headed south again, I mused that, before learning to ride a motorcycle, I had never noticed the diversity within this community. I had always assumed motorcyclists were either the stereotypical young daredevil kids riding too fast on souped-up, screaming rockets, or older, patriotic rednecks, sporting tattoos, beer bellies, and long hair tied at the back of their necks. Now I had begun to recognize many other variations.

Young kids often prefer Japanese sports bikes, specializing in speed. Many wear brightly colored riding suits matching the vivid colors of their bikes. Unnecessary weight has been eliminated from these sports bikes. The bodies are composed of molded plastic and fiberglass with less metal and chrome. These sports riders lean forward over their bikes' engines, keeping their bodies low to minimize wind resistance. The sound emanating from their smaller, lighter pipes is higher pitched and squealing. Typical of youth, this group is more likely to exceed speed limits, weave in and out of traffic, and aggressively test the limits of their bikes and themselves.

Then there's the older patriotic crowd who willingly pays extra dollars for the famous loud-piped rumbling sound of the Harley engine and classic body. This group dresses more casually—often in jeans, vests, and Harley T-shirts. Even in states with laws requiring them to wear helmets, many sport only token half helmets.

BMWs hold a reputation for being luxurious and expensive machines to ride and are often preferred by a wealthier professional population of riders who value engineering over tradition. These riders will tell you that they care more about riding and less about how they look on their bikes, or where they can go to park their bikes and be seen and admired by others.

And then there's the retiree population of husbands and wives who ride what I call an RV version of a touring motorcycle complete with cup holders, air conditioning, heat, cigarette lighter, computer panels, stereo sound system, GPS, luxurious padded seats, running boards, extra foot rests, hard-cover luggage compartments, and every kind of comfort gadget that can be fitted onto two wheels. These bikes are so laden down by weight and bulk that they never take curves fast. They focus instead on the riders' comfort. Many riding companions on these RV touring motorcycles have two-way communication systems fitted into their helmets so they can talk easily and often with each other as they ride.

Whenever I asked Harley riders what they thought of a Yamaha or Suzuki, their responses reminded me of those of Red Sox fans when asked what they think of the Yankees. Despite all these differences, motorcyclists of all types seem to enjoy a shared camaraderie, and now I was one of them. We all face the same challenges when riding down roads on two wheels—our bodies exposed to the elements, surrounded by road hazards and unpredictable traffic that's not looking for us. This kinship among riders is expressed with a left-handed greeting or wave when motorcyclists pass each other on the road. This wave typically is given at handlebar level or lower, the hand is merely held out, not waved up and down. Like a signature, each biker develops their own style.

Even though I had plenty on my mind as a new rider, I enthusiastically took part in this ritual. On the first two days of this road trip my wave was jerky and ambitious, but as I became more of a rider, it became smoother, subtler, and more relaxed. I guess that is true of most gestures in our culture; the more experienced, the more natural and understated a gesture becomes.

I looked up as Ron passed me, pointing at a sign on the side of the highway: WELCOME TO CALIFORNIA. Riding behind Ron I thought about how different he looked on this trip from the way I usually saw him in his perfectly pressed business clothes. Now he wore the same faded motorcycle jacket he had worn for the past ten years. I had kidded him that he should at least get the ripped seam across his shoulder re-sewn, but that wasn't important to him. Every rip and tear was another story and precious memory.

At the restaurant, when I first met Alberto, his expensive silk suit had impressed me, and Eva had dressed in a stunning black dress with bright turquoise jacket and matching large-beaded necklace. Both had looked professional and businesslike, but on this trip, Ron, Alberto, Eva, and I had deliberately left our business identities at home. We enjoyed stepping out of character and into a fantasy world while riding our motorcycles. It was like being at an unending Halloween party where unusual costumes and assumed personas were expected.

It's impossible to look at someone on a motorcycle and know what they do for a living. A man riding an old heritage-style motorcycle, wearing a well-worn jacket covered with skulls and crossbones over a muscle shirt that has seen better days, is as likely to be a corporate executive as a machine welder. And just as at a masquerade party, no one asks what a person does for a living; it's immaterial.

During our unhurried breaks from riding, everyone in our group started conversations with people we met. Whenever one of us began chatting with someone, the rest of us eventually joined in. We'd stay and talk to the person attending the gas station, serving us at the sandwich shop or anyone passing by. In these conversations we shared what we had seen and learned during our ride and appreciated whatever the locals had to offer. Everyone had a story to tell, and we stopped to listen. It was wonderful to savor these moments, knowing we had the luxury of time.

I met young teens covered in tattoos, their bodies heavily pierced with metal ornaments. They came up to me and asked where we had ridden, something about our motorcycles, or where we were from. I was amazed by how easily these conversations started and how much we had to share. Behind their metal and inked façades, they were just curious individuals—as interesting and vulnerable as me.

I was amazed by how little I knew about the world around me. We're surrounded by media pumping out news and information, we interact daily with a variety of people, using email, cell phones, and social media, we travel more widely than previous generations. With all of this exposure, I assumed I was well informed about our country and its people, but on this road trip, it became apparent that I deal with a small sliver of the diverse population represented in our country. Wearing motorcycle clothes and taking time to talk to people along the way was opening a door to some wonderful types of people I had previously excluded.

Later that afternoon at a stop in Crescent City, California, I came out of a gas station. Parked next to my bike was a huge, fully-loaded motorcycle, the kind I call RV-motorcycles. I walked closer to get a better look and stood peering at it as if I were a six-year-old at a pet shop staring at a pen of puppies.

Behind me someone called out, "Isn't she a beaut!"

Startled, I turned around and saw a man and woman walking toward me.

"I'm Bob, and this is my wife Darcie."

Bob and Darcie were the kind of couple you'd expect to meet at a church ice cream social—not exiting a dusty gas station, its walls covered with old calendars featuring scantily clothed women, advertisements for STP oil, and posters hyping the pleasures of chewing Skoal tobacco.

If I had been asked to pick out two people who were married to each other, from a lineup of a hundred, it would have been easy to match up Bob and Darcie. Aside from their obviously similar ages—around sixty years old—and having faces that had morphed to resemble each other over the years, they carried identical jumbo insulated drink cups. But the dead giveaway was their attire: they wore matching fluorescent-yellow leather riding jackets, pants, and helmets that coordinated perfectly with their same-colored vehicle. Their helmets sported microphones attached to the sides for talking as they rode.

"Come, take a closer look at her," Bob said. "She's got everything. I bought her fully loaded."

"We got tired of retirement living and decided to create our own adventure," Darcie said. "We left Indiana six months ago, and we've been traveling ever since. We've even been as far north as Alaska."

"On this motorcycle?" I asked, surprised that they had ridden it so far, over roads so challenging that most cars wouldn't survive.

"Yep, the whole way," Bob said.

"We've stopped along the ride to see our eighteen grandchildren and visit friends," Darcie said.

"Take a moment and sit on her," Bob suggested.

I looked at him, afraid I would damage something if I did.

"No, go ahead. Sit on my seat," he said, patting the large customized yellow-and-black leather covering with the raised initials RLM sewn into the design.

Cautiously, I threw my leg across it, trying not to touch anything. I looked like a nervous first-time parent who had just been handed her newborn infant. I could only imagine how much would break if this bike fell over. I sank into the seat amazed by its plush cushion. It felt huge, almost like being in a car, but without side doors. Bob reached over and turned the ignition key; cold air blasted against my face and more dials lit up than I imagined were on most airplanes. I was sure that on this vehicle I could fly into the air, leaving the roads behind me. This would be a different type of riding. Before sitting in his seat, I'd thought these bikers were missing all of the fun. Now I understood it was a different allure.

After waving goodbye and wishing them a safe trip, the clinking sound I heard as I walked toward my motorcycle wasn't the sound of gravel crunching under my feet, but rather another stereotype shattering on the floor of my brain. It is easy to form opinions with little information or experience. Experts are far less apt to state absolutes. On this trip, instead of *walk a mile in my shoes*, the saying should be *ride a mile on my bike*.

This had been an easy day of leisurely riding and enjoying ocean vistas. Our plan for the evening was to stay in Eureka, California, at an inn located on US 101 in the center of town. John had suggested we book this hotel because it was "biker friendly." Eureka was also near the extensive Coastal Redwood Preserves, so tomorrow morning we'd be fresh when we headed out to see some of the world's most magnificent trees.

As we pulled into the hotel's inner courtyard, I counted at least two dozen other motorcycles in the parking lot. Walking inside the office to register for the night, I thought that this would be another fun evening and another first.

I was schlepping my luggage to my second-floor room when I passed a biker leaning against the balcony railing outside of his room. He looked peculiar as he held a cold cola bottle against his exposed shirtless shoulder on this cool, fifty-degree evening. My eye focused on his bicep, covered by an intriguing tattoo of feathers and a wolf's head done in atypical soft pastel colors.

"That's an interesting tattoo," I said, admiring the intricate artwork.

"I designed it myself in honor of my Native American heritage."

I watched as he rolled a cola can back and forth across his shoulder. "Are you all right?"

"Just hit a monster bee going sixty, that's all," he explained, removing the dripping bottle so I could see the damage.

"Wow!" I leaned in closer to inspect the five-inch red spot on his shoulder with a ruby welt the size of a quarter in the middle.

"Yep, and they always come in twos," he said, pointing to his other shoulder where there was a second one. "They damn near threw me off balance hitting *bam* on one side followed by *bam* on the other." As he spoke he animated his story by throwing back his right shoulder and then his left.

"Looks like you're going to need a second cola," I said, and we laughed. "I'm so new to riding that this is my only souvenir." I pointed to a small knick in my helmet, caused by a flying stone hurled back at me by a passing truck.

"Well, someday maybe you'll get waffles on your leathers."

"Waffles?"

"Sure, you know—those long scrape marks you get on your leathers from skidding on the road when your bike goes down."

"That's one badge of honor I'm hoping to avoid."

We laughed again and wished each other a good ride tomorrow as I walked away still searching for my room.

Wow, that was fun. Off the road and in street clothes, I never would have approached him. He would have looked too forbidding. But he was really a teddy bear—more cute and cuddly than scary outlaw. It was gratifying being both social and approachable.

Just as my sense of being an imposter had made me feel separate from others in my riding group several nights ago, I now saw how assumptions about my accessibility to other types of people had also created another kind of separation. In my daily routine, my conversations were normally directed toward people I needed and wanted to interact with. When was the last time I had lingered at a gas station or convenience store to talk with the person behind the counter? Standing in line at the local Starbucks waiting to order my to-go coffee, why didn't I start up a conversation with the young tattooed and pierced teen in front of me, when I'd regularly engage people dressed in business clothes? Was I unintentionally sending signals of being selectively unapproachable?

Now I was realizing what I had inadvertently eliminated from my life. My new uniform combined with a wealth of leisure time was removing personal limits while expanding my comfort zone. By heading into this blind curve, I was becoming a part of an ever-expanding community that was welcoming and showing me another side of myself. I'd feel less alone after this trip if I continued to encourage this mindset of accessibility and inclusion. It was time to remove my personal guardrails and expand my road.

Sitting on my hotel room bed, pulling off my boots, I looked up to see Eva smiling at me. "Look at your left boot. It's finally getting respectable scuffmarks on the toe. Good for you."

"You're right," I said. "But now I'm going to have to ride even better and quit making so many newbie mistakes."

"Yes, but now the world can see there is yet another woman rider in control of her own motorcycle."

These marks were another point of passage. One of the indications that a person is riding their own motorcycle, not just sitting at the back, is the scuffmark on the left big toe of a rider's boot. These are made when using the front toe section of the boot while shifting the bike's gear lever up and down.

It's generally assumed that men are riding their own motorcycles while the majority of women are sitting behind a guy—or as motorcyclists call it "riding two-up," or worse yet, "riding bitch." These women enjoy experiencing motorcycling, and it's fun to hold onto a person you like. It can be like dancing to lean into the curves, react to bumps in the road, and respond to the same roaring machine together. But the driver is in control and the passenger, as in dancing, is expected to follow. Many two-up riders prefer this role. They are along for the ride and still get to participate in all of the social aspects of riding with a group without having to do the actual driving. On this trip when others learned that Eva and I were riding our own motorcycles, we'd get impressed congratulatory statements from men and women alike.

As Eva and I walked downstairs to meet Ron and Alberto for dinner, I thought about how much fun it was hearing such praise. It reminded me of a six-year-old I had worked with earlier in my career when I had coached a girls' swim team of six- to eighteen-years-olds at the Paoli, Pennsylvania, YMCA. In the youngest competing group of six- to eight-year-olds, the races were only one length of the pool. This age group swam over fifty lengths of the pool in a hard practice and they were seasoned swimmers.

There was one six-year-old, Kimmy, who in practice had beautiful form, but as soon as she was in a race, her stroke fell apart. Kimmy would swim the length, thrashing wildly, looking as though she might not make it to the end of the pool. At away meets I'd often have to walk alongside the pool next to her as she swam, to keep opposing members of the home crowd from leaping in to rescue her.

She came in last in every heat, but when she eventually climbed out of the pool, she received a standing ovation from a cheering, relieved crowd. She would beam widely as she picked up her towel and turned to face her adoring audience. It was useless to try to change this habit, and I was glad that a young girl was at least getting recognition for swimming instead of something less productive.

Well, my scuffed toe and the congratulations it inspired felt similar to Kimmy's standing ovation. My admiring fans, full of praise for my riding my own motorcycle, had not seen how many times I had popped the clutch at stoplights that day, killed the engine and held up traffic. They hadn't witnessed me riding for five miles with my left turn signal on then, an hour later, with my right one flashing away. And now I was being applauded because I had scuffmarks on the toe of my left boot.

I was determined that I would never polish my leather boots. At least not until I quit feeling so unsure of myself and loving the encouragement and respect I was receiving.

13
Sacred Silent Giants

"Where are Ron and Alberto?" I asked, looking up in the direction of their room as Eva and I loaded our motorcycles the next morning in the Humbolt Bay Inn parking lot.

Eva was already on her cell phone. "Hurry up, you guys. We're going to leave and see the redwoods without you."

After four days of practice tying down my luggage, I had developed a formula of precise movements that I further refined each day. I used six bungee cords, each a different color and length. Leaning over I hooked one end of a black and green bungee under my rear left turn signal, wove it through the handles of my backpack and gym bag positioned on the back passenger seat, and stretched it hard as I attached it diagonally behind the right side of my driver's seat. As I was fastening the last cord, Ron and Alberto rushed toward their bikes. Without saying much they hurriedly loaded them.

By now, we all had been late at least one morning, but no one had been brave enough to face the consequences of being tardy on two consecutive days. The trick for escaping harassment from this group was for the non-punctual party to show the right degree of remorse by saying something like, "Sorry to have held you guys up," combined with an equal amount of mock defensiveness, "Hey, it was only ten minutes!"

Soon we were huddled around Ron's motorcycle as he sat holding a map against its handlebars. This was our typical daily two-minute briefing. We rode highly unscripted with only the beginning and ending places acting as anchors.

"We're starting here in Eureka, with Mendocino as our final destination for the day," Ron announced as his finger traced the yellow-highlighted line on the map. "Our primary route will continue to be the Pacific Coast Highway (a.k.a. Route 101) except at the end of today's trip where we'll veer off southwest on Route 1 at Leggett and ride along the coast to Mendocino."

He reminded us that tomorrow we would be taking our only day off from riding to enjoy Mendocino's vineyards, galleries, restaurants, shops, and beaches.

"We'll only have to cover one hundred twenty-five miles today, so we can search out challenging roads and explore some of the redwood forests along the way."

"Wow, this is an easy day. We're getting soft in our old age," Alberto said.

"But the redwoods," Eva sighed. "How could we come so far and not take time to see these magnificent trees? I can hardly wait." *Now it's time for female potpourri of redwoods and pine needle scents*, I thought silently, remembering my earlier Harley machine shop experience.

On family vacations when I was young, we camped in both Yosemite and Sequoia National Parks. I remembered being amazed that the four of us kids could not collectively stretch our arms around a single tree. We were awestruck as Dad drove our Mercury sedan through a tunnel in the center of one. Today I view that adventure differently since we now know that these large holes weakened and destroyed the trees. But as a child, riding through the middle of a tree demonstrated their grandeur better than the park ranger's explanation that some trees reach a height of close to four hundred feet.

At one time in this area of California, redwood forests covered more than two million acres. Sadly, a mere four percent of that old growth remains. Since loggers historically first cut down the most accessible trees to roads, sawmills, and transportation, today's remaining old-growth redwood forests are scattered in remote small groupings.

Eight years ago when I visited Yosemite, I was surprised by the changes that had evolved over the last thirty years. As a result of heavy tourism, personal vehicles were no longer permitted to drive through the park. Instead, visitors rode in tour buses to decrease exhaust pollution and limit tourists' footprints on this over-visited natural wonder.

Today I was curious to find out what these smaller northern redwood parks would be like. My hope was they'd be less popular and wouldn't feel so much like visiting a crowded zoo on a holiday weekend.

Riding south, we pointed out stands of giant redwoods in the distance as we passed them. Even though some of these trees stood over thirty stories high, the ones we had spotted were so far off the highway that their grandeur was diminished. As we cruised past several exits with signs listing redwood parks, I grew impatient, wondering why we weren't exiting. I felt we were missing too much and needed to take one of these opportunities to find roads that would take us into a park.

Just as I was planning how to get the others to agree, Alberto passed us, waving his finger over his head and pointing at the next exit sign as he took over the lead position and led us up the ramp.

At the stop sign at the top, we pulled into a tight two-by-two formation. Turning around, Alberto yelled over the roar of our engines, "I didn't want to ride any further without stopping to see some of these trees. Let's follow the signs to this park and check it out." We nodded enthusiastically. It was obvious everyone had been entertaining similar thoughts.

Turning left and riding several miles on a deserted country road, we entered a redwood park. At the entrance, a ranger booth in the center of the road stood vacant and closed up. There were no park brochures in its empty slots, so we had no information about where to go and what to see. Fortunately, there didn't appear to be any choice with only one main road.

Traveling a short distance inside the park, we discovered what we were looking for. We slowed down, soaking in our surroundings. Magnificent redwoods towered around us. Overhead the trees' branches formed an arched dome, shutting out all direct sunlight. We lifted our face shields, removed our sunglasses, and flicked on our headlights so we could see better as we crept along in heavy shade.

We were the only vehicles on what I surmised must have been an old logging road. My wish had come true—we had a redwood forest to ourselves.

After riding a short distance without finding any designated pull-off areas to stop and explore the forest, we simply parked our motorcycles along the side of the road. We hung our helmets and gloves from our handlebars and turned in circles, gazing upward at the wonder encircling us. This forest was filled with mature trees, spaced about ten to twenty feet apart. It would be easy to walk under them in any direction since their branches were in the upper third of their trunks and the ground underneath them was clear of obstacles except for the occasional fallen tree, branch, or cluster of ferns. Without talking, each of us walked into the woods, picking a different direction—wandering and staring upwards, awed by all that surrounded us. We were in a cathedral, dwarfed by its immense proportions.

With each new step, my boots sank several inches into the deep needle cushion underneath them, giving the impression that this lush, spongy mattress was several feet deep. The scent of needles, humus, and rotting wood was richer than any chocolate mousse I had ever eaten. These trees affected everything in the forest—the dappled light, aromatic scent, textured shadows, and even its hushed silence.

The collective presence of these giants was so powerful that upon entering this domain, I began to vibrate at their frequency and not my own.

My breathing slowed.

Muscles relaxed.

Internal voices fell silent.

Spaces between my few lingering thoughts grew longer.

Listening intently to the forest, I became aware of a faint humming. It emanated from the tops of the trees and was similar to the vibration I feel after a bass fiddle string has been plucked, and as its sound fades, the lingering note still resonates inside me.

I leaned forward and cocked an ear upwards, straining to hear more, trying to decipher this buzzing chorus. It was as if these trees were talking to each other—hundreds of separate instruments simultaneously humming at slightly different bass pitches—all of them speaking at once.

Wanting to further isolate their sounds, I shut my eyes, stood still, and stopped breathing. It felt as though I were in the middle of a giant Jacuzzi, being pummeled by sound jets from all directions. I had read that these trees talk to each other, but was that what I was hearing? I wandered deeper into the woods, looking for other mysteries.

The integrated cycle of life and death was more obvious here than in my normal life. This forest was both a graveyard for past generations and a nursery for new ones—the living and dead integrated and intertwined.

The fallen giants on the forest's floor bared monstrous roots that had once anchored and fed them. One downed tree's root network stretched two stories high. Walking alongside this recumbent elder, I studied the decomposing mass—bark peeling off like strewn clothing, leaving mighty branches bare. But this fallen master was alive too. Sprouting from its rotting interior were a dozen young new trees five to ten feet tall. In this context the dead trees weren't lifeless shells with their souls long departed. They were alive and ever-present— birthing, feeding, supporting, and being reincarnated as the next generation.

I knew that some redwoods are purported to be over 2,500 years old. Staring at the trees around me I tried to comprehend what it would be like to live for over two and a half millennia. I wondered how many generations of my own family had been born and died during the lifetime of one of these elder giants. My projected human life expectancy of seventy to eighty years is superior to most insects, plants, and animals, but here, under these redwoods, I stood young and immature. There are times when I am touched by my own insignificance. Standing amongst this much grandeur and history, I was reminded of the deep integration of all objects, beings, organisms, and cells. It put the last several years of my life back into perspective. It wasn't all about me— my life, my family, my challenges, and my loss.

Singing solo during this past year and a half of mourning, I had closed my world around me, trying to blanket myself in protection. I had made my one voice too important, isolated, and lonely. I had struggled to be enough and failed.

Here amidst nature, my singular alto voice became part of a larger chorus. If I stopped singing for a moment to *just be*, the chorus continued. Later I could choose to rejoin the world's music—rested, refreshed, and ready to contribute again.

That was some of the meaning of this trip, expanding my world to become more inclusive again, fitting back into the larger whole, experiencing life and death as intimate partners.

14
The Gravel Taboo

Surrounded by ancient trees, I wondered what Ron, Alberto, and Eva had experienced in their exploration of this redwood forest. I was concerned that I might not be able to fit quickly back into the group's fun-seeking antics, and I knew I wasn't ready to climb back on a roaring machine and rip through this forest.

I looked up and saw Ron wandering toward me, his face relaxed and softened. He approached and stood silently in front of me. "Incredible," he whispered, and I nodded, relieved that he too was in a subdued mood. He pointed out the shadowy figures of Eva and Alberto in the distance, and without talking, we walked in their direction.

Everyone seemed at a loss for words to describe their solitary exploration. No one tried. It was obvious by our whispered greetings and wide-eyed stares that each of us had been touched by a sense of awe.

In a hushed voice Eva said, "Follow me. We want to show you what we found."

She led us over to a redwood shell that soared fifty feet high. The four of us crawled through a tall split in its side and stood in its hollow core with room to spare. Sunlight streamed in from the open top. Looking upward through the center tube was like peering into a kaleidoscope at a marbled pattern of branches, needles, clouds, and blue sky.

"We've got to take pictures of these trees and one of all of us standing inside this one," Eva suggested.

We pulled out our pocket-sized automatic cameras and began snapping photographs, but as we reviewed our digital images, we realized the essence of this place was beyond our talent and equipment. Despite our cameras' impressive array of features, there was no way to convey and communicate the trees' immense proportions.

In this dimly lit setting, trying to photograph each other also produced amateurish results. In the heavy shade with only small patches of filtered light, the reflective strips on our clothes showed up in the photographs as bursts of exploding white light. A photograph of Alberto standing inside the hollowed-out tree could have been titled "Beam Me Up, Scottie" because there was so much white glow reflecting from his clothing.

"Let's get back to our bikes and see where else this road takes us," Ron said.

"I'd like to look for an even more remote back road to lead us deeper into these forests. I'm ready for more," I added.

According to our map, the road we could take to find more redwood stands inside the park was a continuous thirty-one mile loop that circled the park and ended at the entrance. There were no other roads turning off this singular loop, so it would be easy to follow.

After riding about five miles into this circle, the redwood trees disappeared and our park road became one-way. Taking advantage of two lanes of pavement, we cruised in both, enjoying a road free of other traffic. But slowly the sides of our wide road tapered inward until it became so narrow that we were forced to return to our normal single-file, riding pattern.

About twenty miles into the loop, the pavement shrank to less than the width of a VW bug, and the quality of its surface deteriorated from firm blacktop to crumbling, cracked concrete. I had read that most national and state parks' budgets had been severely cut and assumed that the vacant booth at the park's entrance and this unmaintained road were results of that squeeze.

As our road wound through valleys, over hills, and around numerous blind curves hugging mountainsides, I anticipated discovering more mature redwood stands. But normal pine and broadleaf trees continued to surround us. Still, it was a serene setting, and we enjoyed this remote wilderness undisturbed by any visible signs of human civilization—no houses, structures, vehicles, people, utility lines, or even simple road signs.

After traveling thirty miles, we expected to find the park entrance around each bend. Instead, without warning, we could see in the distance that our dilapidated road was about to turn into a dirt one. I questioned whether I should pull over and stop. I had never ridden on an unpaved road and wondered if I'd be able to control this heavy motorcycle. I shifted down to first gear and slowed to ten miles per hour as I cautiously studied the approaching surface.

It was smooth and hard-packed without significant ruts. As Alberto and Eva's motorcycles crossed onto it, their bikes continued to ride normally, so I tenuously followed their lead, griping my handlebars much harder than necessary. It turned out to be a firm enough surface to ride on, so we continued forward, anticipating our momentary return to the promised main gate and highway.

Looking down at my odometer fifteen minutes later, I calculated that we had now ridden at least thirty-five miles.

What's going on? My odometer might be off by a few miles, but four miles seems too many.

Our diminishing dirt road narrowed further and became a lane barely three feet wide. As it continued to climb, descend, and curve through the forest we became leery of what lay ahead. I had no faith that the promised thirty-one mile loop on our map existed.

We crawled forward, traveling now almost entirely in first and second gears.

I wondered, *What happens to RVs and regular-sized cars on this loop? We must have made a wrong turn somewhere. But there had been no turn-offs or other choices.* This was no longer a passable road for anything larger than a motorcycle.

Riding through a broad meadow ringed by trees and hills, with grasses as tall as our heads, we came around yet another blind curve. Abruptly we braked and halted.

Ahead of us was a climb up a steep hill with four sharp hairpin turns in the lane as it wove back and forth across a grassy, precipitous slope and then disappeared at the top. The road ahead was not only covered with loose gravel, it also had deep ruts running through it, probably caused by heavy rains and erosion.

Sitting on top of our four noisy motorcycles, we pushed up our face shields and looked at each other. Heads shook no way, shoulders shrugged, and eyebrows arched high on foreheads. The question that didn't need to be spoken out loud but was on everyone's mind was: *What now?*

We sat still, each contemplating possible alternatives.

I was sure none of us wanted to turn around and retrace our last thirty-six miles, especially with most of them going the wrong direction on a one-way road. There were too many blind curves, rises, and falls to do that safely. If we had a collision with unaware traffic coming from the opposite direction, more innocent people would be affected.

But even if we all made it up this hill unharmed, it was impossible to know what lay ahead. Would this trail lead us back to civilization and the park entrance, or simply vanish over the top or disappear in the middle of the next field? So far we had every reason to believe that it would continue evaporating. Obviously, our map was inaccurate about the road's length and condition. With such faulty information, how could we trust it any longer?

Our dilemma was clear—our discomfort intense. Our obstacle loomed one-hundred yards in front of us. I squinted, studying the hill and passage up the steep trail, trying to figure out how hard it would be to climb it on my motorcycle. The path cut back and forth across the slope four times. It started off to our right as a hundred-yard approach before the first sharp curve. The long run before this first and then the second curve as well as their wide bends would offer time to control the speed of the bike and choose where on the road to ride, avoiding the deep ruts and exposed larger rocks. But the third and fourth turns concerned me. The steeper climbs between these curves would require more speed to get up them, but the tighter loops demanded slower speeds to get around them safely.

As I questioned whether any of us was proficient enough to climb it, I felt the muscles of my shoulders and chest tighten, a knot formed in my throat, and my stomach churned. *How could I have encouraged this remote exploration?* I stopped myself mid-thought. This wasn't a voice I could afford to listen to now. Looking back at events, it's always easy to be an expert and criticize decisions. *Stay present and deal with what's here.*

The sudden loud rumble of a motorcycle engine startled me and interrupted my thoughts. Ron, without consulting anyone, had decided his course of action. He roared across the meadow, slowing slightly as he headed into the first curve. He eased his motorcycle through the second curve. But in the middle of the third, his back tire skidded. Alberto, Eva, and I stared, amazed.

"Oh, no!" I gasped, barely able to watch but unwilling to look away. I held my breath as he slid around the fourth one, before he sped to the top. In unison the three of us let out sighs, relieved that he was safe and his ride was over.

I shouldn't have been surprised by his choice. Ron never was a person to over-analyze a situation when quick action could resolve it. At the top he had vanished, then reappeared and sat facing us on his bike. At such a distance he looked small, his facial expression unreadable, but his fists pounding into the air above him in celebration were easy to understand. He waved, signaling us to ride up and join him. Alberto looked at Eva and me to see if we were willing to follow Ron's lead. I knew Alberto wanted to tackle the hill, but he was too considerate and protective to leave us behind.

Since we had already agreed that we would stay together, I realized the decision of whether we rode forward or not rested on the less-skilled riders—Eva and me. I was sure if we turned around and retreated, Ron would ride down and rejoin us.

Eva and I glanced at each other, knowing the influence we held with each other. So far on this trip, whenever either of us held back or pushed forward, it emboldened the other to follow suit. A first act by either to go ahead or turn back would most likely engender a similar vote from the other.

Again, I was facing a decision with no clear black-or-white answer. There were many persuasive arguments for attempting to ride up this perilous hill, as well as equally strong reasons to turn around and pursue the dangerous reverse ride. In this remote area there was no accessible medical help or mechanic if any of us crashed on the hill. It would take hours to get help.

If we turned around, we'd be breaking a traffic law by riding the wrong way. My mind whirled with pros and cons and endless scenarios. I wanted to do the right thing. *But what?*

I couldn't stand the suspense much longer as I have never been able to sit still in a time of portending doom. As a child playing hide and seek, as soon as I hid in a good spot, I'd get fidgety and have to go to the bathroom. While watching Disney's *The Musketeer Show* as the young Hardy boys entered the haunted house, I'd cover my ears to block the foreboding music, unable to bear its terrifying effect, and pace the room.

I rarely went to thriller movies, and when I did, friends found me more terrified and entertaining to watch than anything happening on the screen. Bill and I had worked out a routine: I'd cover my eyes and ask when I could look again. I've seen a lot of movies through the cracks of my fingers. Afterward I'm sure I lost ten pounds and definitely a good night's sleep.

My friends often think I am brave as I tackle challenging obstacles. Really, like Ron, I am impatient, preferring any action to being paralyzed by dread or fear.

I had felt enough tension while staring at this hill and experienced enough indecision this past year to last many lifetimes. I was exhausted from endlessly trying to figure out optimal courses of action—always asking, *What now? What's best for everyone?* It was time to either take this hill or turn around and re-ride the loop.

So I flipped a coin in my head, and without waiting to see how it landed, roared off in the direction of the hill, ready to just get this over with, regardless of the outcome.

As I approached the gravel surface, I slowed. I knew from driving cars over similar country lanes that I'd need to keep up enough speed to maintain momentum, but not so much that I'd lose traction on this uneven surface. *Copy Ron's speed*, I told myself.

I flinched, startled by the sound of popping gravel crunching beneath my tires and spitting out behind me. It sounded like industrial-sized popcorn exploding inside a copper drum, but even that noise was drowned out by my thunderous heartbeat and hysterical screaming inner voices.

My motorcycle teetered back and forth in short side-to-side movements as it struggled across the top of the uneven road surface. Instinctively I leaned forward, clenching my handlebars and putting more weight over my pegs, while using my body to counterbalance the bouncing bike beneath me. As I experimented to find the best speed— slow enough to quit spinning my tires on the stony surface, but fast enough to smooth out the ride and maintain momentum—I reseated myself, saying: *See, I can do this; I've got it under control.*

Heading into the first curve I braked briefly before, but miscalculated and gave the bike a burst of gas coming out of the turn. The motorcycle's front tire leaped up in the air slightly. "OHHHH!" I shrieked, startled as my body jerked backward, accelerating my speed as my right hand pulled unexpectedly harder back on the throttle. *Oh my God, my first mini-wheelie! They're going to think I'm showing off instead of trying to survive.*

During the approach to the second curve, I asked: *Why do I always bite off too much?* But I cut myself short: *Concentrate on this next curve. Ride high on the outer edge. Stay away from that crevice down the center.*

As I entered the bend I called out: "Brake . . . Now accelerate . . . Yep, that's a better rhythm." I was used to this kind of oral self-coaching. It kept me focused on an immediate single action instead of panicking at the whole ordeal. But the momentary feeling of relief disappeared as my bike turned and started the steeper, shorter climb up to curve number three.

I muttered, "Oh, no," and held my breath. When you're preparing for imminent death, air isn't required. Breathing had become an unnecessary distraction. My eyes stopped blinking, replaced by a frozen stare on the path ahead. I couldn't afford to miss identifying one rock, rut, or hole in a millisecond blink.

My bike slowed and the engine sputtered from the strain of the steeper climb. I had no choice but to give it more gas.

Come on girl—don't fail me now! Everyone's counting on us. Entering the tighter third curve with too much speed, I braked mid-turn causing the back tire to slide as the bike leaned precariously into the hillside and skidded. My body recoiled in panic, realizing this long slide could mean I was going down.

I counter-leaned in the opposite direction and gave it more gas, hoping to straighten it out again.

Thank God, it worked.

We sped towards the final curve.

Curling my body over the bike, we became one. There was no time to think. Just *be*.

The bike and I rounded the hairpin turn—bouncing, rebounding, sputtering, and spitting stones and grit into the air in all directions. Opening the throttle for the final straightaway climb, we raced through the golden hue of grasses toward the sky's blue ribbon stretched across the finish line at the top of the hill. I wanted this over, *now!*

Surrounded by glorious sky, we circled around, pulling alongside Ron. We had made it—the bike and me. Victorious! And in one piece.

I planted my feet on the ground as I gasped, sucking in huge breaths to make up for ones I'd neglected to take while climbing the hill.

My muscles were still tightly contracted, and every part of my body still screamed *ALERT!* I repeated to myself, *It's over. Relax!*

As my body began to respond, the tension was replaced with sweeping exhaustion. Completely spent, I collapsed over my gas tank like a wet rag doll, unable to hold my body up any longer. I lay there, performing a quick mental inventory to reassure myself that all body parts were still present and functioning.

Not trusting my quivering legs to support my heavy motorcycle much longer, I willed myself to sit up, kick down the bike's sidestand, and crawl off. I wasn't sure my legs would hold even me up as I tried to balance and stand alone.

Ron bounded over to me, delivering a high five and a crushing bear hug.

To Ron and the group I was a real trouper, but my view of myself was more like a roll of used-up caps on a sidewalk that had been beaten on by kids with stones until each dot had exploded, then abandoned when they had no sound left to give, the paper strip tattered and blackened. But gathering my dormant acting skills to play the role of triumphant athlete, I joined Ron's lead in waving at Alberto and Eva, signaling them to come up and join the victory party.

Secretly my motivation for encouraging them was impure. *They've got to come up. There is no way in hell I am driving back down this hill!* My body could never be conned into that action twice.

Ron's and my festive mood evaporated, as we watched Eva move her motorcycle into position at the bottom of the hill. It could only be a victory if everyone made it unharmed to the top. I felt guilty and responsible for her fate as she started to ride. If she got hurt, I'd blame myself.

Eva's determination and riding skill were apparent as she rode through the first three curves, but in the last curve she too fought skidding as she spewed up dust and stones. One thing I admired about Eva was that she hung in there determinedly and competently whenever things got tough. As she arrived at the top of the hill, her flushed face radiated joy. I was relieved that my bold move had cost her nothing.

Startled by the roar of yet another motorcycle, we turned, and there was Alberto cresting the hill. At last, all four of us were at the top. Eva hopped off her motorcycle, spinning in circles as she shouted, "I did it. I did it!"

I raced over to her, leaping and hopping as if I had industrial springs attached to my feet. Alberto came up behind me and slapped me on the shoulder, saying, "Way to go." Caught off-balance, I stumbled forward. We all had so much adrenalin flowing that I am sure we could have lifted our motorcycles over our heads while dancing and twirling.

It was glorious to feel so silly. We raced around in circles with arms out like airplanes as we hollered and roared.

"Hey, Linda, when you skidded in that third curve, I thought you were a goner," Eva yelled. "But you pulled it out and even flew through that last one like a pro."

"I don't remember the last curve. I just remember racing to get to the blue sky," I said as I stretched out my arms and pulled back on an imaginary throttle while yelling, "Vroo-om, Vrooooom!"

Eva and I embraced each other and soon found ourselves encompassed by Ron and Alberto's arms. It was a well-deserved group hug. Giddy and saturated with exhaustion, our group fell over in a heap onto the ground. We sprawled in the grass and lay on our backs, looking up at the sky as we enjoyed a moment of triumph and rest.

Eventually, thirst sent us hunting through our luggage for water bottles. Fortified, we were ready to examine our narrow road ahead. We celebrated our immediate good fortune. The lane remained at this higher elevation traveling along the edge of the forest. At least there was no immediate steep decline to navigate and our road was continuing and not disappearing.

We pressed forward. The road began to widen, and within the next mile, we whooped with joy when we spotted the park entrance. We had made it back to civilization.

⚬

Back on Highway 101, we were surrounded by mainstream drivers. Happy for the segue and adventure, we were now ready for a more predictable, and yes even a more boring ride. None of us was a daredevil needing constant adrenaline rushes to feel alive. It was the contrast we enjoyed. Life needs its mix of excitement and routine—too much of either is exhausting.

As often occurs after a frightening event, the significance of what could have happened, as well as other possible outcomes, suddenly struck me. During a crisis, I normally remain calm and turn into a problem solver and a leader. I feel my greatest fear retroactively after a crisis has passed, sometimes weeks later.

Aside from the obvious danger and risk of injury, this whole experience could have resulted in some serious consequences for our happy group. *What if we hadn't all been able to agree as a group to either go forward or turn around and ride against traffic?*

Even though we had previously agreed to stay together and not to ride on gravel, the decision of whether we should break the rule rested not on the adventurous members ready to take the hill, but rather on the more conservative, risk-averse members, who had lobbied and succeeded in getting a group rule made against gravel. Both choices, going up the gravel hill or turning around, had safety consequences.

Rarely have I found myself defending tradition and sitting in the conservative seat, but today I could have easily sat there. Conflict could have surfaced among us about which rules were more important— violating state traffic laws with the consequence of tickets and points from riding in the wrong direction on a one-way road or breaking our group's *no gravel* and *riding together* agreements.

At the beginning of this trip when we agreed on our rules, this situation with two risk-laden choices hadn't existed. Even if Eva and I had turned around and chosen to ride against traffic, Ron and Alberto might have justifiably felt that their safer choice was to go up the gravel hill that wasn't a hazard to them. This is one of the dilemmas with all

138

rules. They are formulated to deal only with situations *imaginable* at the time they are created.

Luckily, we were all safe and still happy as a group. In fact the bond among us was stronger as a result of our individual and group successes today. I, too, was finding out that I was stronger than I thought as well as shocked by my ability to respond to the unknown on that hill. Gratitude filled me for the wonderful way this side trip turned out. I had been lucky this time with my coin-toss decision, but what about next time?

15
Mendocino Intermission

We arrived in Mendocino late in the afternoon. Following signs, we exited the highway toward what we assumed would be the center of town. Not sure what we were looking for, we selected streets that ran closest to the ocean. Eventually we saw a cluster of shops, restaurants, and a church, so we looked for a place to park our motorcycles.

At the end of Main Street sat a series of compact two-story wooden buildings, looking more like small houses than traditional business establishments. Thirsty from the drive, we strolled into the Mendocino Hotel, a historic three-story Victorian establishment. The air in the lobby divulged some of its history—the smell of old smoke from years of burning wood in fireplaces and stoves; a musty fragrance of old books, wallpaper, and leather, and the dusty aroma of heavily upholstered antique furnishings.

As we climbed up the twisting, narrow oak stairs to the second floor bar, they creaked, protesting our clunky motorcycle boots. We sounded more like a herd of prancing buffalos than a cadre of thirsty travelers.

Rather than sit in the lounge with its delicate antique furniture, Persian rugs, and Tiffany lamps, we sought out an open-air second-floor balcony running across the front of the building. The black wicker chairs more appropriately welcomed our leathery outerwear. Ron and Alberto were already sinking down into these seats, ready to order cold beers and gaze at the panoramic ocean view. But Eva turned to me with another idea.

"Let's go shopping. I can't believe we've been traveling for five days and haven't been in a single store. I can't go home without gifts for my daughters and husband."

The small stores located on the first floors of these quaint houses did look interesting, although the ocean scene in front of me was an equally strong magnet. "Let's just take a quick look. We'll meet you guys back here in thirty minutes," I said.

We hurried off, convinced that a town like this must have a few buried treasures waiting to be discovered. We passed an expensive jewelry store, a vineyard showroom, a couple of catchall gift shops, and several clothing boutiques.

There's nothing like riding a motorcycle to make spending money on items found in gift shops seem superfluous. After all, who needs a crystal-and-feather dream-catcher meant to dangle in a window, a long backscratcher carved out of wood, or a snow globe that says Mendocino? And what does snow have to do with remembering Mendocino or a lot of other places?

We entered one of the clothing boutiques. I froze, staring at hangers adorned with lacy dresses and sequined tops that were inappropriate for anything we'd be doing in the next five days. They seemed frivolous and unnecessary. Whatever I bought would have to be stuffed and carried in already over-packed bags for the rest of the trip to be used in the future—one still undefined by me.

So far on this trip, I had escaped the worries that had routinely awakened me in a panic around three o'clock in the morning and accompanied by the question: *What now?* For the past five glorious days, I had thought only about this trip and had slept peacefully through the whole night. For the first time in a year and a half I had been happy again, leaving my hurt in the past.

I wasn't ready to think about my unsettled future. At least not yet. It was time to get back to the present—one with enough challenges to fully engage me and plenty of enticing scenery.

"I can't get in the mood to shop today. I'm going to rejoin Alberto and Ron," I said.

"Wait, look at what I found. Look at this cute pink T-shirt that will look great on Heather. Oh, and check out this small, darling sequin-covered clutch. Won't this be perfect for Kimberlee?"

"They're nice," I said, feigning as much enthusiasm as I could.

"This is a great place. I'm going to look for more," Eva said.

I was glad Eva was having fun, but I wanted to flee and reconnect with the textures I associated with a motorcycle road trip and north-western adventure. This whole shopping scenario felt strange and uncomfortable. It reminded me of similar feelings I'd had when I went wilderness camping and passed a camper with a TV blaring inside. This invasive man-made noise drowned out all of the desirable natural sounds of wind rustling leaves, birds chirping, tree limbs creaking in the wind, squirrels protesting another's infringement on their territory, and the many other sounds of nature I had come so far to hear.

To me shopping and road trips were opposite worlds colliding. I wanted to re-enter the adventure and leave behind this commercial interruption. My needs on this trip were simple—sturdy clothes, food, drink, a comfortable bed, engaging conversation, interesting scenery, reliable motorcycle, and great company.

I still had fifteen minutes before I was due back at the hotel porch. Wanting to sort out my feelings, I crossed the street and headed toward the ocean. This was what I had come on the trip to experience.

I sat hidden in the tall grasses of the rocky headlands, staring out at the sea. White daisies as tall as my head bounced on tall stems in the wind, welcoming me. I thought back to the driving impetus for this journey—the forces that had made me hunger for anything new—a trip to the opposite coast, immersion in nature, learning something different, new friends, an adventure with bass undertones, doing the unexpected and hanging out with a fringe community It was so opposite to what I had been doing, but it felt so right.

How had I ever figured out that this was what I needed now? Leaving traditional wisdom behind. Creating my own path away from the well-touted road of how to eat, sleep, and exercise. Erasing the old boundaries I had drawn around myself, defining the "old Linda."

As I leaned back, observing my random thoughts, the silly image of the Mendocino snow globe from the gift shop floated by. Snow globes brought back pleasant memories from childhood when I had been filled with delight as I shook them to make a snowy scene. I loved the reaction I could create with a twirl of my hand and was disappointed if the snowflakes fell too rapidly back to the globe's floor. It was the swirling chaos that I loved, not the serene scene that followed once the individual flakes joined the others on the ground. I could create instant blizzards and whiteouts. I was all-powerful!

Before this trip I had been sitting in the middle of my own serene scene, waiting for the right answers to come and tell me what to do next to re-create my life as a single woman. I was ready to take action but just needed the right direction that I could be excited about before proceeding. I was waiting, waiting, ever waiting for the perfect idea to appear and feel right. Then I'd have enthusiasm to move forward again. Then I'd have energy to commit myself to making life happen again.

I'd had a number of short "aha'" ideas that flurried briefly with potential, but as soon as I started to initiate them, they'd fizzle out and the fragile moment of certainty would evaporate. Not wanting to be cynical, I believed that eventually the right ideas and direction would materialize, I just needed to be receptive and keep visualizing their stage. I practiced positive thinking and affirmations about their arrival, but daily I kept awakening to more of the same and adding additional pages of written possibilities that didn't seem quite right.

Now I knew that what I had needed to do instead of waiting for these winning answers to come to me was to create *fuel* to birth them. I needed to create snowflakes of possibilities—even bits and pieces of them—in a wondrous blizzard of energy swirling around me inside the globe of my life.

First, the creation, fun, and play in my self-created blizzard, later I could look more closely at the flakes and maybe even combine some into snowballs while allowing others to fall on the snow-covered ground around my boots. I could always bend over later and re-examine the snow-covered ground if the snowflakes I chose melted or blew away.

Until I created this playful momentum, which naturally accompanied any new activity like motorcycling, and erased my former boundaries defining my now-outdated self, I wouldn't have this rich fuel necessary for rebuilding something new. Without joyous activity as a part of creation, every new effort felt like more work—just another item on my already overloaded to-do list.

The day Ron suggested that I go on this trip, my world turned from quiet and sedate to a flurry of possibilities. My being had been rocked with my rebellious decision and the single flick of my wrist. Suddenly life was filled with enticing new thoughts, covering worn-out ones. At first, all I saw was lots of commotion and disruption of my normal routines. But it was fun too, frolicking with all of the exciting changes.

From past experiences I knew that a complete life answer rarely appears all at once. I didn't know at the beginning of learning to ride a motorcycle and this ten-day road trip how both would influence my future, but I had faith that somehow they could and would. Life has always made more sense looking back on it, but rarely as I experienced it day-to-day.

My intuition told me that, for now, this trip was all I needed to think about. What I was doing in life was creating momentum, fuel, and joy again. I was out in the world trying, failing, and succeeding, but in the midst of it all, laughing, crying, making new discoveries, and having lots of fun.

⌘

Auberge Mendocino Seaside Inn and Cottages was run by two former New Yorkers. Cheerful yellow walls covered with large colorful artwork painted by local talent greeted us as we walked into the living room. Sitting on the coffee table in front of the fireplace was a plate of chocolate cookies just taken out of the oven and waiting for guests to enjoy. This bed and breakfast was another great choice and the only place where we would be staying two nights. Warm cookies or brownies, we were told, appeared magically every afternoon. They had a very happy cook in the kitchen. We tromped off to find this generous baker and say thanks.

After checking into our rooms and changing clothes, we met to plan visits to several local vineyards on our travel-free day tomorrow. Ron arranged for a customized half-day wine tour so we could leave our bikes behind. Then we went out to find dinner in town.

Mendocino presented a problem—there were too many choices. We made our restaurant selection that first night based on two factors:

Would they take us without reservations, and could we sit outside with a view of the ocean? Having found a place that fit our needs, we were seated on a deck under a hanging basket of the cheeriest orange-and-yellow nasturtiums I had ever seen. They draped down several feet over the containers' sides. It was impossible to sit under their blooming cascade and not beam back at them.

Being in wine country, our waiter was as enthusiastic about helping us pick out the best wines to go with our dinner as he was in recommending the superlative choices on their menu. This was a great ending to a day spent first in the majestic redwoods, and then achieving victory in the perilous gravel hillside climb. Twilight found us savoring a village of connoisseurs of art, wine, and food.

The next morning, although we had reserved the last breakfast seating, we straggled downstairs still half asleep and took our places around the dining room table. Breakfast arrived, beginning with fresh berries and hot walnut bread, continuing with a ratatouille with apples and sausage, followed by crepes in a Parmesan cream sauce, and concluding in a triumph of bread pudding with spiced rum sauce.

We woke up and dug in as if we hadn't eaten in days. It was the appropriate prelude to a wine-tasting morning. At least we would be following the rule about not heading out to sample wines on empty stomachs.

Our limo arrived early. Steve, the owner, was a likable guy. He suggested that we start our half-day tour with a medium-sized winery, then move to more obscure smaller ones. While we were enjoying the first one, he'd call and arrange a private tasting at the next.

It was nice having a local person tell us about our surroundings. He explained how Mendocino had originated as a small logging community. As we drove south, Steve pointed out several remaining old-forest redwood stands. In the 1940s the logging industry along with Mendocino had gone into decline. Luckily, the art community discovered the town in the 1950s, and the addition of an annual music festival in 1987 added further visibility.

The first vineyard we visited reminded me of similar ones I had been to in the Napa and Sonoma Valleys. Passing under a veranda draped with vines, we entered a large tasting room with a wine bar in its center. The wine steward methodically recited memorized verses about each wine we sampled and then turned to serve others.

Leaving the first establishment, Ron, Eva, and I were eager to get to the next vineyard, anticipating that the experience there would be more friendly and enjoyable. We figured Alberto, who had walked outside moments earlier, would be waiting in the limo. Instead, he was sitting under the trees at a picnic table engrossed in a conversation on his cell phone.

"Not again, he's always on that thing," Eva said.

We stood outside our car, trying to be generous, giving him a few more minutes, but when I turned around to ask where we were headed next, Eva was walking in one direction and Ron in another, both on their cell phones.

I stood alone without agenda. I had no one I needed to call. It felt lonely being unattached—no husband to share small trip updates, no family needing daily guidance, no clients or staff waiting impatiently for my constant input. I couldn't think of another time in life when I had been so unattached from everything. Many over-committed people would have envied my freedom, but it didn't feel like a luxury to me. It felt lonely.

Alberto joined me beside our limo. "Well, where is everyone? It's time to move on to the next vineyard."

"We can't," I said, pointing to Eva and Ron, still on their cell phones.

Throughout the morning ringing phones continued to interrupt our activities. For the first time in days we were reachable. Without the roar of engines, we could hear and be tempted to respond to their rings.

Bill and I had never agreed about the advantages of technology and its impact on people's lives. In the early 1990s when email and the Internet began making inroads, Bill was the first among his peers to spend hours trying to get connected and explore the limited rewards and extreme frustrations of those early days. Even then he could see how it would revolutionize business, as he excitedly focused on its benefits. I, on the other hand, enmeshed in businesses that easily expanded into hundred-plus-hour workweeks, focused on how technology would soon destroy our ability to escape and have lives separated from work.

We both were right—technology allowed us to forward our business phones, leave work early, and even telecommute. While awaiting a critical call, there was no longer the need to stay in the office all day. But email, text messages, voicemail, phones calls, and social media all interrupt critical blocks of thinking time at work and personal recovery time afterwards.

Vacations are meant for escape, downtime, and renewal. An advantage of a motorcycle road trip was that everyone (clients, associates, families, and friends) accepted the fact that while we were riding our motorcycles, it would be impossible to hear our cell phones ring and dangerous to talk if we could. So we had acceptable excuses for turning off our phones and relaxing.

By mid-morning tensions had built over too many cell phone interruptions, so we turned them off. In the afternoon we would no longer be tethered together, and everyone could catch up on calls then without disrupting the group's activities.

Riding in the limo toward the third vineyard, I was convinced that I would enjoy an afternoon of lying on the beach more than this wine tasting morning. I hadn't found any special interest in the wines we had sampled thus far, and the people serving them weren't interested in chatting with us.

By contrast, as soon as we pulled up at the Esterlina Vineyards & Winery, we were greeted by a young woman in a bright, flower-covered sundress. She was warm and welcoming and wanted to know what had brought us to this part of the country.

She led us upstairs to a small second-floor wine-tasting room, but suggested that since it was such a nice day, we would probably enjoy sitting outside on the balcony at the table under a large umbrella. She placed cheese doodles, crackers, and an assortment of cheeses and fruit on the table. When we looked askance at the cheese doodles, she laughed and promised we would be surprised how well they went with certain kinds of wine.

Since this vineyard was so small, she had only four wines to offer that day for tasting. They were at the end of last year's inventory and this year's crop was still on the vines below. She said they used only their own grapes in all of their wines.

The first wine she poured was a Sauvignon Blanc. She encouraged us to smell its fruity perfume before tasting it. I have never appreciated Sauvignon Blancs, but this one reached out with warmth and richness that surprised me.

It was hard to know if it was the wine, the perfect view below us of grape vines, wild flowers and the valley with silhouetted mountains beyond, the delicious warm weather with a gentle breeze, or the warmth of our wine hostess, but the combination was wonderful.

To complete this perfect picture, an affectionate black kitty appeared on the porch deck and insisted on jumping up and settling in my lap. Holding a purring cat that luxuriates in response to each pet across her back or scratch under her chin melted my heart. We had lost our family cat, Peaches, the previous year and I still missed this kind of soft interaction. I was being set up to have a sensational experience.

Next, our hostess served a Riesling. Having lived in Germany for two years where Vati—my German host father—had gone to great lengths to turn me into a connoisseur of Rhine and Mosel white wines, I had learned to avoid all Rieslings here in the states. I found them too sugary and weak. But this Riesling was amazingly dry with great flavor.

She opened the third wine, an Estate Pinot Noir. Of all wines, I enjoy Pinot Noir the most and was disappointed when others discovered it about fifteen years ago, driving prices higher. Our hostess explained that this wine was so flavorful because the area weather and soil created great grapes. Again she was right. I had never been to a wine tasting where I liked and was ready to purchase three wines in succession.

The fourth wine I was sure would break this perfect run, especially since it was a port wine. We were all unenthusiastic about trying a port on such a hot summer day, but wanting to be polite, we acquiesced. Again we were surprised. It was smooth and at the same time complex. It would be wonderful with desserts, or as she said—the magic word—chocolates!

We were so pleased with our morning that we told Steve we were ready to return to our bed-and-breakfast. Any additional winery would have suffered by comparison.

A luxurious afternoon with no plans spread out in front of us. At the Inn we agreed to meet for dinner and straggled off in separate directions to enjoy our free afternoon. I didn't know about the others, but I knew exactly where I wanted to go.

16
Life's Blind Curves

With my face burrowed deep in the corner of my bent elbow to block blowing sands stirred by ocean breezes, I floated between distorted consciousness and seductive slumber. The sun's mid-afternoon rays fought to pierce slivers of sliding clouds. Basking one moment in the sun's caressing warmth, shivering in the deep shade the next, I'd once again try to convince myself to wake up long enough to pull on the jacket crumpled beside me on the beach. But the remnants of a morning spent tasting wines, a body exhausted from five days of being issued nonstop orders while motorcycling, and a head that started to ring every time it was moved, made the effort seem monumental.

"You awake?" came the muffled voice of Eva as she approached from the hillside behind the beach.

"Just barely," I said as I lifted my head several inches and squinted in her direction. She placed a covered cardboard cup next to me in the sand.

"Brought you a cappuccino from a coffee shop in town."

My hands welcomed its warmth as I dug it out of the sand and held it between both palms. Spreading her blanket next to mine, she dropped her magazines and book onto it and sat down.

"I'm reading a great article about married couples who found each other through newspaper personal ads. Ron said that's how you met Bill. Is that really what happened?"

"Yes. I answered just one personal ad in my whole life and married the guy. With Bill it was love at first sight."

"That's a story that doesn't happen often. What made you answer his ad?"

"It was another one of life's blind curves. You know, one of those times when you're so desperate for change that you're willing to do anything different to shake up your life."

I explained to Eva how, after seventeen years of being single following my divorce, I was ready to be married and knew my current choices weren't getting me there. It was a Friday evening and the first week the local *Lancaster New Era* newspaper had begun to run personal ads. These ads were the kind that encouraged you to call in and pay five dollars to listen to a writer's recorded message.

As I quickly surveyed the page filled with short, four-line profiles, one ad stood out from the others. It started out: *International business consultant, father of a six-year-old daughter, living in a 250-year-old farmhouse.* This spoke to me because, as another business consultant, he'd understand my crazy, demanding work life. The word "international" told me that he had at least traveled outside of Lancaster County. The sentence about being a father meant that he knew how to love and continue to care about others.

Curious to learn more, I decided for fun to listen to what he had recorded. At the end of Bill's message, an operator's pre-recorded voice said, "And now at the sound of the beep, leave your message."

It all happened so quickly, I was caught off-guard. I had no idea that I'd have a chance to leave my own message. I had nothing prepared, but I've always been good at impromptu speeches, so I left a rambling message along with my phone number.

Bill had stated in his audio message that he'd be out of town at a conference in Dallas, Texas, until the following Monday morning when he'd return all calls. I spent the rest of the weekend scared that he might call and worried that he wouldn't. But he did call on Monday—first thing, at 8:30 in the morning. Seven months later we were married.

"Your story is better than any of these. They should have interviewed you!"

As Eva picked up her book, I sat staring at the ocean, thinking, *that was another time in my life when I willingly steered my life into a blind curve.* That first blind curve, answering the personal ad, took me into two more significant blind curves—marrying a man I had only known for seven months and becoming a first-time mother at the age of forty-five to a six-year-old. These were huge, life-altering changes, but it had felt natural to break with convention and marry so quickly.

There had been such certainty for both of us about our joint future together that Bill never proposed to me. Somehow our discussions moved naturally toward talking about our impending married life together. We even planned our formal engagement date. When he gave me a ring two months after our first meeting, I presented him with an engraved engagement watch inscribed on the back: "IF, Linda." It was our shared secret that IF stood for "infatuated forever." We both wanted to keep that initial passion in our life with each other.

I smiled as I thought about how much energy we had channeled into keeping our relationship fresh—recreating the exciting qualities of infatuation while balancing them with ever-deepening feelings of appreciation, respect, and love. Taking another sip I thought about our "IF code" and what a woman at our local coffee shop had said about us eleven years later.

⁓

Something tickled the back of my neck. I flinched and reached up to discover what it was. As I turned around, there was Bill, laughing at my startled response. He had seen my car parked outside our local South Lakes Starbucks on his way home from the Sport & Health Club and decided to stop in to join me. He still wore his workout shorts, muscle T-shirt, and running shoes.

"Gotcha," he said, laughing, pleased with himself.

"What are you doing here?" I asked, startled but delighted to see him. Blue eyes twinkling, he planted a quick kiss. "I saw your car. Thought I'd come in and surprise you."

At times like this he looked more like a schoolboy of twelve than a sixty-two-year-old businessman. As he talked, he jumped back and forth in small hops from one foot to the other with mischievous energy. I called this his "Billy Dance." He stood much closer than he needed to as we waited in line, but he was feeling playful and flirtatious. I couldn't help joining in. His energy was contagious.

"Enjoy your workout?" I said, already knowing his answer.

"Power Yoga class was hard, but I kept up with Cynthia." Cynthia was his favorite yoga instructor who loved to push her students, and Bill was proud that he could hang in there with her, holding each pose longer than most others in class.

"You're out early," I said.

"I know. For some reason I couldn't finish the ninety-minute kick-boxing, so I left before class was over. That's been happening the last couple of weeks. I just run out of air."

"Having your usual?" I asked.

"Yep, I'll grab us a place." With that he turned, feet still dancing, to find us a table.

"Mind if I ask you a personal question?" the woman behind me in line said. "How long have you two been married?"

"Eleven years."

"Oh, I thought maybe you were newlyweds."

As I picked up our two cappuccinos and headed toward the tables, I thought, *It's better than being newlyweds.* Not only was Bill my husband, he was my business partner, best friend, most honest critic, and staunchest supporter.

It took us several more months to find out what was causing Bill's shortness of breath. On the kind of January morning when regrouting your bathroom tile seems more appealing than venturing outside into the gray, wintry air, I sat in the large outpatient surgery lobby of the Inova Fairfax Hospital, twenty miles from our home in Reston, Virginia.

The weather report had predicted freezing rain throughout the day, turning into ice storms by evening. Each time the main lobby door opened, a chill blew across the floor, sending me burrowing deeper into my down-filled coat.

Whenever a name was called over the loudspeakers, I strained to hear if it was mine. After each announcement, the person walking toward the desk was met by a surgeon who brought news about a completed operation.

Bill had been wheeled into surgery several hours earlier. For the past two months he had seen a variety of specialists to find out why fluid was gathering around his heart in his pleural cavity. Scary test after scary test had come back normal. His pulmonary specialist decided he needed to have exploratory surgery so they could place a small video camera inside his chest to see what was causing the problem.

We were told it was probably a rare, difficult-to-diagnose virus. This morning they would finally discover which one, so it could be treated. We were ready to quit holding our breath.

Finally, my name was called. I stood and walked toward Bill's pulmonary surgeon. He didn't mince words. With both of us standing in the middle of the lobby filled with commotion and people, he delivered the news.

"Your husband is in an advanced stage of cancer. Most probably mesothelioma. I'm sorry, there's nothing more we can do."

"Are you sure?" I asked, trying to get my mind around the news.

"Yes, his life expectancy isn't long, perhaps four months. There's no known cure for this type of cancer. If you have questions ask your oncologist," he said, shoving several photographs of the offending tumors at me as he continued talking about their sizes and locations.

Ripples of fear clenched my chest, my shoulders coiled forward, and my knees began to buckle. I wanted to flee and find my "real" life and not this one. Instead, I reached out and grasped onto the edge of a tall planter box on my right, hoping to steady myself. All I had heard were the words, *four months* and *no known cure*.

I took a deep breath to catch up with his conversation.

"Talk to our oncologist? We don't have an oncologist. We didn't know we needed one. You're a surgeon. You're an expert in pulmonary function. You know more about mesothelioma than most doctors. Please, what can be done to save my husband? Surgery? Chemotherapy? Radiation? Experimental drugs? Something? . . . Anything!"

"You'll have to talk to your oncologist," he repeated, turning and striding away.

I reached and stepped in his departing direction, wanting to ask more. In shock, I stood motionless, staring at the NO ADMITTANCE sign on the closed door he had just walked through.

After an indeterminable amount of time, I stumbled, dazed, to my seat and collapsed. Alone in the middle of a hectic reception room, I sat gripping the arms of my chair, trying to comprehend what had just happened.

The world whirled around me, out of focus, as if I were on a merry-go-round that had begun spinning so furiously it had broken off its spindle and was careening through space.

Several years earlier after a chest X-ray, a doctor had told Bill that he had scarring on the front lobe of his left lung that was typical of asbestos damage. He was reassured there was no reason to be concerned because mesothelioma, cancer resulting from earlier asbestos exposure, was so rare that few pulmonary doctors saw even one case during their lifetime.

Two hours later my name was called over the loudspeaker, and I was escorted to Bill's bed in post-op. He was still groggy from sedation, but it was reassuring to see him. I instantly relaxed, leaned over his bed's side guard, touched his arm, kissed him, and told him I loved him.

Bill smiled up at me.

After a brief conversation he asked, "So what did they find? Is it a virus like we thought?"

Shocked that no one had told him the results of his surgery, I tried to disguise my inner panic. It was up to me to deliver the diagnosis no one ever wants to receive or report. I knew Bill would not want me to tiptoe around the truth so I told him as gently as I could.

"The doctor said it's cancer, probably mesothelioma." I awaited his response, unable to predict his reaction.

He pondered for a moment, then smiled up at me and said, "But I haven't had my fifteen minutes yet."

"What?" I said.

"I haven't had my fifteen minutes yet."

"What?" I asked again, still not comprehending Bill's answer.

"Everyone's supposed to have their fifteen minutes of fame before they die. I haven't had mine yet."

Bill never got his fifteen minutes of fame in the traditional sense. He did get eleven more months of life. He did get loving support from his family and friends.

That last year our home was opened to our children, our families, and a host of supportive friends, often over-filling our guest room, sleeping on couches and sharing our meals.

Bill became an incredible diplomat, helping frightened family and friends relax and laugh in his company. In spite of what was happening, he was still the Bill I had fallen in love with—the Bill we all loved.

Life during his last eleven months became more meaningful, scary, real, tenuous, and precious. We discovered wonderful gifts on this final journey together—experiencing love's strength, communicating without words, and shedding useless protocols as we re-funneled our energy into what mattered most.

Much *healing* took place in all of our lives—family, friends, mine, and Bill's—we came together, cried, loved, and lived as never before. But no one could *cure* the cancer.

Bill and I spent every day and many sleepless nights together. I dedicated myself to doing everything and anything that would make his life more comfortable, memorable, and overflowing with love.

During his remaining time, we grew even closer, operating seamlessly as one unit, appreciating each other, each day, each precious moment.

Now, looking at the ocean and watching the crashing waves, I knew if I had it all to do over again, I'd still answer that personal ad. Nothing in life is a mistake! My inner certainty had led me through a blind curve to Bill. That same internal voice had known this trip held more than a good time.

With the trip half over, I wondered what other treasures I was supposed to find. Would I know all of its meaning by the end of this adventure, or would I need years to understand it?

17
The Longest Day

After an early dinner we huddled around multiple maps spread across the inn's dining room table.

Ron announced, "Tomorrow's our longest day. It's three-hundred-fifty miles, but very doable. With lots of back roads at the start of the morning, and with the extra rest stops we'll need to make to recover from the hundred-degree midday heat, we won't average much more than forty-five miles an hour for the day. So prepare yourselves for a long, extended day of riding."

"Let's check the maps to make sure your distance is right," Eva said.

Alberto began reading off the mileage on his map, tracing the route from Mendocino, California, to Crater Lake, Oregon, as Eva added up the numbers.

"That's not three-hundred-fifty miles. It's more like four-hundred-fifty," Eva said.

"That's at least ten hours of riding tomorrow," Alberto said.

"Maybe longer. Look, there are several hundred miles on Interstate 5 during the heat of the day. There may be some heavy backups. Linda, this is really going to be a test of your riding ability," Ron said.

I gulped. As a former Californian, I knew about the trials of riding on the dreaded Golden State Freeway, the main interstate going north and south through California. It was always heavily traveled. Even at two o'clock in the morning it could get backed up with stalled traffic.

So far on this trip, we had avoided interstates, but now, to get to Crater Lake where we had reservations at the National Park Lodge, there was no way to avoid traveling on Interstate 5.

Riding on a six-to-eight-lane freeway, aside from being monotonous, was dangerous. It's hard monitoring so much traffic in multiple lanes, and our small group could easily get separated by cars moving into our lane, even if we rode in a closer-than-normal formation.

Using different maps, we each began searching for alternate routes that could shave off mileage and time from tomorrow's journey. We all agreed that our zigzag beginning route contained too many unnecessary miles going the wrong direction. It headed first north to link with a back road that ran diagonally southeast before finally connecting with I-5 where we would turn north again.

"I'm going to check with our innkeepers to see if there's a way to avoid this southerly sojourn to I-5," Alberto said as he started toward the kitchen.

He returned a few moments later shaking his head. "There's no faster way. We're stuck."

I checked my spreadsheet of nightly lodgings and verified that our Crater Lake Lodge reservations were pre-paid and nonrefundable, even if we were to call now to cancel them. We understood the reasons for pre-booking our lodging with guaranteed reservations. It was dangerous after a hard day of riding to go in and out of hotel parking lots, checking to see if they had rooms available, and no one wanted to be riding late into the night because all lodging was full.

The trade-off for these pre-paid arrangements? If we didn't arrive at our booked destination, we'd end up paying double lodging that evening. Also, if the lost distance couldn't be recovered the next day, successive nights could be affected. So there was always some suspense about possible illness, mechanical breakdowns, bad weather, and traffic delays.

Evaluating alternatives to simplify tomorrow, our longest day of riding, we concluded that going to bed early and hitting the road no later than eight o'clock the next morning was our only choice. After a day filled with wine tasting, shopping, beachcombing, and dining, a nightcap of reading a book and going to bed early felt right.

After arranging with the staff for a seven o'clock breakfast, we retired to our rooms. Tomorrow promised to be a test for even the experienced riders. I wasn't sure I wanted to understand how hard the longer distance and more challenging roads might be for me. Being a novice with its accompanying naiveté was a blessing at times like this.

⁂

Frustrated, still standing in my nightgown, looking at a pile of folded clothing on my bed, I turned to Eva and asked, "How do we dress for today?"

"I don't know. It's hard," she responded. "Look outside. It's cool now, but it's going to get a lot hotter by midday. Then tonight it'll be chilly again. Better just dress in lots of layers and be prepared to take off what you don't need and put it back on later."

We were starting the day with crisp coastal temperatures in the mid-fifties—twenty degrees colder yet on a motorcycle with wind chill created by riding. By noon, traveling through Northern California, we'd have to endure near hundred-degree searing heat. Finally, by evening, after crossing back into Oregon, we would be riding in mountains, possibly with snow and ice on the ground. So my choice as I got dressed was whether I wanted to be too cold or too hot. There would be little "just right" today.

After eating a hearty breakfast we emerged into the cold, gray outdoors. So far on this road trip we'd been lucky and hadn't experienced any coastal fog, but this morning we were surrounded by a thick, heavy mist. This meant we would be starting our longest day traveling even more slowly than anticipated.

"This fog's going to make everything more dangerous," Eva said, shaking her head.

"We've got to keep our speed down until we're out of this soup," Ron cautioned. He pulled his bike to the edge of the driveway and stopped as we lined up behind him, preparing to enter the highway. I looked back at Alberto in last position and was grateful his jacket was bright yellow, so he'd be easier for other vehicles to see. It was generous of him to assume that vulnerable line position. As we pulled onto the highway, we could barely see each other, let alone the road and oncoming traffic. I was thankful to be riding in a group and not alone. I felt like a beginner all over again, worried and unsure of what lay ahead.

The cold morning winds sent chills through me even though I was wearing heavy leather pants with another Lycra pair under them, thick knee socks over my regular socks, a long-sleeved T-shirt over my sports halter top and a fleece zippered jacket under my lined heavy leather jacket. With all of this, I still regretted not having added yet another layer, but where would I have put it?

After riding north on Highway 1 for twelve miles, we found our cutoff road to the southeast. This was the type of winding road we normally celebrated, full of complex curves, but on this morning we found ourselves behind lethargic pickup trucks and dawdling cars that were going well below the speed limit, unhurried on this Friday morning. Our only choice was to relax and accept that we were part of a slow-moving parade.

It was new and intimidating riding on my first interstate, traveling at faster speeds with heavy traffic in all of the lanes around me. Until now, riding on a motorcycle with a less powerful engine and fewer luxury features had created little impact on my riding enjoyment. However, on an interstate where our pace was maintained at a consistent speed with no shifting, stopping, and starting, I understood the downside of not having several basic upgrades. Without cruise control, it was tiring to grip and turn the throttle hard enough backwards, at enough rotation to produce our consistent sixty-mile-per-hour speed.

After holding my right hand and wrist in the same twisted position for extended periods, the inseam of my right glove started to produce a blister from its repetitious rubbing and pulling against my right palm. I tried to push small bits of Kleenex into the space, but this offered little relief. The skin was already too raw.

At these higher speeds, the vibration of my motorcycle's engine was unrelenting and resonated throughout my whole body. The extra-padded mounting below the engine on more expensive models, advertised to reduce engine vibration, was now an addition I'd welcome.

The other more elaborate motorcycles in our group contained a second footrest positioned straight ahead of the rider and higher in the air. Additionally, they had running boards five inches wide by twelve or more inches long to rest their feet on as they shifted and braked.

I only had a single set of round pegs four inches long by two inches wide for my feet to rest on, located directly below my body. The only way to stretch my legs was to kick a single foot momentarily out into the air around the bike. It looked funny but offered a brief respite from a singular, tiring position.

I knew that most serious riders upgraded to more powerful and luxurious bikes. Until now, I had assumed their motivation was primarily status-driven. Today, riding on the interstate on this more basic motorcycle, the upgrades made sense.

On my next trip, I'd be ready for better engineering, more power and additional features. Riding comfort on long trips could easily be translated into a safer ride, since these shortcomings were becoming both distracting and exhausting.

⟨⟩

Although we had started the day freezing, now the midday temperature in central California was over one hundred degrees. With open fields on both sides of the interstate, there was no tree cover or building shadows to diminish the sun's unrelenting rays, so we cooked in California's kitchen three different ways as we rode: *Broiled* by the sun's rays beating down upon us from above, *baked* by the scorching heat of our own motorcycle engines and exhaust pipes beneath us, and *fried* by the ambient heat rising from the road underneath us, searing our feet and lower bodies like hundreds of blowtorches.

Even the normally cooling winds produced by our speed offered no relief. Instead it felt as if we were riding straight into hair dryers switched on high, their hot air blasting our bodies.

Ther-wack . . . ther-wack . . . ther-wack . . . was the repetitious sound of our tires riding across joints in the highway filled with sticky tar that had liquefied in the heat. It was as if each tire was being pulled into the tacky substance only to finally break free and be caught by the next crack. The motion repeated with the uncomfortable sound of a band aid being ripped off a wound thousands of times.

Scientists claim that wearing an extra long layer of clothing actually is more cooling to the body than going shirtless in the sun, but I would have welcomed their riding with us in today's heat and seeing if they still agreed with their controlled laboratory findings. My long-sleeved jacket and pants were not cooling anything. I looked enviously at other motorcyclists we passed on the road—no jackets, dressed in sleeveless shirts, jeans or shorts, and wearing half helmets without face masks.

I understood the reasons for our heavy, protective gear, but it was hard to adhere to this logic under these miserable conditions.

I noticed that Alberto, Ron, and Eva had lifted their face shields on their helmets, so I pushed mine up too. The air trapped behind them had simply become too unbearable. Even with my clear shield up in the air, it still felt ten degrees hotter behind my sunglasses, but I kept them on as some form of eye protection was needed against possible flying objects.

Draped in heavy black protection, we fought sleepiness and thirst, so we increased the frequency of our breaks to wake up and rehydrate. At every stop we re-soaked our railroad bandanas and re-tied them around our necks.

We had already peeled off as many layers as we could. I was down to a halter-top underneath my jacket. My leather pants had long zippers up the side running from my ankles to the tops of my legs. I unzipped these at every rest stop, ignoring the plentiful suggestive comments and stares from others.

It was hard to feel sexy when I felt more like a piece of charred beef than a Barbie doll. No, feeling sexy was the furthest thing from my mind. Comparing the desirability of hot, steamy, torrid sex matched against a cold, frigid snub combined with frozen glares, for once I would have opted for the frigid fantasy. Anything cold was desirable! Even the words icy, chilly, frosty, and arctic were soothing.

For the first time on the trip, the riding was truly miserable; our breaks became our treasured time. Subway restaurants were our stop of choice due to one earlier good experience laughing and joking with the young girl behind the counter. We had even convinced her to concoct a special sandwich just for us. Now, each time we stopped at a new one, we'd anticipate repeating the fun and order our custom sandwich. With such expectations, we were rarely disappointed. Their pumped-up, noisy air conditioning, combined with ridiculously-sized jumbo drinks, made the shops seem like heaven.

I held my current icy drink against every patch of uncovered skin and sighed, relieved by the cooling sensation.

It's amazing how the definition of heaven changes during challenging times. Heaven was unzipped leather pants, frosty drinks in tall waxy paper cups, noisy air conditioners belting out cold air, a sopping-wet handkerchief tied around my neck, and perching on a plastic chair around a rickety, unbalanced table that easily toppled any drink resting on it when bumped. *Yes, this is what heaven must feel like!*

⋘∘⋙

Back on the interstate again in the early afternoon, we were confronted by yet another unanticipated delay that would extend our longest day even more. All four lanes of the northbound freeway slowed, jamming up and eventually coming to a full stop.

Balancing our heavy bikes with our legs, as we sat on them with the sun beating down from directly overhead, we had no way of knowing how long we'd be stuck there. Concerned that we might run out of gas if we ran our motorcycles continuously, we turned them off and sat until traffic had moved forward enough to merit turning them back on again to close the thirty-or-so-foot gap. For over an hour we endured the heat, repeating this awkward routine.

Mile after mile it continued. Creeping forward. Then parking. Turning the engines off. Waiting. Turning the engines back on.

Twenty feet forward. Repeat.

Fifty feet. Repeat.

Thirty feet more. Every minimal gain was hard earned.

Eventually, we quit fighting this routine and simply replayed this motor-on-and-off charade mechanically with ever-increasing skill and efficiency. With emotional resistance gone, our suffering dissipated. The one thing we controlled was our attitude.

Finally, after what seemed like an hour, our speed reached a consistent fifteen miles per hour. I silently cheered, thinking the ordeal would soon be over.

Off in the distance I could make out a cluster of flashing lights and sadly surmised that an accident, not roadwork, must have caused this delay. As we rode closer, I could distinguish lights belonging to several emergency vehicles—three police cruisers, an ambulance, and a fire truck off on the far right shoulder of the highway.

As my curiosity escalated along with concern, our speed accelerated, forcing me to return my focus to my motorcycle and the erratic driving around me. All traffic was being funneled into the far left three lanes, with the right one blocked off by state police cars and flares.

As we passed the accident, I could only afford a quick glance in its direction. I gasped, shocked to see an elaborate black and silver motorcycle lying on its side in the far right lane of the highway facing the wrong direction. A dozen motorcycles were parked neatly in a singular line along the shoulder.

At the rear of the ambulance, a group of bikers stood shoulder to shoulder in a semi-circle around what I guessed must be rescue workers attending to a body in its center.

I quickly returned my eyes to the road in front of me, wailing: *Oh no!*

A wave of panic clenched my heart. *Someone's husband has died. Someone's son is hurt. Someone's brother, someone's best friend, someone's colleague, someone's riding buddy is fighting for his life.* I clenched my handlebars tightly, identifying with all of the hearts that would be pierced by news of this accident. I knew this pain of sudden devastating loss intimately. I whispered a quick prayer asking for protection for the biker and everyone who loved or cared about him or her.

I attempted a second hurried glance. The scene appeared somber and serious, the motorcyclists' eyes staring downward, as they stood motionless, looking more like artificial mannequins than living bikers.

I wanted to quit driving and freeze in time and space. But instead I returned my attention to my own driving and the hazards around me. On my left a white Mustang's white-walled tires drifted over the dotted white line, dangerously close to me. The brake lights of the red Dodge pickup in front of us lit up as his tires screeched. Distracted drivers alerted by this sound began to over-correct their wandering vehicles.

I reprimanded myself: *There's too much imminent danger to process these emotions now. Pay attention to your own motorcycle.*

Having just witnessed my first motorcycle accident, I was painfully aware of my vulnerability, riding so exposed to the chaotic traffic around me.

Our speed soon accelerated to our previous sixty-mile-per-hour rate, and the compacted traffic began dispersing. I grew concerned as my red gas warning light started to flicker. I knew others in our group were probably low too. Thankfully, a sign indicated an exit in two miles.

We signaled each other that we needed to get off the interstate for gas and a much-needed chance to discuss what we had seen. This was a memory none of us wanted. It was time to talk about it instead of riding alone with its images and imagined consequences replaying in our heads.

I would only need to hold it together a little longer. Stoically, I flicked on my right turn signal and followed Alberto and Eva up the ramp with Ron following behind. Pulling into a restaurant parking lot, I turned off my motorcycle but remained sitting. I breathed deeply and cried silently. *Life is so fragile. It can end or be altered forever by a whiff of a moment.*

Eva and Alberto walked toward the restaurant. I pulled my face shield back down over my face, wanting to retain some semblance of privacy as I bent over my motorcycle and felt the weight of the horrors of the accident now flashing in my mind. The fallen motorcycle lying without rider, alone in the lane. The huddle of bikers—solemn, not moving, heads dropped, shoulders curved, vulnerable. No longer a band of fearless warriors charging down the road, playing and hollering. Now they stood silent . . . Castrated . . . Lifeless . . . Someone might have been maimed for life or died. Lives were forever changed.

We had all just viewed the nightmare of every biker and everyone who cares about someone who rides. Death had been in full view. It was close-up and personal, not just a photo or story of some faraway disaster. The victim was a biker riding a similar motorcycle to ours, dressed like us, most probably our age. He or she had been riding on the same highway, been tested by the same searing heat we were fighting. *That driver could have been any one of us. It could have been me.*

Salty tears streamed down my face; my chest heaved in silent crying. My empathy was for the biker's family and friends.

One fleeting mistake, a minute miscalculation in riding, lapse in concentration, or maybe a pending health crisis had kicked in—a heart attack, heat exhaustion, a stroke—and now gleaming motorcycle and decorated rider were down.

I continued sobbing, barely making any sound as my breathing caught and my chest rose and fell. Since Bill had died, I had felt totally unprotected from such scenes. My compassion for others was no longer distant or separate. It was instant, and I was there.

When stories about tornadoes, tsunamis, fires, hurricanes, and other tragic losses appeared on TV, I'd flip it off, unable to watch as reporters thrust microphones in survivors' faces, creating the color of terror to entertain us viewers. I quit going to suspense movies, reading much of the newspaper, or knowingly picking up a traumatic book.

I was too raw. Too exposed. My pain united quickly with the universal pain of all experiencing losses. It wasn't a story or entertainment. It was real. It was life.

I felt a hand placed gently on my back and looked up. It was Ron. "Let's go inside. We all need to talk about what we saw back there."

He said more, but I didn't hear his words as I lifted my head, breathed deeply, and began the steep mental journey from my past back to this present. At least now the past no longer felt more real than an undesirable present. At least now I wanted to be a part of this current life. I had rebuilt the bridge between the past and the present. I crawled off my bike, peeled off my gloves, pushed off my helmet, and wiped my wet eyes with the backs of my hands.

As we turned toward the restaurant, Ron placed his comforting arm around my shoulder and left it protectively as we walked. He didn't speak, and I was grateful. I didn't need someone else's thoughts at that particular moment, but I did appreciate the company of a special friend.

Alberto and Eva had already gotten their soft drinks and had grabbed a booth. Ron and I ordered our food, then walked over to join them. Eva's face was flushed, and she ignored the food in front of her as she sat staring out the window. It was obvious from her matted hair that this was one time she hadn't immediately refreshed her looks after she took off her helmet. Alberto's brow was furrowed and his head was bent forward as he sat staring at the tabletop, not moving. Ron and I slid in on the opposite side of the booth.

At first no one talked. We sat almost motionless, lost in our own thoughts. But as soon as Eva began to talk, we all joined in speaking on top of each other as no one could wait and merely listen. There was too much energy to be released.

"What could have happened?"

"Do you think he hit something?

"There weren't any skid marks and the motorcycle seemed fine. It was lying on its side without anything else nearby."

"No other vehicles seemed to be involved . . ."

"Maybe he had a heart attack . . ."

"How about a stroke?"

"Lost his concentration or passed out from heat?"

"Or maybe he fell asleep? I was having a hard time staying awake myself. That interstate was hot and monotonous."

"Could he have run out of gas and lost control?"

"At least there appeared to be plenty of medical help."

"Hope it was enough . . ."

"This is exactly the type of thing you never want to see, and we all dread," Ron said. We all nodded and retreated back into our personal thoughts and discomfort.

"Look guys, let's ease up on our plans for today. It's our lives that really matter. I've got a husband and daughters," Eva said. "Who cares if we make it to a silly National Park tonight where we have reservations. There's always tomorrow."

"You're right," said Alberto. "We can all afford to pay for a second hotel room tonight. If it's too far or too late, we'll just stop and find another place."

Ron, Eva, and I nodded.

The accident had shocked all of us. It repositioned our road trip's significance as a mere stone amongst a greater life filled with richer treasure.

If we could not make it to Crater Lake this evening, we would simply find another hotel and stop when it made sense. All of us wanted to ensure the group's safety. That was the higher goal over merely completing a logistical agenda.

Once again, no longer was the destination more important than the journey.

18
Vroom!

A mesmerizing, snow-capped mountain appeared in the distance. It stood solo and regal, unaccompanied by foothills or other mountains. Riding on a motorcycle, it was impossible to grab a map to see if we'd be riding past it. From road signs we soon learned that this stunning, eye-catching, roughly 14,000-foot volcano was Mount Shasta.

When I first saw this mountain, I mistakenly thought we'd be next to it in ten or so minutes. I had forgotten lessons learned as a child riding in the West, about size, distance, and travel time. It was over an hour before we came close enough to decipher its multiple peaks. Our highway passed over Lake Shasta, but we couldn't see the Shasta Dam from the interstate. We'd need to take one of the exits to visit what I later learned was the second tallest dam in the world—twice the height of Niagara Falls.

Part of the challenge of any trip is making the decision to pass up some spectacular sites to have adequate time for others. My sisters and I still gently tease my mother for having pointed at maps while on our earlier annual camping trips across the United States, saying, "Oh, look Ed, we could stop and see 'x' (fill in any possible attraction), it's only two inches off our route on the map." The four of us Crill kids would respond in a chorus of overly dramatic groans, knowing that the mere two inches could easily equate to another two hours of riding cooped up in an overloaded car.

Today I extend yet another apology to my mother for my childhood antics, as I now understand the allure of missing an attraction by a mere two inches, as well as the desire to experience it all. Life is too short to waste any part of it.

But realizing the wisdom of balancing quality against quantity, I didn't pose the two-inch plea to my riding peers, especially on this longest day.

As we motored past Mount Shasta on I-5, we could only longingly look at the turn-offs to the mountain as we continued northward toward the Oregon border. We were all skiers, so we lustfully viewed its snowcapped top, wishing for a quick chance to swoosh down on its summer snow, enjoying a different kind of speed and thrill. But this was our longest day—the only trip day without extra playtime.

As we finally rode across the border into Oregon, the temperature continued dropping, traffic thinned, and views of the Cascade Mountain Range returned. Riding became easier again as the probability of reaching our destination of Crater Lake Lodge seemed certain.

A short while later as evening approached, we turned off our interstate onto the kind of two-lane, winding backcountry road we loved.

Dog-tired, we felt as if we had stepped into a sensual shower. Entering forest-covered hills, our eyes were soothed by colors softened in twilight's encroaching haze. We inhaled the rich musky smells of humus, grass, and pines. Our muscles relaxed, realizing the battle against heat and pounding winds was over for the day.

Running parallel to the road was a fourteen-foot wide mountain brook that raced around boulders, cascaded over rocks and collided against its own banks in its many turns. The rushing sound refreshed ears weary from a day spent in thunderous traffic. The stream played a childhood game of peek-a-boo with us—viewable and noisy one moment, hidden and whispering the next.

Even though it was the middle of June, patches of snow lined the sides of the road as we slowly climbed in elevation and drew closer to the park. These snow banks appeared old and packed down, with softened edges from daily meltings. In spite of the snow's probable age, it was still surprisingly white.

Darkness softly enveloped us as we turned onto our final road of the day, and our headlights lit up a split-timber National Park sign with carved-out, bright yellow letters stating: Crater Lake National Park.

I had never ridden in the dark with my headlights pointing out the way, and smiled as I added yet another first to my now crowded list.

We pulled up and stopped at the entrance gate to the park ready to pay the fees and get directions to the lodge. We were smiling, congratulating ourselves and proud that we had finally made it. The longest day of riding was almost behind us.

A female park ranger sat in the booth. She leaned out her side window and motioned to us to come even closer. It was obvious she wanted to address our whole group. We pulled into a tighter formation, shut off our engines and lifted our face masks so we could hear her better.

She reported that most of the park's roads were still closed, buried under deep snowdrifts. The recently plowed road winding up the side of this steep volcano to Crater Lake Lodge at the top would be challenging riding for motorcycles in the dark. The ride would take about twenty minutes, and she cautioned that we should be prepared for steep ascents, hairpin turns and patches of snow. Most importantly, we should be on the lookout for hard-to-see black ice.

Our faces dropped. We were tired—our bodies exhausted. We were finally almost to our destination. We were already celebrating a shower, change of clothes, drink, and dinner. Now we were told there was yet another unexpected challenge. Our reserve of stored energy had already been robbed. Little was left.

Turning back didn't feel like a possible alternative. The last motel we had seen was over an hour ago, back near the main highway. We didn't have the stamina for that long ride or the uncertainty of available rooms once we got there.

We thanked her, and then gathered at the side of the road to discuss our next steps. No one had strength left to explore other options for tonight's lodging. We had come so far and battled so hard to get here. We at least had to attempt this mountain road.

As we remounted our bikes, Alberto, Ron, and Eva talked on top of each other, shouting tips to me about how to avoid the beginner's mistakes on hairpin turns combined with steep ascents. My head spun as I tried to make sense of their disjointed coaching.

I recalled the story Ron and Alberto had told on the first evening of this trip, about climbing a mountain in the Alps, when all six members had dumped their bikes in the middle of a particularly tight upward mountain turn because they had misjudged its challenge. They had laughed as they retold that story, but I knew from personal experience at the rider training class how much it hurt to have your body slammed against the road surface and then crushed by your own motorcycle. My body was already moving towards panic from just its memory alone.

The discussion inside my head became noisy and jumbled. I was new to riding in the dark where the motorcycle's headlights only lit up what was directly in front of the bike's handlebars and not what was around a sharp turn. I'd be riding blind to what was on the road ahead of me as I made those precarious tight turns.

Also, I had never ridden a motorcycle on snow. The thought of riding up a steep mountain road with difficult hairpin curves at night, possibly coated in black ice and slippery snow, had one voice inside my head shouting: *It's simply too much. Quit before you get hurt.* A calmer, more reasonable voice, reminded me: *After all you have been through these past years, this is a piece of cake. You can do it.*

I tuned out the first voice, took a deep breath and addressed it. *This was nothing. I know what hell looks like. This isn't even close. I can do this.*

With Ron leading and Alberto riding shotgun behind, we motored off into the darkness. Inside I also shifted my body into its own kind of neutral gear where I quit thinking of the dangerous climb ahead and concentrated only on what my motorcycle's headlights were showing me. This whole climb still felt overwhelming, but this in-the-moment focus was manageable.

Twenty minutes later we rode around another blind curve and found ourselves in the Greater Lake Lodge parking lot. We parked our motorcycles and stood shaking our heads, sharing our joint surprise at our unexpected arrival.

We had prepared ourselves for such a horrendous climb that we continually assumed the impossible turns that the ranger had described were still in front of us. Instead we must have ridden through them as we waited for the more formidable ones to appear. We had made it to the top, turn by turn. We had survived. All were accounted for. Our bikes were still intact. Today's longest ride was over!

Before the road trip had begun, John had estimated this day's ride as three-hundred-fifty miles. Last night we had recalculated it as four-hundred-fifty miles. But now, as we looked at our odometers, we realized we had ridden five hundred fifty miles today. Our misinformation had made this longest day ride an attainable goal. VROOM!

We checked in at the lodge's spacious combination lobby-lounge room called The Great Hall. We were delighted that this space was filled with many large, comfortably overstuffed chairs and sofas. The cathedral three-story ceilings showed off substantial rustic log beams. In the center of the inside log wall stood a huge river-rock fireplace with a roaring fire.

Along the outside wall of the Great Hall were rows of windows and French doors that looked out onto six-mile-wide Crater Lake below. A full moon reflected on the water and gleaming snow. Tall pine trees, silhouetted on the rocky ridge around the water's edge, completed the majestic picture.

Inside the lounge, people sat everywhere, enjoying conversations and the relaxing scenery. Through expansive glass doors at the far end of the room was a dining room, crowded with evening guest.

After showering and changing we flopped down on the first empty chairs we could find, directly in front of the grand fireplace. *Finally, it's satisfying to have something that roars that doesn't come from a motor.* Our waitress told us there was an unusually long wait for dinner in the neighboring dining room, so we ordered generous appetizers and drinks.

If heaven earlier today had been an over air-conditioned Subway restaurant with mega iced drinks and a wobbly table, tonight this national park lodge replete with crackling fire, lush overstuffed chairs, and extra-dry cold martinis had to be Elysium, Shangri-La, and the Garden of Eden rolled into one.

This was another best evening of the trip, as I kept redefining the word "best." We were so happy to be at the lodge, and the setting was magnificent. We laughed and retold stories about the trials of the day—the fog, the snail-paced early morning parade on the winding road, the unbearable heat on the interstate, the motorcycle accident, the exquisite beauty of Mt. Shasta, the relief of riding next to a playful mountain brook and lastly, the dark, icy climb to this lodge.

We were so noisy, animated, and jovial that we instantly made friends with our waitress and everyone seated around us.

Rarely have I had more than one martini in an evening, but I added another new experience to the many firsts of that day and had three.

Throughout the trip, every day had been special in its own way. We all had remarked at the end of each day, what a great time we were having. But on this night, we were exuberant. Sharing the same daunting experiences made celebrating together so much more gratifying. Confronting difficulties together, we had learned a lot about each other's character. I would trust any of these riding companions with my life. Such deep bonds are hard to form in everyday life.

The coffee table in front of us told the story of our evening's celebration. It was cluttered with a menagerie of empty glasses, stacked appetizer plates, an array of empty bottles, and weird animals crafted out of twisted straws, lemon zest, and drink skewers poked into martini olives. The dining room had shut down an hour earlier. We were one of the last remaining groups lounging in the Great Hall. Even the fire was reduced to a few embers that could barely toast a lone marshmallow.

"They're closing shop around us," announced Alberto. "We have another ride ahead of us tomorrow. Shall we call it a night?"

We agreed, picked up our things, and climbed the huge pine stairs to the second floor.

Eva's and my room was tiny and not luxurious, but the view out our window of Crater Lake made it seem immense.

"Do you mind if we sleep with the curtains open tonight?" I asked, not wanting to be separated from the lake's beauty.

"As tired as I am now, I could fall asleep with lights glaring and music blaring. Go ahead. Treat yourself."

I pulled back the curtains, crawled into the bed next to the window, and peeked beneath heavy eyelids at the moon's reflection on the shimmering lake below.

The strenuous day, topped off by three martinis and a spirited celebration, made it easy to fall asleep. But as often happens after drinking, I awoke several hours later.

Finding it impossible to fall back asleep, I sat up in bed in a crossed-legged meditation pose and stared out the window. The lake was mesmerizing.

After spending the last seven days exposed to nature and using all of my senses to experience my surroundings, I was irritated by the sensual barrier and limited view imposed by this window. I wanted to smell the pine trees, feel the brisk wind whipping against my body, and view this panoramic attraction unobstructed—from above, below, and all sides. Looking at this flat picture, I felt as if I were in a museum, standing behind a velvet rope, staring at a static scene inside a wooden display box with a thick Plexiglas front.

Unable to silence my disgruntled feelings, I crawled out of bed, slid into my clothing, and picked up a room key. I glanced at Eva, feeling relieved that I hadn't awakened her, and crept downstairs. I tiptoed through the lobby—its lights had been turned off or dimmed and the front desk stood vacant. I slipped out the side lobby door, checking the locks first to make sure I would be able to re-enter later.

Outside in the dark, standing on the porch off the Great Hall, I pulled my jacket tightly around me as I moved forward to the railing, gazing at the postcard-perfect setting of lake, mountain peaks, trees, snow, sky, moon, and stars.

There was an unfamiliar stillness, void of the normal daily accompaniments—traffic, machinery, motors, people, pets, and sounds of wildlife. Highways were distant, guests asleep, staff retired and hotel operations shut down for the night. Everything had ceased moving and now rested.

Here, on the top of a dark volcano, separated from normal light pollution, the sky stretched away black, punctuated brilliantly by stars. It was a sky I rarely saw living in a city.

In the far distance a lone satellite carved its way through the sky, leaving a thin trail of flickering light that promptly faded.

Watching for shooting stars, I saw one, but when I tried to make a wish, all I felt was a heart filled with deep, intense desires. But I couldn't find words to express even one. Instead of a wish, I whispered the mantra I've been repeating daily for over thirty years: *I am surrounded by the white light of God. May nothing but goodness come to me, and may nothing but goodness flow from me.*

Some scenes in nature are definitively masculine or feminine. Looking at Crater Lake in the moonlight I was viewing a grand woman. As I gazed downward at the lake in front of me, she responded by hurling a cutting gust upwards at me, highlighting her frigid dominance. Very different from her volcanic past when she spewed hot lava, rocks, and fire, tonight she stood a frozen beauty, reigning over the terrain—regal, exquisite, and untouchable.

At first nothing seemed to move. But as I, the watcher, became still, slowing down my breathing, feeling at one with all that was around me, I started to notice a scene filled with activity—clouds moving in front of the moon, snow blowing off tree branches, stars twinkling, wind swirling. Reflected in the silvery rippling waters of the massive lake below me appeared the face of a magnificent woman, smiling and winking one of her deep violet eyes flirtatiously at me.

Breaking the night silence she spoke: "I am worthy of your travels. Quiet your mind. Be still. And you will be amazed by what my beauty stirs inside of you."

The leading lady, sharing the stage with no one, she presided regally, dressed by the night in her blue-black sequined shimmering formalwear. Surrounding her face, the snow-encrusted trees formed a dazzling diamond necklace that cast a sparkling glow across her face, lighting up her expression. The sky and stars formed her dark hair held gently in a glittering net sprinkled with stars. The moon was the spectacular diamond barrette in her hair that gleamed brightly and served as a spotlight to further illuminate her beauty.

She didn't move from center stage. Like many sirens, she stood desirable but untouchable, able to be viewed only from afar by her many suitors and admirers.

Following her suggestion, I quieted my mind and felt my inner being.

In the stillness I realized I was ecstatic, bursting with wondrous energy on a night when I should have been passed out in bed. Instead my spirit soared as I felt a union of both worlds—internal and external. Everything from my past and present was connected. I was one with all, and at the same time nothing held purpose other than this moment.

There were many parallels between this day and the day I'd finally passed my motorcycle test and received my license. Once again I was radiantly happy. On both occasions I had tackled daunting tasks that seemed impossible, and against all odds, had completed them.

Taking it easy, resting and pampering myself hadn't made me happy. Walling myself off from the world and protecting my fragile heart had failed. Over-achieving at implementing the Survivor's Trilogy had left me unfulfilled. But tackling the difficult, learning something new, accomplishing a feat most people wouldn't try—these were the sources of a new vitality inside me.

I searched for the right word to describe this vibrant energy surging around inside of me—joy, passion, trust, love, confidence, courage, zest—none of these words alone was right. I decided that no single word existed, and that I would have to make up my own name. *I'll call this energy . . . "Vroom!"*

Vroom is such a contagious high that I was sure Ron, Alberto, and Eva had not only felt its power but also expanded, multiplied, and spread it further last night.

Yesterday morning when we had looked at the difficulty of the longest day, we were concerned about whether we'd be able to complete the ride. And even if we could cover the distance, we were worried we'd be exhausted and unhappy with each other by the day's end.

Instead, we managed the journey's endless hurdles well as a group. We supported and helped each other in a host of small and large gestures throughout the day. As we overcame each successive challenge, we grew to trust each other and ourselves more than before.

As I thought back on our group celebration last night, our collective spirited jubilation had come from being proud of all we had faced and survived in style. It was a noteworthy accomplishment. No one had needed individual congratulations. Each of us was bursting with our own *vroom* energy. This glow made us attractive to each other and the people around us in the lounge. It expanded and became abundant and self-perpetuating.

I bowed and gently thanked the lake for her counsel and resplendent beauty. Turning, I opened the heavy door and headed back to bed. I looked forward to seeing what magic this diva would offer in the bright morning light.

19
Road Runner

Daybreak arrived, the first tinges of the rising sun turning the blue-black sky of night into dawn—bands of gold, orange, and crimson fading into each other as they rose above the volcanic ridge and were mirrored across the lake's vast, still surface below.

Looking out my window I smiled. Like a true beauty, the lake and all her exquisite features were only enhanced by bright daylight. Her uncontested reign continued.

There was no great rush to have an early breakfast on this eighth day of our trip. Before joining Ron and Alberto in the dining room, Eva and I strolled out onto the lodge's long stone patio to enjoy the view of Crater Lake in morning sunlight.

Park brochures and guidebooks in our hotel rooms had characterized her water's coloring as "vibrant, brilliant, deep, and indescribable." This morning her intense blue exactly matched the color of the cloudless sky. I wondered if her waters were gray on days when it was overcast.

Eva and I were still not completely free of sleep as we joined Ron and Alberto in the dining room for a leisurely breakfast.

"Have you guys been out on the patio this morning? The mosquitoes are vicious. We've got to buy some bug repellant after we eat," Eva said.

"Save your money, nothing works. Slap and cover up are your only true defenses," our waitress offered.

"You should see my welts from last night's bites," Alberto said. "I've counted over thirty. Some are swollen as big as quarters."

"You're just too sweet," I teased, and then added, "At least the mosquitoes are big and slow. If you pay attention, you can brush them off before they bite."

"Brush them away so they can live to attack again? No way. Show them no mercy." Ron demonstrated his retaliatory killing slaps in the air around him.

After we had ordered hearty breakfasts to make up for our missed dinners the previous night, Ron turned to me and said, "Okay, tell us about this lake. Show us what you've learned."

Ron knew I couldn't resist learning about the natural scenery wherever I went. Before this trip, I hadn't known anything about Crater Lake.

But since arriving last night, I had gathered brochures from the stand next to the front desk and glanced through the National Parks Guide on the night table in my hotel room. I was curious to find out how such a large, clear lake could be located at the top of a mountain without a glacier, river, or spring feeding it.

Marketing material boasted that it was the deepest or second deepest lake in North America and the seventh or eighth deepest in the world, depending on who was doing the math. *Why hadn't I heard of this lake before?* In my parents' attempts to take us to every national park, this one had been missed. It must have been one of those extra two inches on the map that we kids kept vetoing.

I explained to my riding partners that we were on top of a destroyed volcano, posthumously named Mount Mazama. Through a series of eruptions, explosions, implosions, and subsequent collapses of the volcano's top cone, a large crater in its top had been formed. After centuries of harsh eight-month winters, producing heavy snows followed by summer rains, the empty caldera filled, creating Crater Lake. Its beautiful blue color is the result of its pure, still waters that allow its volcanic sediment to rest undisturbed on the bottom of the lake.

This park had escaped the superfluous forms of recreation that seem to encroach on most natural attractions and public spaces. There was nothing to do here but hike, bike, fish, camp, or take a volcano boat cruise on the one boat allowed on its water. Even though people requiring powerboats, snowmobiles, multiple restaurants, shops, music, movies, and other forms of entertainment weren't drawn to this park, it still attracted close to a half million visitors each year during the short season of passable roads from mid-June through early October. This is the kind of retreat I treasure—just stillness, beauty, un-manicured nature, fireplaces, friendly staff, and martinis.

After breakfast we walked outside on the balcony but were attacked again by an onslaught of ravenous mosquitoes. Quickly retreating inside my leather jacket, gloves, and helmet, I found myself as protected as a beekeeper working under a netted suit.

Without the mosquitoes' presence, we would have been tempted to linger on the porch in one of the many rocking chairs and fritter the day away. We played with the idea of finding snowshoes so that we could take a walk to the highest peak around—Mount Scott, a mere 1,500-foot rise, but a strenuous climb, nevertheless, through deep snow drifts.

Luckily, the mosquitoes encouraged us to hide inside our gear and retreat to our bikes in an attempt to outmaneuver them. We agreed to explore part of the thirty-three-mile Rim Drive around the lake, dotted with numerous scenic viewing spots all focused on seeing the sole star of the show, "Crater Lake."

Our checkout clerk explained that only five miles of the drive was open today. It would probably be another two weeks before the whole road would be cleared for vehicles. Usually, the Rim Drive wasn't completely drivable until the end of June or beginning of July. We were several weeks too early.

It was strange to see snow on the ground in summer. The morning air whipping around the sides of my window shield felt brittle as we set off on our motorcycles. After stopping at a second scenic pull-off point to view Wizard Island, a small volcanic island sitting in the western part of Crater Lake, we rode out of the park and made our way over to Highway 97 north.

Our destination today was The Dalles on the Columbia River, located on the southern side of the border between Oregon and Washington. It would be an easy day of only 190 miles, so our late start would not be a problem. Most of the day would be spent on the same highway, unless we got bored and veered off to investigate some exciting detours.

The latter could be counted on.

By midmorning we were rolling through the grass-covered hills of Oregon without much traffic or many towns to interrupt our flow. It was time to take out the iPods and enjoy music as we traveled. Earlier in the trip, I had avoided this amenity, as I needed to hear every sound made by traffic and my motorcycle while learning to shift gears and ride. But now I felt more relaxed and confident.

It was a treat, having a rich musical backdrop to add to my riding. Ron suggested I try listening to his blues and oldies play list, and I did. The great basses of these songs, distinctive rhythms, deep and often rough singing voices, and stories of unrequited love, heartbreak, and hard lives were enriched by the accompaniment of my motorcycle's own raspy baritone voice and vibrating cadence. Listening to the thundering bass sounds of "Riding with the King" by Eric Clapton and B. B. King or "Sweet Hitch-Hiker" by Creedence Clearwater Revival on a motorcycle is an experience similar to watching fireworks with a symphony orchestra accompaniment—music always makes the other more vibrant.

Perhaps if I were riding a luxurious touring BMW, Natalie Cole singing her jazz rendition of "Route 66" would have been more appropriate. But in this dusty western setting replete with tumbleweeds and roaring pipes, blues and oldies with throaty, deep voices were better.

While riding, absorbed in the scenery, I kept hearing each familiar song with new ears. How could anyone listen to Janis Joplin belting out, "Oh Lord, won't you buy me a Mercedes Benz" and not laugh. Better yet, singing along with her at the top of your lungs, because no one will notice—including you—whether you're in tune or not.

At rest stops we'd trade iPods, ready to listen to someone else's collection. Next I tried Alberto's iPod. He suggested I select his classical music list, and with masked reluctance, I politely agreed. I was about to discover the problem with having too many conflicting tastes. My former definitive statement about blues and oldies being the best was about to make a liar of me. Listening to Alberto's selections, I quickly experienced how Beethoven and Vivaldi's fully orchestrated music became even richer and fuller on a motorcycle. It was like being in a motion picture with a full orchestral soundtrack to enhance the movie-like set I was riding through. This second fantasy accompanied by dramatic phrasing worked well too.

The problem with how my mind works is that while I'm great at brainstorming and thinking about infinite possibilities when I get excited about anything, I'm not good at deciding on one choice, one route or one direction. Instead I reason, *Why not this AND that too?*

I was now busy mentally assembling other collections of music for my next western motorcycle trip, making a note to myself to find the soundtrack to "How the West Was Won," then "This Land Is Your Land" sung by either Bruce Springsteen or Woody Guthrie, and what about Ferde Grofé's "On the Trail" from the Grand Canyon Suites? . . . more blues, more oldies, more classical, more popular songs, more movie themes. This was how I ended up buying over one hundred CDs in the previous year—the desire to always experience more.

⚬⚬⚬

There are some wonderful back roads in Oregon, filled with twists and turns. We'd laugh sometimes and point out familiar road signs with the yellow diamonds and a black-arrow line zigzagging back and forth to signify curves ahead. But instead of showing one or two bends in the road, these signs showed many. Sometimes there would even be an additional smaller rectangular sign below stating, "Next twenty-eight miles," or some other similarly long distance. That's when you know you have found an excellent motorcycling route.

On roads with a lot of curves, I was learning to follow Ron and Alberto's coaching. Sometimes I fell into a wonderful rhythm of first leaning into a curve in one direction, and then returning upright, and without stopping, leaning in the opposite direction around the next.

My body and motorcycle were like a pendulum swinging first right, then left, and then right again. It was magical to swoosh back and forth through a series of turns using this kind of repetitious arcing motion.

Add to this a rhythm of braking or shifting down before and accelerating out of each bend, and the experience is raised to an even higher plane.

This feeling of being "in the zone" isn't unique to motorcycling. Athletes, artists, professionals, craftsmen, gardeners, meditators, and many others learn to find this ethereal state. It's a glorious feeling when it happens and is something we all desire to repeat again and again. But this feeling can't be commanded to appear. A natural combination of skill, focus, and relaxation allows an individual to fall into the activity's natural rhythm.

As soon as I'd start to think too much, tense up or even feel, *I don't want this to end,* the state dissipated.

This is another occasion when over-thinking hinders rather than helps the flow. I've learned that being in the zone is the ability to participate completely in the *now*, without worrying about what happens next. There is no past, no future. There is only recognition of the present.

It takes courage and experience to ride into a blind curve or approach the crest of a hill without being able to see what lies beyond it. Knowledge of where to position the motorcycle for greatest safety is only part of overcoming this fear of potential obstacles.

At the motorcycle training, they taught us new riders to minimize curves by carving through them using a straightened travel line, but today I wanted to experience every turn fully, minimizing nothing, so I rode through the full curve. I was now more relaxed, cheering when we found challenging back roads with lots of zigzags, bends, and hills.

I practiced leaning my body and motorcycle into each turn more deeply. Initially, the thought of tilting my body and bike to the side was scary. I was sure this extreme lean would cause the motorcycle to fall over, but motorcycles are bottom heavy with a low center of gravity. As I dipped into curve after curve, these physical traits accompanied by speed made for a smoother, more natural ride around each one.

Ron had gone to a professional motorcycle track where he learned how to take corners at speed. He explained that they were coached to tilt so far into each curve of the track that their inside foot pegs scraped against the road surface. The instructors rubbed chalk on the sides of their motorcycle tires starting at the tread and going inwards five or so inches toward the center spokes of each wheel. The object was to rub the chalk off the tires' sides by slanting their motorcycles into the turns and scraping the road.

I had said earlier that I was proud of the scuffmark on my left boot toe. Despite what Ron said about scraping the bike's foot peg against the road, I was not yet ready to earn that mark.

By this point in the trip, when we found good motorcycle roads, I was no longer hidden at the back of the pack. It was easier to be out in front than try and calculate how others ahead of me would respond to each change in the road.

On these back roads, we purposely wanted the group to spread farther apart. This happened naturally as we all had varying levels of comfort with different terrains that changed with our moods throughout the day. Now, toward the end of the road trip, even Eva and I occasionally took the lead position when we were feeling particularly rambunctious and strong.

I have always loved speed. Several years ago, while training for the MS bicycle ride, Kris, one of my Virginia bicycling partners, gave me the nickname "Downhill Crill." On a bicycle I was slower than most and easy to pass while pedaling up hills, but on the other side—racing downhill—few people could catch me as I passed almost everyone. On these descents, I was fearless and would occasionally watch my speedometer reach forty miles per hour.

Doing that kind of speed riding on a lightweight bicycle with thin one-and-a-half inch-wide tires, wearing no protection other than a bicycle helmet, felt far more risky than riding a motorcycle on similar roads, wearing significantly more protection, with fatter tires and stronger brakes.

During one of our afternoon breaks, as we discussed the great roads we were riding, Eva suddenly looked up, her face bursting with excitement as she addressed the group.

"I've got it! Know what we should call Linda? She's 'Road Runner.' Even though she's on a less powerful motorcycle, no matter what happens in traffic, no matter what transpires on the highway, no matter how difficult the terrain, you can't lose her! She's like the roadrunner in the cartoon. She keeps going 'BEEP BEEP!' If she falls down in one frame or runs off a cliff in another, she always comes back, unscathed and passing us all."

Ron and Alberto began laughing, nodding, and repeating my new nickname, "Road Runner," and saying "Beep Beep!" and laughing.

They all thought that the name fit and so, it stuck. I had earned my own nickname.

It was a cute name. If I was to have a reputation, this was one I could laugh at and enjoy. Road Runner had always been one of my favorite childhood cartoons.

The beep-beep part was especially funny, because that is exactly how my motorcycle horn sounded. Often when we passed each other and wanted to laugh, we'd sound our horns twice in a short beep-beep repetition. It seemed so funny that these ear-deafening machines making their loud VRROOOMing noises were only equipped with little beeping horns. Our motorcycles' horns sounded similar to the ones we had on our bicycles during our elementary school years.

I have never understood why vehicle designers give huge trucks the loud blasting horns and little cars and motorcycles the silly squeaky ones. I think it should be the other way around—the smaller the vehicle, the bigger and louder the horn.

Soda bottles were raised, clicked together, and I was christened "Road Runner" by the group.

20
Gray Heaven

Beep, beep, beep! It was Eva passing me on the left, pointing at a sign that said "Columbia River." We were almost at our eighth day's destination—The Dalles in Oregon. After gesturing to call attention to the roadside marker, she continued with an exaggerated one-armed shrugging movement that clearly indicated her concern about what we were doing.

Jolted from my own concentration on the road ahead, I recalled that we had planned on turning left onto Interstate 84 West, which runs parallel to the Columbia River on the southern Oregon side. Instead we were heading north across the bridge into Washington State a day earlier than planned.

Nevertheless, it was a treat riding across the mile-and-a-half bridge spanning the Columbia River. How could anyone greet such a celebrity without joy and excitement? For a second time on this trip I was riding across the grand Columbia River!

We entered Washington State and immediately turned west onto Highway 14. We'd simply backtrack to The Dalles along the northern side of the river and take the next bridge south back into Oregon.

Our hotel for the evening was located near the intersection of Highway 197 (a north and south road) and Interstate 84 (the east and west one we had just missed). We had picked this hotel so we could have a view of The Dalles Dam from our hotel rooms. "Dam, flowing water, Columbia River, what could be more dramatic and picturesque?" we had thought.

At this point Eva was leading, having given up on the belief that Alberto—formerly in that position—knew where we were going. We never lacked for willing, competent leaders in this group.

As focused as Eva was on getting us back on track, she never missed an opportunity for a great detour, and one was just presenting itself. In the middle of no visible commerce, surrounded only by bare, soft-rounded, light-brown sugar mountains and a distant ribbon of a river, suddenly on our left was a large multi-story building. Next to it was a patio with many tables and chairs and an expansive parking lot. A sign hung high over the drive leading into the establishment: *Mayhill Winery*. This was a place that yelled, "Stop and come in!" With Eva as point person, there was no question about what we were doing next. She already had her turn signal on and was pulling into the left lane, slowing and getting ready to turn. The rest of us fell in behind her.

It was mid-afternoon, and there were only a few other vehicles sitting in the large parking lot as we four pulled our motorcycles into a row, parked, and dismounted.

"Look guys, it's only three-thirty, and we're just a few miles from our hotel. We got the time; let's check this out," Eva said as she turned and headed toward the building, not waiting for our response.

"But Washington wines?" Alberto said, stating my thought and probably Ron's. As East Coasters, we were well versed in the reputation of California wines and had only days earlier been spoiled by the excellent quality of those in Mendocino, but none of us had heard anything about Washington wines. Not ready to pass up a new adventure, we followed Eva's lead. At the very least we'd walk away with another good story to share.

Inside the building was a large room that began with a gift shop stocked with gourmet cheeses, crackers and snacks, as well as the typical wine-related books, glasses, and gifts. Along the left side of the long room was a continuous series of floor-to-ceiling windows showing off the river and valley below. On the right side was a long, rich wooden bar with stools lined up across the front. The young man behind the counter welcomed us and explained the price for different tastings.

We selected the choice that included three of their wines. We asked him about the success of local wines, and he told us that a major wine industry had developed in Oregon and Washington. Naturally, showing great local pride, he expounded on their quality and taste, influenced by the Columbia River Gorge and Cascade Mountains. The river moderated the temperature extremes in summer and winter, while the mountains blocked excessive precipitation. This unique combination produced great conditions for growing grapes.

It's unfortunate how expanding world food markets are changing local farm products across America. In the last ten years in my current home state of Virginia, many traditional apple orchards have moved from being profitable businesses to financial disasters as they try to compete with China, which is cornering this market. As a result, many Virginians have turned to growing grapes, and now vineyards dot the countryside across northwestern Virginia, producing very respectable wines. Sadly, here in the West the stellar reputations of the Washington apple and cherry industries are facing similar global challenges. So it makes sense that they too are looking for new products to keep their precious farmlands from turning into more housing developments and strip malls.

We began our tasting with a white wine and followed it with two reds. The third was surprisingly good, and we liked its flavor. Since it was a beautiful day and we hadn't had much to eat Ron suggested we sit outside around the tables, enjoying a late lunch along with the splendid view of the Columbia River and the vineyards and cherry orchards in the valley below. Eva and I selected cheeses and crackers, while Ron and Alberto chose a bottle of wine.

After yesterday's long, stressful day riding from Mendocino to Crater Lake, it was good to have an easier time again and to be ten miles from our destination by mid-afternoon. We relaxed into our wine and cheese picnic and stared at the peaceful, almost calendar-like scenery below our high perch on the vineyard patio. But something wasn't quite right.

I'm not sure what I was expecting to experience at our destination today, but when I thought first about the significance of the Columbia River, The Dalles being the end of the memorable Oregon Trail, and finally the historic significance of Lewis and Clark's expedition through this area, images of the "Wild West," untamed nature, jagged terrain, and hearty pioneer folk came to mind. But here we sat, wine glass in one hand and aged cheddar on top of rosemary cracker crisps in the other, as we gazed down at a peaceful scene similar to Mendocino's artist community, with small well-kept vineyards outlined by beautiful trees and wildflowers.

Order was everywhere.

Nothing was rugged or wild.

Everything had been neatly arranged, almost as if nature had hired an accountant to reorganize this area into precise categories, rows, and columns. The pieces on this scenery spreadsheet conformed flawlessly, fitting together in straight lines—horizontally and vertically—lining up perfectly at right angles—straight rows of fruit trees, grapevines, roads, river, horizon, and sky.

When I think of a famous powerful river like the Columbia, I immediately conjure up images of thundering water cascading over and around mammoth boulders and jutting multi-directional stone slabs. The river and terrain competing to dominate the space as the water aggressively swirls and surges into other waves and anything else in its path. I think of dangerous currents, eddies, whirlpools, and rapids.

The Columbia River is the largest river by volume in the western hemisphere, flowing 1,240 miles from British Columbia, Canada. It empties into the Pacific Ocean between Oregon and Washington. It is known for its significant elevation drops, making the resulting flow an excellent source of energy captured by fourteen hydroelectric dams.

But sitting here looking at it from this veranda a half a mile away, it was just a plain wide band of smooth water. No ripples, no whitecaps, and no sign of power or movement. It looked more like a long piece of shiny blue ribbon than a dynamic, majestic river. Through years of re-engineering by dredging, constructing locks, and adding dams, the Columbia River's wild nature has been forever altered and diminished.

Even the salmon that used to run up the river jumping its falls and rocks now have neat little progressive square steps along the sides of its many dams to jump one at a time. That is, if the fish are lucky. Some dams didn't add this necessary solution to their walled-off waterways and the declining salmon population sadly reflects this critical omission.

Next I focused on the vineyards situated a mile directly below us on the right, between the hill we were on and the river. In Virginia along the bicycle paths where I ride, wild grapevines often take over the terrain, growing prolifically in all directions. They immediately dominate and expand over any landscape where they root, draping their leafy blankets overtop bushes and shrubs, allowing nothing beneath them to view the sun. After climbing electric poles and reaching their tops, these grape vines extend along the wires. They creep straight up timber, leaping tree-to-tree as monkeys do when they swing from one to the next. But here the grapevines were contained in neat, well-maintained rows, vines fastidiously pruned and tied along taunt, straight wires—like well-trained soldiers parading in full-dress for inspection, no hair untrimmed or out of place.

On the left below was an equally straight-rowed orchard of cherry trees. Again, each tree was pruned to the same comparable size and shape.

Lastly, there was the solid blue sky starting at the horizon with a slightly lighter color and subtly turning into an ever-darker shade overhead. Not a cloud or wisp of white haze interrupted its clean, pristine surface. It appeared neat and perfectly sky-blue.

Still, the view was serene and beautiful—just not what I had expected. But time changes everything, and history is more easily preserved and maintained in books and stories than in the physical world. My impressions of "West" just needed to catch up, expand, and become contemporary. But where was the "wild"?

❧

Following our afternoon interlude of wine and cheese, we returned to the highway to find our hotel. Soon we approached our turnoff onto Highway 197, taking us south across a bridge over the Columbia River, back into Oregon and the intersection where our hotel was located.

The bridge had two sections—a gold-painted, steel, cantilevered bridge contained two pointed peaks, rising high into the air, followed by another long, lower concrete addition. The first metal section of the bridge looked similar to one we would have built as kids using a metal erector set.

Unlike the first day when I panicked as I thought about riding up a metal grate onto the ferry, I was now so comfortable with riding that I didn't even think about this bridge's steel lattice surface, so I was caught off guard.

Riding across its metal roadbed, I tightened my grip on the handlebars as they wobbled, made frequent minor rebalancing corrections with my body, and constantly redirected my front wheel forward to keep it going in a straight line. It wasn't scary, only disconcerting, as I realized I was involved in a mild game of tug-of-war with the bridge's iron surface over who got to control the direction of my motorcycle. Ultimately, I won, but I wasn't ready to volunteer for a rematch anytime soon. Tomorrow morning, when we headed back into Washington, I'd vote for the interstate and the paved bridge we had gone over earlier that afternoon.

As we drove across the lower part of the bridge, I could see the Dalles Dam. I remembered visiting Grand Coulee Dam on the Columbia River as a kid and had expected a similarly impressive and high structure complete with crashing waters. But from the bridge, the Dalles Dam fell short by comparison. It wasn't very high and water flowed from only two of its twenty or so low gates, so that neither the dam nor the river pooling below it exuded much drama.

It was still early as we got off our motorcycles at the Shilo Inn Suites Hotel. We decided to check into our rooms quickly, but before even unpacking our cycles, we'd take another short ride along the Columbia River. We still believed this river and scenery had more drama to offer. We just needed to head further west to locate it.

We pulled out of the parking lot, turning onto Interstate 84 west. The fact that the road on this southern side of the river was an Interstate should have given us a hint of the disappointment ahead.

Instead of seeing the Columbia River flowing furiously through deep gorges with waterfalls cascading down from cliffs above as other rivers joined its rushing currents, we caught quick glimpses of brownish-green water, flowing without a ripple, through gently sloping hills covered by dried grasses. In other areas pine forests lined its peaceful banks. But mostly, we encountered lots of impatient five o'clock commuting traffic, exit signs, the four-to-six-lane cement highway beneath our bikes, while concrete bridges crossed overhead.

We drove as far west as the Hood River, thinking that maybe we'd see the powerful dynamics of two big rivers surging and flowing together.

But again from the cement confines of the Interstate, we found nothing impressive.

We finally agreed to call an end to our search for drama and turned back toward our hotel.

Drained by the challenges and adrenaline required to complete the previous day's long ride, we viewed this evening's scenery through exhausted eyes. Last night's celebration that had culminated in a joyous crescendo of drinks, socializing, and storytelling had spent any final reserve of energy not consumed by our longest day.

Today had been a quieter time of easy riding, music, wine and cheese, and finally serene views of the river and valley. But this simpler day had not been enough correction for our exhausted bodies. We still needed to come back further toward center to rebuild our depleted energies.

Today, The Dalles, as beautiful as it supposedly is, was greeted by our passive, drained bodies. The subtle beauty of the countryside and river couldn't pull our exhausted mood upward during the evening. Without rushing white-capped waves, turbulent whirlpools, and roiling rapids, our own energy waned and bottomed out. The river's wide brown expanse, flowing massively without splash, reflected our own dark, lumbering spirits at this hour.

Tonight, finally, when we returned to our hotel rooms, we looked to the television to see what movies were showing. We gathered in one room and ordered in pizza from a local chain store, too tired to venture out again. We could have been Anywhere, USA.

Sitting on the hotel room floor, staring at the TV, eating unmemorable chewy, mildly-warm pizza off a paper plate with a watery iceberg salad drenched in too much vegetable oil and dried oregano, washed down with a barely-cool canned beer, left me feeling blah.

Even the movie was blah.

It was time to shut down all channels and sleep, hoping the depressive exhaustion would naturally lift during the night and leave me refreshed by morning.

I excused myself from the group and retreated to my room.

As I turned out the lights and crawled into bed, I thought about what I had learned about gray moments and days while living in Southern California.

When I moved to San Diego in the mid-eighties, my cousin Kevin explained to me that I would learn to enjoy the occasional gloomy day and especially June-gloom periods that lasted several weeks.

As a newcomer fresh from living for five years in Manhattan, I was confused. I had seen enough gray days. I was there for the sunshine. During the following years, I woke up gratefully every day there was bright, sunny weather. I had quickly learned to not tell my New York clients about the great weather when they called in February, exhausted from their freezing drizzle and gray winter. When they asked about our California weather, if I had told these New Yorkers that the weather was bright and sunny, out of spite they would never have given me business. So I had announced to all of my East Coast clients and friends that I would lie and always say it was gray and miserable. I needed their business and support.

After I had lived in San Diego for several years, Kevin's prediction came true. When a gray day finally arrived, it was almost a relief not to be continuously cheerful. Instead, it was fun to allow my spirits to go inward, find a soft warm blanket, curl up in an overstuffed chair and savor a hot cup of ginger tea.

That's what tonight felt like—a time for nesting. The theme of balance repeated itself. It felt good to stay in, pull on my flannels and crawl into bed, snuggling deep under the covers. Eva could tell me tomorrow how the movie ended. Tonight was just another kind of gray heaven. Using its dark blackout curtain, sleep could and would be wondrous.

As I slowly drifted off, I thought about how tomorrow was not only another chance to explore Washington, it was also an opportunity to reconnect with the state where I had visited my relatives so often as a kid.

As my thoughts continued along this vein, my inner soul started to smile, and I said a silent prayer of thanks. I fell off to sleep happy with this moment, loving its dull color and ready for new adventures in the morning.

21
A Fistful of Pennies

"Let's go! It's time to get on the road," Alberto called out as he started his motorcycle and rode to the stop sign at the edge of our motel parking lot. I had been impatiently sitting on my bike, wanting to get started this morning, and was glad to see someone else take the initiative. I quickly lined up behind him. Eva fell into third position, and finally Ron pulled up behind her. This was our normal way of entering traffic as a group; we lined up behind each other on the side of the road, then merged into traffic in single file, each person making sure it was clear before entering the road.

To my dismay, Alberto turned right, heading toward Highway 97 and the same bumpy-surfaced bridge with the metal grate bed we had struggled on yesterday. His choice was another sign that the group was no longer coddling me. The washed-out gravel climb, the longest day's trials riding to Crater Lake, the Road Runner nickname, and most recently the rhythm, leans, and speeds around curves, had dissolved their protective blanket that had swaddled me during my infancy, cocooned in the center of the group.

I hadn't quite made it to adulthood as a rider—never having ridden in falling snow, rain, hail, or severe winds—but at least by now I was an adolescent, with the typical indomitable confidence one minute, wavering skills the next, and ever-changing mood swings—highs and lows.

At the next corner, the sign for Washington pointed right. Washington State and my Crill family have always been deeply linked in my mind. My father, Ed Crill, had lived in this state as a teen. When I was a child, his mother, brother and sister, and their spouses still lived there with their families. Every three or four years, we'd drive across the United States to visit them, taking a month to camp and visit other relatives along the way.

I am glad my father wanted us to learn about his western family, as all of these grandparents, aunts, uncles, and even my father are gone today.

Although these western family vacation trips probably had included some unhappy times, I have long since edited them out. What I've retained are pleasant memories about riding horses, eating dark Bing cherries, and enjoying huge, homemade pancake breakfasts prepared by my Aunt Mildred on her cast-iron, wood-burning cookstove. She loved catering to us kids as it gave her an excuse to play too.

As we passed an old, slow-moving car driven by a white-haired woman who looked at least eighty and barely able to see over her steering wheel, I thought of my own Grandma Crill and her miniature house that sat high up on a little hill. It was small and cramped when all six of us visited her, and there weren't many things to play with, so as children we tried to invent our own amusements.

During one of these visits when I was six years old, I wandered into her bedroom and noticed a collection of stick perfumes sitting on her dresser. These beautiful glass bottles were about the size and shape of today's pharmacy prescription pill containers. Inside each was a scented, congealed stick of cologne each wrapped in different colorful imprinted foil. They sparked my curiosity. Grandma had let us four Crill children play with eight or so of these—smelling each scent and rubbing many of them on our skin as we sampled and shared them with each other. Soon we were drenched in their overwhelming aroma.

I can only imagine how badly we must have collectively smelled as we piled back into our car, returning to Aunt Mildred's house. It may have actually been worse than the smell the car already exuded. Days earlier Mom had hit a skunk. In its final retaliatory act, it left a not-so-fond fragrant farewell. The car's stench was already barely tolerable. Now we added perfume, producing a disastrous odoriferous concoction that would have made having a head cold with a stuffed-up nose a blessing.

My attention was quickly pulled back from my daydream as we motored across the bridge's metal grate roadway. Today, it was easier riding across it. I simply let my arms and legs do the work of steering and buffering the vibrations while relaxing my core body. Resistance wasn't a part of my nature on this beautiful morning.

In the middle of the bridge, Ron passed Alberto to take the lead, since he had studied the maps and was in charge of today's routes. Although most of the day we would be traveling north on Highway 97, he had found some great motorcycle back roads for us.

Our ninth day's destination was Leavenworth, Washington, near the town of Wenatchee. The best way to describe the location would be to say it's situated almost exactly in the middle of the state. Leavenworth was about 200 miles away, but with deliberate side trips, our final day's mileage would be more.

As we came to the intersection of Highway 14, I was surprised when we turned west instead of east to continue on Highway 97. We were already taking a detour. *More roads with curves ahead,* I thought gleefully.

Soon we were turning north again, and I waved goodbye to the Columbia River and majestic Mount Hood in the southern background. Eva, noticing my gesture, waved too.

We had grown used to having a silhouette of one of these dramatic Cascade volcanoes in the background. I counted the grand ones we had seen so far—Mt. Rainier, Mt. Shasta, Mt. Mazama, and Mt. Hood. Today in southern Washington I wondered if we'd be able to see Mount Rainier again, along with two new ones—Mount St. Helens and Mount Baker. These Cascade volcanoes all stood majestically over eleven-thousand feet high, dwarfing other smaller mountains and hills around them.

About ninety minutes later, I got my wish as we pulled off Route 97 north at the Santus Pass. From this point we could see all four of these Cascade Range volcanoes to our west. What was equally surprising was how few vehicles were on the road this morning, and so we enjoyed this spectacle with minimal interference.

Back on the highway as I thought about today's destination, I wished that I had called Mom last night to see if she remembered where Dad's relatives had lived in Washington when we visited them. As a kid I associated destinations with who was there to play with and what there was to do. Names of places were of secondary importance. I vaguely recalled that they lived in the Wenatchee and Lake Chelan areas. Even though there was no one living there today, it would have been nice to have more information, but while preparing for this trip and learning to ride a motorcycle, I'd had little time to consider my Washington family connections.

⁂

Now that the trip was in its final days, the unavoidable started to happen. At the beginning and middle of this road trip, we enjoyed the luxury of unlimited time and a sense of freedom, having been released from the responsibilities of our daily lives. Now, occasional thoughts of home, work, and the future began to filter in. Whenever that happened, I'd abruptly pushed these thoughts away, pleading, *Not yet! It's still vacation time.*

Arthur Frommer said in his travel books that the purpose of a vacation is to provide contrast. To me the best vacations were ones that offered a change in weather, location, activity, food, and routine. This vacation had certainly succeeded in doing that. I had chosen a radical departure from my solitary life. For the past nine days, I had spent few moments alone.

Over the past couple of years I had added lots of new things to my life, but all of them contained the same kinds of solitary and gentle energy. I must have knitted forty unique scarves, each with a new combination of patterns, stitches, and colorful yarns; bought countless jazz, guitar, and world music CDs; surrounded myself with a mountain of comfortable fabrics (soft throws, goose down pillows, and bedding with high thread count); read stacks of books on surviving losses, spirituality, and the meaning of life and death; and associated with family and old friends who protected me, letting me dictate the length, content, and type of interactions.

Despite this variety, its collective energy was skewed—lots of yin, not much yang; mostly feminine, not much masculine; all treble, little bass. I had become bored with a life filled with so many palatable activities in an attempt to soothe, comfort, and restore myself.

Initially, after Bill's death, softness was the only energy I could tolerate, but eighteen months later I was now rebelling, yearning for excitement, noise, sweat, toughness, physical challenge, and grit. I had reined myself in too long as I tried to figure out: *What Now?*

But why such a radical over-correction and not something less intense?

One of my close friends, Yvonne, is a decorator as well as a trained counselor with hospice expertise. After my husband's death, she had insisted that I redecorate the main floor of my home and my master bedroom to create a new environment reflecting the single me. From her I learned that for a room to be welcoming there could only be so many focal points. Not everything in the room could demand attention. It's the dichotomy, the balance of opposites, that creates interest, she told me. So if I chose a carpet with lots of texture, colorful activity and motion, elsewhere in the room I needed to have solids and plain textures to create the contrast of a more serene feeling.

The hardest step in taking any action for me has always been leaving behind many attractive options as I move forward with a singular selection.

As a small child I loved watching the Art Linkletter Show when he interviewed young elementary-school-age children. On one show, a child was told he could put his hand into a jar filled with pennies and take home as a prize as many pennies as he could grasp. How I envied that child—a fist full of pennies. At that time one penny could buy at least five pieces of candy at the corner store. With a fistful, I'd be rich!

We often talk about abundance and the ability to create bounty, but in decorating, as in life, each decision affects and eliminates other future choices.

I often find myself facing the dilemma of a jarful of alluring possibilities. As an adult, my jar of riches is no longer filled with pennies. It's filled with nuggets representing how to spend my time and energy. But this adult jar has another major difference—the container's mouth is so small that I can only get my adult-sized fist out of the jar by letting go and leaving behind all but a few nuggets.

It's tempting while holding onto all of these precious gems to drag around this heavy jar with my full fist clenching my riches, which can't be spent while they're still trapped in a jar.

I hadn't realized when I decided to go on this road trip that I was making a major commitment of time and resources. This decision added the much-needed correction or counterbalance of energy to my life, but it had also absorbed me so completely that other significant routines were dropped.

It was as if my brain were a telephoto lens on a camera, and I had zoomed in, focusing on one priority—this trip. In two days, I'd be zooming this lens back out, bringing everything else back into the viewfinder again.

I wondered as this vacation approached its end, what I would do when I returned home to integrate my new and old lives. I had chosen to reintroduce adventure and fun into it. I knew that maintaining a focus on health with physical exercise and nourishing diet was wise.

People talk about leading a holistic life, but I find it impossible to keep everything balanced, all of the time. Often, trying to manage everything creates overwhelming stress. As I'd review my daunting list of activities to be balanced, I'd realize how easy it is to become immobilized, defeated and simply walk away, doing nothing.

Maybe the focus shouldn't be on activities. More critical might be paying attention to the dichotomy of requirements within me that needed to be addressed.

❧

Back when I was still trying to decide whether to go on this motorcycle trip, I was at a local knit shop, picking colorful yarns for my next project. During a conversation with the saleswoman, I discovered she too was a widow. It had been eight years since she had lost her husband. She confessed that she hadn't even gone out of her house much for the first five years. But from her short, asymmetrically-cut, flame-orange hair, purple-green glasses, and sassy attitude, I knew something had changed.

When she asked me how I was doing, her appearance gave me courage to speak more frankly than I normally would have to a stranger.

"I am so tired of following all of those traditional rules about how to live as a widow. I'm tired of taking care of everyone else's needs—always looking at every decision as to what's best for others," I confided. She smiled and nodded her head in quick repetitions. Encouraged, I continued, "It's time to put myself first for a change. I've decided to break free of my self-drawn boundaries. I'm ready to do something completely out of character and rebellious. I'm even thinking about learning to ride a motorcycle!"

As we continued talking within the tight confines of this small knit shop, other women stopped shopping and started to cluster around us listening, joining in, saying they felt the same way too. A commonly repeated statement was: Why are we always taking care of others and not ourselves?

When I mentioned that I was looking for a local place to learn how to ride a motorcycle, these women joined in.

"You have to do it!" said one.

"Quit putting others first, it's your time," said another.

"A motorcycle, way to go!" beamed a third. "Just think of what my husband and grandkids would say! Whoa boy, it'd be worth it just to see their faces."

"I've always secretly wanted to ride. It looks so exciting."

Swept up in their own enthusiasm, they began scribbling their names and email addresses on slips of paper, stuffing them into my hand and begging me to let them know when and where I was going to take my lessons. They wanted to join me and to learn too.

Leaving the shop with names and addresses of these accomplices, I had smiled as I thought what an improbable group of women to want to ride motorcycles. They looked like ladies you might find in a church sewing circle, volunteering at the local clinic, or running the town library. These were not women you could easily imagine donning tight leather pants, straddling a heavy metal machine, and roaring down the street on an intimidating chrome chopper.

The contrast was too much. I shook with laughter, shaking my head. *This could become a new business to replace the one I was still closing down after Bill's death.* But I quickly pushed this business idea aside, not ready to be responsible for others' safety; worrying about my own was laden with enough guilt.

But here again, found within these women from the knit shop, was a desire to counterbalance life. They were looking for the vroom type of invigorating energy and fuel I had found on this trip. Erasing old boundaries, expanding horizons, facing fears, testing beliefs, risking it all for something new—these were the impetus-drivers for choosing *blind curves.*

A mundane life eventually becomes its own prison.

In our homogenized world, we crave the stimulation and excitement that comes from exploring and discovering something new. Vicariously watching from the sidelines as others "do it" (or as on many reality TV shows or other entertainment, "fail to do it") doesn't fill this basic need. We must find ways to put passion and excitement back into our lives that we create on our own.

My spectator days were over. Placing the expertise of others above the intuitive guidance of my soul was gone. The adventuresome Linda had been re-discovered. This might be my only trip wearing leathers, but the desire to continue to open more doors formerly labeled "not me" and head into more blind curves with different risks and rewards would definitely continue.

22
Nostalgic Reunion

We pulled off at a gas station in Yakima, Washington, in the late morning. After filling up, we bought sodas and sauntered over to the picnic tables in the shade of several fruit trees next to the station. I tossed my helmet and gloves on the table, unzipped my leather jacket, and started rubbing my back left shoulder and the back of my neck. The muscles were tight and had been aching all morning.

"Is your neck stiff?" Eva asked, reaching up to knead the same place on her shoulder. "Mine's bothering me too."

I walked over behind Eva and started to massage the back tops of both of her shoulders, digging my thumbs into her tight muscles in a circular motion. I have always enjoyed sports medicine, and sports massage was something I had become known for among my athletic friends.

"We're next!" Ron and Alberto demanded.

"What about me?" I said, pointing to my own complaining shoulders.

Soon, having peeled off our jackets, we were all sitting in a circle rubbing the shoulders of the person in front of us. After nine days of wearing heavy helmets, our necks were protesting their added weight.

It felt good to have these sore muscles massaged, and we all enthusiastically groaned and moaned, expressing our relief. I'm not sure what the locals thought of our strange circle, but other motorcyclists would have recognized our activity and readily joined in. However, our vocalizing might have been mistaken for the soundtrack of an X-rated movie.

"A little more to the left . . ."

"Oh yeah . . . Even *more* to the left . . ."

"Now *down* a bit."

"Go deeper . . . Rub harder . . ."

"Oh, yes . . ."

"Oh, God . . ."

"More. Don't stop."

"That's it! . . . Ahhh . . . Oh, yes!"

Taking advantage of our riding break, we began pulling out our cell phones to call family members and check for messages. I tried to call Mom to find out more about the Crill relatives' locations but only got her answering machine.

Back on the road again we rode through countryside that felt familiar. I love these low, rounded mountains, covered with golden dried grasses, tumbleweeds, and few trees. We had just passed roads named Horse Heaven Hills, Sagebrush Ridge, Cowboy Lake, Cowiche Mountains, and Rattlesnake Hills. They made me smile. No Candy Cane Circle, Azalea Court, Cozy Corner, Lilac Way, or Spicewood Drive in this area. I'd have to wait until I was back East in my suburbs for those gentle names.

❧

Most of the time, we only see the results of wind—flags furling, branches swaying, hair whipping, doors banging, windmills spinning. Since wind traveling alone is invisible, it is hard for us to prepare for the blowing air's unexpected force as the wind lifts off our hats, steals our napkins, or scatters our unguarded papers.

This afternoon, as the air began gusting more forcibly around us on our bikes, wind lost its normal anonymous façade as it picked up open-range dirt and highway debris. The prankster had become easily traceable.

As I watched its amusing antics, the wind's random patterns reminded me of first graders out for recess—each separate breeze seeking something to play with and create its own game.

As these playful children scampered across fields on both sides of our road, several sucked up dozens of tumbleweeds, aimed their weapons at our motorcycles, and sent them bouncing up and down across our expected pathways. We dodged their attacks, and then taunted them afterwards by throwing victory punches into the air above our heads with clenched fists, pleased that we hadn't been tagged. At least not yet.

Around us, dust-devil funnels rose upwards over twenty feet tall by several feet wide. It was amusing watching these mini-tornadoes and their resulting disruptions caused by their whipping circles. We tried to predict their erratic paths as they crossed our highway. We were triumphant when we anticipated their random courses correctly and avoided them, but less pleased when caught—their fine debris making high-pitched clinking sounds as it scoured our windshields, pelted our bikes' metal bodies, and glanced noisily off our helmets.

Several swirling breezes combined in force, sending a gritty blast across the highway. As it slammed against the solid bank on the opposite side of the road, it broke up into mini-whirlwinds, some surging high into the air while others plunged back onto the road in a reverse curlicue motion.

And just as nature's gales had surprised us by arriving out of nowhere, the wind mysteriously retreated, and once again, the only breeze we now felt was the self-created wind of riding.

⌘

By mid-afternoon the terrain had made another dramatic shift. We rode amongst dark-blue-green mountains, with precipitous jutting granite surfaces at their tops, long rockslide ribbons winding down their sides, and soaring pine forests cloaking their bodies. It felt as if we were in the Alps of southern Germany. Cottonwood trees grew along the sides of many of the untamed, noisy creeks that rushed down the mountainsides.

These streams had probably started at the tops of the mountains as mere trickles of melting snow, joining together with similar small runs, growing in volume with each addition until they had become a sizeable brook, and finally, rushing chilly rivers at the bottom of the mountain. In the wide, flat valleys below were grassy meadows, orchards, small farms, and towns.

This feels like Aunt Mildred's country, I thought. We were riding through the Wenatchee National Forest.

This familiar terrain stirred up faded and forgotten childhood memories. A sign advertising an apple-packing plant reminded me of how Aunt Mildred used to work packing apples in Wenatchee from August through late fall of every year, making extra money that never seemed to reach far enough.

It was mid-afternoon, and we were approaching a major T-intersection in the town of Peshastin. Ron had put on his left blinker. We were finally ready to turn off Highway 97 onto Route 2 west. A sign indicated that Leavenworth was three miles to our left. We were almost at our destination for the day. Now it was my job to get us to our hotel. I pulled my motorcycle up beside Ron's at the stop sign, so I could take the lead position after the turn. My written directions indicated that our lodging address at the Enzian Inn was on Highway 2, so I'd just have to pay attention to the street numbers to guide us there.

As we turned the corner, I noticed a large rushing stream on the right-hand side of the highway. Next to it was a sawmill that looked like the one where Uncle David used to work.

Suddenly the name Peshastin clicked. Uncle David, Aunt Mildred's husband, had worked in Peshastin. That meant that Grandma Crill's earlier house had to be somewhere nearby.

On my left was a series of small houses sitting on a hill about thirty feet above our road. Something about them felt vaguely familiar. Suddenly I noticed a house that could have been her home. My mouth hung open as I quickly glanced at the house, then back at the highway, and then back up at the house again. With traffic around me, I didn't dare look again, but I might have just passed Grandma Crill's old home. The last time I would have been there was when I was nine years old. I could hardly wait to get the group to our hotel so I could turn around, ride back, and take a closer look. My head whirled in the disbelief and excitement. I might have found a place that had been alive only in my memory and heart.

Riding into Leavenworth, I searched the buildings for street numbers and began noticing that most of the hotels had German names—Bavarian Lodge, Der Ritterhof, Innsbrucker Inn, Linderhof Inn, Edelweiss Hotel, Bavarian Orchard House. Slowly, even my travel-dulled brain perked up and took notice. Not only did most of the lodging have German names, but even the Holiday Inn, Quality Inn, and Best Western Hotel were built to look as if they were located in an Alpine village somewhere in Germany.

Painted on one sidewall of the Holiday Inn was a large scene of young women dressed in Dirndl Kleider and men in Lederhosen. I smiled, remembering how often I'd seen similar murals on the sides of old German hotels and restaurants.

Many of the buildings were styled to look like German *Fachwerk*— the German building style similar to British Tudor that left some of the wood framing visible. It almost looked authentic, except these buildings were too geometrically correct, missing the charming askew shifts that happen with true aging and settling over hundreds of years.

In what seemed like the far end of town, we found our hotel and pulled into the Enzian Inn parking lot. We lined up our motorcycles near the front door and dismounted.

"Where are we? What's with all of the German names and buildings?" Eva asked excitedly.

"I don't know, but it feels like *Bayern* (Bavaria, Germany) to me," I said.

"This should be fun!" Alberto added.

"Did you know about all of this German influence when you selected this stop?" I asked Ron.

He shook his head no, looking as bewildered as the rest of us.

We walked into the hotel lobby to register. It was boldly decorated to resemble a Bavarian home with heavy overstuffed oak furniture, elaborate cuckoo clock, oil paintings, and chests decorated with stenciled folk-art.

I smiled. This looked more like the furnishings of the generation of my German host family's grandmother than anything her children or grandchildren would want in their homes today.

As we walked up to the registration desk, I noticed that all of the hotel staff members were dressed in Dirndl Kleider or Lederhosen. We laughed at this unexpected touch. Eva fell naturally into her mother language, greeting the staff with: "Guten Tag!"

"Oops, I can't speak any German," responded the wide-eyed young woman of about eighteen with long blonde braids, standing behind the desk.

"That's all right, we speak English too," said Eva.

"What's all this about, with so much German stuff everywhere? Where are we really?" I asked.

While we registered we learned that Leavenworth had struggled for forty years after their railroad was rerouted, the logging industry collapsed, and the town's sawmill closed. In the 1960s the town decided to take advantage of its accessibility to Seattle (less than two hours away). Building on their alpine setting, they launched "Projekt Bayern" and converted Leavenworth into a replica of a Bavarian village.

Before this transition Leavenworth already had many local mountain resort activities such as skiing, fishing, biking, hiking, and birding. But to strengthen its appeal for tourists, they created a bunch of annual festivals: Maifest, Oktoberfest, Accordion Celebration, a Christmas Lighting Ceremony, and Autumn Leaf Festival. As a result Leavenworth turned itself into this fairytale-like German town.

Since it was only 3:30 in the afternoon after we checked into our rooms, Eva, Ron, and Alberto decided to go for a swim in the hotel's outdoor pool. I politely declined, indicating that I was anxious to go back and have a second look at the house that looked like my Grandma's, check out the sawmill, and drive around the countryside to see if I might stumble across Aunt Mildred's and Uncle David's old farm.

Heading back on the Highway toward Peshastin, I enjoyed the independence of riding alone for the first time on this trip. On my right the small cottages perched on the hill looked like the one where Grandma Crill had lived, forty to fifty years ago. The expected changes over time to these houses, along with my own cryptic childhood memories, made it difficult to know for sure if this was one of her true former addresses.

I decided that it didn't matter. It was fun just remembering Grandma Crill, and this setting was bringing back a host of forgotten connections.

Every time I make a meringue today, I still hear her voice inside my head coaching me to add sugar at just the right time to make sure it dissolves completely before spreading it on top of a pie.

My Grandmother Crill couldn't balance her own checkbook. Her favorite literature was *Reader's Digest* and *The Upper Room*. She was confused easily by health issues. But she cooked hearty meals, created beautiful hand-sewn quilts, and crocheted intricate designs with the thinnest metal crochet hook and fine ball of thread, without looking at her work or counting her stitches as she talked to us. For each of her grandchildren, she crocheted large, one-of-a-kind lace tablecloths with delicate patterns. When I was nine and received mine for Christmas, I was disappointed, but now it's one of my most cherished family treasures. Every Thanksgiving, Christmas, and on special occasions I smile and think of her as I spread it across my dining room table.

I turned left across the bridge in front of the sawmill, unsure which direction I should ride in my attempt to find Aunt Mildred's former house. But again, I decided this didn't really matter. It would be fun simply to enjoy the countryside as it was today.

As I meandered along small roads in this valley, the landscape seemed greatly changed from what I remembered. I recalled small fields of alfalfa and wheat, with the occasional old, white, two-story house with steep-pitched roof to shed the heavy snows, and heavily-weathered, dark-colored barns.

Now there were many cottages on small lots with little orchards—rows of apple, cherry, peach, and pear trees—and even miniature vineyards.

Everything appeared excessively cute, almost like a scene from a children's Walt Disney movie—sunlight streaming through green leafy trees, birds singing overhead, bees buzzing, and so many vibrant flowers blooming everywhere that I was waiting to see if they would break into a chorus and dance the way they did in cartoons of the 1950s and '60s. The valley ahead was even called Icicle Valley. It couldn't get much more adorable.

I easily understood why people from Seattle might enjoy building retreat vacation homes on these properties. The picturesque, serene setting would be a great break from hectic city living.

As property values rose with this booming tourist economy, I was sure that Uncle David and Aunt Mildred's farm had been sold and divided into many smaller, unrecognizable pieces.

Thinking about my uncle as I explored the countryside, I remembered what a renegade character he had been, even forty years ago. He always had a knife out, whittling something, woodchips scattered everywhere either from his carving or his endless chopping and splitting of logs to fuel the wood-burning furnace and cast-iron cookstove.

In this area of the country, men proudly had shown off their large, meticulously stacked woodpiles, the way men elsewhere might have presented their new car or golf clubs.

Uncle David enjoyed working with wood so much that one year he made a violin. He had never played an instrument—just made it because it was a challenge that would display and expand his skills. He later gave it to my mother because she was a music teacher and the only person he knew who might truly appreciate it. Mom said the violin's sound was distorted since the wood was too thick in many places and some of the dimensions were wrong. But it certainly did look like a violin. It was one-of-a-kind, and it was an accomplishment for a non-musical farmer to have built.

Although Uncle David worked at the local sawmill, stoking its furnaces, he also relied on his farm to supplement his income and provide food for his family.

Being a child at their place was fun.

Uncle David had several cows that roamed freely on the open range. Every evening he went out into the mountains, accompanied by his dogs, to round them up. Bell, the lead cow, was named after the bell hung around her neck to help the dogs locate her and the rest of the cows every night. Working with the dogs, Uncle David would bring the cows back to the barn to milk.

We Crill kids ran along with Uncle David on this chore, carrying sticks and whooping up a storm, trying to get the cows to obey our overly zealous commands. We celebrated that we were allowed to carry and wave branches freely, but the truth was we were really pretty scared of these big lumbering animals, and those switches made us feel less afraid. There were also chickens, four to six calves, sheep, several horses, and a goat or two. We'd go with Uncle David to feed the chickens and other animals and watch him in the evening as he hand-milked the cows once they were in their stalls.

My Washington relatives believed that kids were meant to explore and learn. No one stopped us from trying most things, and Uncle David personally decided to stretch the boundaries of our town-only living experiences.

One night when he was ready to milk Bell, he turned to us kids and asked, "Want to try?" He stood up and backed out of the way.

"Sure," I said, jumping at the chance. I walked over, pretending to be brave. I sat on the teetering, three-legged stool, grabbed a hold of one of Bell's teats, and pulled downward as I had seen Uncle David do. When nothing happened, I tried again pulling harder, but still no milk. Finally, I yanked and squeezed as hard as I could. Bell mooed loudly and kicked her right rear leg forward, knocking over the bucket and sending it clattering across the cement floor. In a single leap, I jumped back out of the way and stood shaking, shocked at the commotion I had caused.

Uncle David roared with laughter, saying, "Now you know what *not* to do."

That was his theory. Let kids find out what worked and what didn't. There was no finer teacher—that is, if you survived the experience. This way no kid had to be told anything twice. It turned you into a survivor, an astute observer, and an imitator of how things were done.

The next day, in answer to my many brazen hints, he saddled up one of his horses. After leading the horse and me around the paddock a couple of times, he handed me the reins, opened up the corral gate, pointed at the path going up the mountain where we looked for cows each evening and said, "Take Bullet for a ride up that road."

Happily, I kicked the horse's flanks as I had seen cowboys on TV do, and yelled, "Giddy-up!"

But Bullet, defying his name, refused to alter his leisurely pace no matter how often or how hard I kicked. I was more scared than I'd admit, grabbing tightly onto the saddle horn with both hands while still trying to hold onto and maneuver the reins. I'd pull hard first on one rein and then the other, trying to get Bullet to go in my desired direction, but he was only interested in eating and walked to wherever the grass or leaves looked best.

Although this horse was slow walking away from the barn, he made up for it once he turned around an hour or so later and headed back toward home. Starting first at a trot and quickly moving into a full gallop, he was bounding for the barn with unfettered enthusiasm.

Pulling on the reins while frantically yelling "whoa" had no effect on his speed. He had had enough of my nonsense and was ready for the oats he'd get once he was back in his stall. I bounced wildly all over the saddle, trying desperately not to fall off.

There was still one more obstacle I had to overcome to get out of this experience unharmed. Heading into the barn through the still-open corral gate, Bullet had to go up a large singular step to pass through the side barn door to reach his stall. I realized in the middle of this maneuver that the barn door wasn't high enough for both Bullet and me to pass under it. At the last possible moment, just before getting scraped off the horse's back, I jumped and grabbed onto the corral fence's top rail on my left.

Again, Uncle David watched, amused, and said, "I wondered when you'd figure that one out."

I never had to be told again that horses won't listen to a rider who doesn't know what they are doing. They'll run when they're returning to the barn. And you shouldn't ride a horse into Uncle David's barn.

I wonder how often this kind of instruction happens today. We teach young children rules, but often they have no appreciation for their context. We lecture, we demonstrate how something is done, but where is the background understanding for why this knowledge is necessary and wise? Where is the initial exploration that creates the necessary motivation to want to learn more? Maybe this is why technology is so attractive to youth. It's something they can learn on their own or from each other, without rules and instructions controlled by grown-ups.

My Washington relatives expected us to learn by doing—by being engaged with the world around us. We weren't shielded from much as we tagged along everywhere, watching and copying the adults.

Thinking about these stories helped me appreciate my father more. Dad's greatest wish for his four children was always that we would learn to take care of ourselves in any circumstance. Maybe that was where some of my *macha* energy came from. From my mother I had learned to pick my battles carefully because, as she said, there would be many to choose from. And from my father I had learned to survive the battle once I had chosen or was given one by life.

Thinking about Dad, I suddenly remembered something he had said to me as a child. He told me that when he lived in Washington as a teenager he had ridden a motorcycle and smoked cigarettes. As a small child, I couldn't imagine either of these things. They were so out of character for the father I knew. But if he'd tried to predict which one of his three daughters might eventually want to ride, I guess he would have known it would be me.

As a kid I didn't get tossed from a horse the first time I rode one, and so far, I'd kept up with the group on my motorcycle. Being determined has its upside. My mother and three siblings always said I was a lot like my father. Thinking of today's memories, I wondered if my adventurous spirit, my ready-to-try-something-new attitude, was one reason I enjoyed the Washington I'd learned to know briefly in my childhood.

❧

That evening as the four of us walked on Front Street into the center of town, we found Bavarian-style Leavenworth delightful. It reminded me of happy times touring southern Germany. *How had the leaders in Leavenworth ever managed to get every hotel, store, and business redecorated with Fachwerk, balconies, shutters, gingerbread woodwork, and painted plastered exteriors?* Even the streetlights were designed to look like gaslights, and many were adorned with huge baskets of hanging flowers.

Since it was Sunday evening, all of the stores as well as most of the restaurants were closed and few people were on the streets. There was a shop filled with just music boxes; another with hundreds of nutcrackers and incense smokers; others where you could dress up in Bavarian clothes and have your picture taken; a woodshop with handcrafted toys, puzzles, and Christmas ornaments; a sausage and fine imported foods store; and many more gift and clothing shops.

The Germans gave us the word we use for the so-called art displayed in many of these stores—it's *"kitsch,"* or, as my German family translated it into English, "junk-art." When I lived in Germany in the late 1960s, many of the nutcrackers, music boxes, incense smokers and toys were hand-carved. Now they all looked machine-made, lacking the originality, detail, and imperfections that add charm to true handiwork.

With all the stores locked and lights out, Eva and I could only press our noses against the glass windows and look at each other with wistful resignation. If we couldn't amuse ourselves strolling through these stores, connecting memories with familiar treasures, we'd simply have to move onto another passion—German food and beer.

215

As we read through the menus posted outside several recommended restaurants, Eva and I both were looking for one that would have some of our favorite dishes. I was hunting for Eisbein (smoked pork ham hocks). Other German dishes I enjoyed—Rouladen, Sauerbraten, and many kinds of Schnitzel—I could make myself, but I could never find the large-sized smoked pork hocks in the United States that are required for Eisbein.

We finally chose a place and walked down the steps into a Bier Keller. We each ordered a different German beer that arrived in appropriately large steins. The food portions were unbelievable, and in that sense more American-style than German. My ham hock was larger than any I had ever seen and would have made any Texan smile. It was served with hot potato salad, sauerkraut, and dark pumpernickel bread with unsalted butter. Others ordered Gulash with Spätzle noodles, Wiener Schnitzel, and Bratwurst. In a very short period of time, none of us could eat another bite. After Chinese food it is easy to be hungry in an hour, but that never happens with traditional German food. We were stuffed, happy, and barely able to climb the steps leading back up to the street outside the restaurant.

Tonight Eva and I walked back to the hotel European style—arm looped into arm—singing songs and rattling on with each other in German. It was too hard to try to talk about what we were seeing and remembering in English. German was easier, and Ron and Alberto politely left us to our own conversation. I guessed they might even have been relieved that they didn't have to feign interest in what we were chattering about.

The day had started out as just another road trip day. This afternoon and evening I felt as if I were in Charles Dickens' *A Christmas Carol*, visiting past lives.

When I am asked if I believe in reincarnation, I have often answered: *Yes, but so many lives have been lived during this one lifetime.* Today, as I thought about my Crill relatives, I had revisited feelings and stories of a Linda who was four, eight, twelve, and fourteen. Tonight I traveled back to being an eighteen-year-old high school graduate, and then a twenty-one-year-old college exchange student living in Germany. How precious these times were in my life, but how distant they felt from the Linda of today.

Tonight, as I thought about a Linda who had been willing to ride a horse up a mountain, milk a cow with no experience, and travel to Germany as an exchange student to live with a new family for a year, not knowing more than a few words of German, I began to think that maybe deciding on the spur of the moment to enter this blind curve—learning to ride a motorcycle and taking a road trip with so little experience—was not out of character for me after all.

The blind curves faced on this road trip had been filled with fears that needed to be surfaced, heard, and then gently honored as they faded, leaving room for new feelings and discoveries. Around these cures previous self-created boundaries were erased. Each day on this trip my world became wider. As a motorcyclist, I viewed my world with beginner eyes.

It's impossible to go back home again or relive childhood memories; many things change significantly. The treasure I had been given on this day was a new appreciation for some of my childhood history and its influence on the present. The real significance of it all was being able to view my past as an adult and to say thanks.

I fell asleep with a smile on my face, pleased that my sometimes suit-wearing, church youth leader, college professor, psychologist Dad had once ridden a motorcycle on these mountain roads. *Hey Dad, Vroom!*

Before drifting into deep sleep I thought there was one more thing I needed to do before I left town in the morning. And I would need to get up early to do it.

23
Shadow Trip

I was awakened as the first rays of sunlight streamed through the filmy white curtains of my hotel window. I have always loved this time of year because there is so much daylight—it comes early and stays late. I looked over at Eva sleeping soundly in the other bed and decided to quietly get dressed in my motorcycle gear, slip downstairs, and head out on my personal errand before the others awoke. As I walked through the hotel lobby, I was surprised to see Ron already sitting outside next to the pool, reading a newspaper. I walked over to greet him.

"Good morning. Guess I'm not the only one who couldn't waste another moment of this last day by sleeping in," I said.

"I rarely get to leisurely enjoy a newspaper first thing in the morning. This is heaven," he replied. "What brings you out so early? I thought you loved sleeping in late."

"I'm on a special mission. I saw a German bakery on the edge of town yesterday when I was out exploring and thought I'd go check it out. Want to help me pick out some pastries?"

"You bet," Ron said, throwing down his beloved paper and standing up. "I'll drive. You ride behind so you can hold our food on the way back."

Ron started his motorcycle and backed it out of the parking space. I jumped on the back and pointed out the way.

Both years I lived in Germany I had gained twenty-five pounds, and part of the blame went to the irresistible German baked goods. Thankfully, I had lost the extra weight each time I returned to the States. But what could just one morning of sin cost? We were off to discover the level of temptation they offered.

In the parking lot outside the bakery as we dismounted, we realized we were in trouble. The air was dancing with smells of baked breads, cinnamon rolls, roasted nuts, vanilla, melted butter, and coffee. We were engulfed in pastry heaven. As we entered, the screen door slammed shut with an abrupt bang, and the bell hanging over the door jingled noisily. The startled young girl behind the counter turned around and walked toward us.

We looked at each other, giggling with delight.

"Okay, how many should we get?" Ron asked as he strolled the whole length of the fifteen-foot display case assessing the trays of tempting delectables shielded by a chest-height, curved Plexiglas cover.

"Oh, my goodness." I barely breathed as I recognized some favorite choices. They had *Apfelstrudel* (apple strudel), *Bienenstich* (bee sting cake), and *Mohnkuchen* (poppy seed cake). There was also *Krapfen* (jelly-filled doughnuts), *Stollen* (Christmas bread), *Spitzbuben* (almond cookies), and a host of other tempting confections, breads, and baked goodies in the cases, encompassing us on two sides.

Ron and I knew too much about each other and could predict the probable outcome for this escapade. On a similar venture thirty years earlier, we had gone into a donut shop together. To my surprise Ron had immediately picked out a dozen without asking for my help in making any of the choices.

I protested and asked, "What about what I want?"

He had replied, "Oh, these are all just for me. Pick out yours and I'll pay for them." So I ordered six more—many more than I had planned to eat—so as not to let my choices be dwarfed by his. Alone, each of us would have left with a more reasonable number—but collectively our enthusiasm fed on each other and was disastrous. Neither of us needed much encouragement to have fun, and together we often pushed the limits of common sense. During the next six hours we had demolished fifteen of the eighteen donuts and then, deciding we needed something less sugary, cooked a seafood dinner together.

"How do we decide?" I asked.

"We don't. We just buy," responded Ron, leaning forward while rubbing his hands back and forth together in front of him as if revving up his engines for the imminent attack. "Get out a big box," he told the young woman behind the counter.

But I leaped in, determined to make the first move this time. "Please, we'd like a piece of the *Bienenstich*, a *Spitzbuben*, and a *Krapfen*," I said to the young woman, pointing to each choice once I realized that she didn't recognize my German names, and I wasn't sure of the English ones.

Ron followed without hesitation, pointing to more pastries, cakes, and cookies, not caring what they were called. We walked out of the bakery carrying a huge, wide box of goodies tied shut with string.

Before leaving the bakery parking lot, I called Eva and Ron called Alberto to suggest they meet us by the pool for breakfast, but we were surprised to discover they were both already in the café eating a *full* breakfast.

"Take it easy or I will be wearing all of these," I said as I slid in behind Ron, trying to figure out how to keep the fifteen-by-eighteen-pinch box level while holding onto him.

Ten minutes later we joined Eva and Alberto at an outside table next to the pool, and I untied our box of cakes and cookies. Eva squealed with delight as she recognized some of her German favorites. Alberto and Ron didn't care what things were called or about our past connections to these tempting beauties. They jumped in ready to try everything without a plan. I grabbed a knife and began cutting corners off items I wanted so I could at least have a taste of these memories.

Twenty minutes later, our faces covered with powdered sugar and frosting; fingers sticky from sugar, honey, and fruit; fronts and laps covered with dropped pieces, we assessed the crumbs strewn everywhere and several remaining half-eaten pieces still in the box. No one could force down another bite. Small birds hopped around us, waiting impatiently for us to leave so they could have the second seating.

"I shouldn't have done that. I'm going to really have to do lots of extra running next week to make up for this," Eva said.

"After all of that food last night, how could we find space for all of this?" I added.

"Hey, it's our last day. We're allowed some transgressions," offered Alberto.

Men are so lucky, I thought. *We women fall into guilt much more quickly after eating than they do.*

"Well, what's our schedule for today?" Eva asked.

We all turned and looked at Ron.

"We've got a simple two-hundred-mile day, but it's hard to predict the traffic north of Seattle or how difficult it may be to cross the border back into Canada. Let's pack up, check out, and meet at our bikes, ready to roll in a half hour."

⌘

As we tied our gear onto our bikes for the last time, Ron explained that this final day was deliberately planned to be the least ambitious of the trip. In determining the route, he and John had wanted to ensure that today's distance would be easy to cover in case there had been any earlier problems with our weather, traffic, health, or motorcycles. Our flights back to the East Coast didn't leave until almost midnight, and we expected to arrive in Vancouver by late afternoon. This extra eight or so hours would leave us plenty of time to absorb any unexpected hang-ups today.

Ron quickly recited the route to our final destination in Vancouver. We'd start out riding directly west on Route 2, which would eventually take us almost to the Pacific Coast north of Seattle. Then we'd continue on other smaller northerly roads as long as we could. Close to the border, we'd need to hop onto I-5 north to go through the border checkpoints and customs. Once we crossed into Canada, we'd only have a short thirty to forty-five-minute drive to the same Sheraton Hotel in the Richmond area of Vancouver where we had started our journey ten days ago.

Route 2 turned out to be a beautiful scenic road running directly through the mountains. On most of this trip, while cruising on fairly flat terrain, we had seen the Cascade Mountains off in the distance. Today we were finally riding right through this range, enjoying beautiful vistas from on top of them instead of from the valleys below.

Our highway was a starved motorcyclist's banana-split sundae overflowing with mile-high scoops of yummy custard, crowned with heavenly whipped cream oozing downward in all directions, and peaked with maraschino cherries adorning its highest summits. This road offered delectable opportunities to display my hard-earned riding skills as I pressed my two-wheeled partner to flaunt her power. Beneath me she purred, exploded, and vroomed with vigor at finally being freed to broadcast her sexy and robust assets.

About thirty miles west of Leavenworth, we drove through Steven Pass. Again we were in great skiing and hiking country, and I was trying to figure out how in the future we could carry our own skis on our motorcycles, so we could do everything. I couldn't imagine how, but I was sure some clever person must have found a way to do it all.

We enjoyed romping on this road, waving at everyone and weaving in and out of successive curves. Our riding formation changed constantly, each of us passing the others freely in a rolling game of leapfrog. It felt like one endless amusement ride.

When I used to jog in my twenties and thirties, there were times when I'd seem to float as I ran. In such magical moments, I barely felt my legs or was even aware that I was moving them as the integration was so complete between me, the runner, and the motion I was creating. Well, today, that was how it felt on my motorcycle. Earlier on the trip I had operated this rented cycle directing it to do actions and hoping it would be obedient and respond. Now there was no discernible division between rider and motorcycle. Shifting, braking, slowing, accelerating, turning, and swerving just happened.

Together we soared around curves, flew past vehicles, glided over mountaintops, and dove down their backsides. We were one enmeshed, interconnected unit. It's similar to the aftermath of making passionate love, when you find yourselves tangled amongst arms and legs, not knowing or caring which limbs belong to you and which to your partner because it feels as though you are one.

Later in the afternoon, when I would need to return my motorcycle, I'd feel lost without this familiar extension of myself. I'd miss riding so openly and exposed to the world around me. After this experience, driving in an enclosed car would feel like living inside a plastic bag!

As we approached the Canadian border in the early afternoon, traffic slowed and eventually halted. This was the delay we had anticipated in passing back through the checkpoints from the United States into Canada.

Halted in traffic, we spent the time pleasantly chatting with each other and the motorists around us. In contrast with our longest day, I was now accustomed to the practice of turning my bike off and on between the short forward gains. In several short weeks, motorcycling routines that had been overwhelming were now automatic.

Even my earlier, ever-present companion—Fear—had retreated to doze on the back of my seat. Fear's voice had become an endearing friend that I would now smile and greet whenever she appeared and spoke. I had learned it was useless to order her to go away. Actually, she played an important role.

Like an over-protective parent, she'd surfaced anytime I ventured outside my familiar neighborhood to deliver her warnings. I had come to realize that her greater value was hearing what she had to say before I went into action. That's when I could consider Fear's ominous concerns as I assessed my future choices. If I decided to proceed, I would benefit from the heightened sensory awareness she rallied inside me and the adrenalin she stirred up that could be used as fuel.

But, once I became immersed in any challenge, her hysterical voicing became a dangerous distraction. As I climbed the washed-out gravel road, rode to the top of a volcano in the dark with patches of snow and black ice on the road, or passed the scene of a recent motor-cycle accident, I needed all of my attention focused on the present, processing what was happening in the "now."

Before this trip I hadn't realized how much I had tried to protect myself, afraid that I couldn't survive more disappointment. I walled myself off from most of the world, needing to control every aspect of life—who I interacted with, what events I attended, what news I heard, what activities I tried, what changes I considered. As I pursued any new direction, such as building a new business, I required the plan to be perfect without possibility of failure. No wonder I was asking, "What now?" and not finding the right answers. I had let Fear become my compass in life.

This vacation turned out differently than the frivolous escape fantasy I had rebelliously imagined. The road trip did deliver on its promise of a ride through beautiful places—Victoria Island, Washington's Olympic National Forest, the Oregon Coast, redwood forests, Mendocino wine country, the Columbia River Valley, Wenatchee apple country—that provided endless eye-candy and entertainment.

But the real journey—starting with the decision to learn to ride a motorcycle up to and through the ending of the road trip this evening—brought me face-to-face with my full repertoire of fears: of failure, injury, no-escape, lack of selfworth, inadequacy, heights, being alone, success, survival, discomfort, and being an imposter. As with most fears, once they are faced, they lose their power and voice.

On this journey I had faced Fear dressed in her many costumes and befriended her. We could now ride together with clearer respect for each other's roles and company. The compass had been returned from Fear's hand to my own.

When we finally rode into the hotel parking lot in Vancouver where we had started our journey ten days earlier, we felt a bit nostalgic but not sad. We pulled our motorcycles up next to each other in a neat row and parked them. The trip had been short enough that we still enjoyed riding everyday through to the end, but long enough that we were ready for something else.

Getting off our motorcycles we felt a flurry of emotions. Ron, Eva, Alberto, and I went around in a circle giving each other long heartfelt embraces, unable to say much as we did this round robin. Words were both unnecessary and insufficient in expressing what we were experiencing and had shared together. Silence was a much richer expression of what we felt.

John and T. J. were there with a pickup truck and a trailer hitched behind it to transport three of the bikes back to his home. The fourth would be ridden. As we began unpacking our motorcycles, they came over to join us.

"Looks like everyone made it back in one piece," John said. He walked over and gave each of us a hug along with multiple enthusiastic pats on our backs.

"Well, almost in one piece. Look," I said, pointing to my broken turn signal light, the one that had busted on the second day at the gas station when I forgot to put down my sidestand.

"That? That's nothing. It's only about fifty dollars worth of damage. At least you're okay. You're the one I was really worried about. You're one brave woman."

"She was awesome. We call her Road Runner. You can't lose her. You should see her on curves and hills; she eats them up!" Eva said.

John nodded, smiling broadly at me.

"How's your weather?" T. J. asked as he rolled the motorcycle Eva had ridden onto the trailer.

"Unbelievable! Didn't rain once," Ron answered. "Really didn't have much wind either—nothing like what we had several years ago when we went with you. We did ride with snow on the sides of the road and fried in the sun on I-5 in the middle of California, but all in all, it was better than anything we could have wished for. This was definitely one of our best trips."

"Your luggage you left with me, it's over there," John said, pointing to a pile of black bags next to his truck. "I've already confirmed your hotel rooms, so you can shower, pack up, and relax until you have to leave for your flights tonight."

We sauntered over to pick up our things.

Walking seemed unnatural and primitive after spending ten days on my motorcycle. It felt strange to be moving forward on legs instead of riding on top of motor-driven tires. The transition from integrated motorcyclists, fused with our bikes, to ordinary human beings propelled solely by our own more-limited legs and internal engines—circulatory, digestive, neurological, muscular-skeletal and adrenal systems—had begun.

Since our return flight was a red-eye, I knew that it would be a long, uncomfortable night and hoped I'd be able to sleep through part of it. Exhausted physically, mentally, and emotionally, I wished there was more room to spread out as I slumped down in my seat, wedged my pillow between my neck and the window, and let my heavy eyelids float shut.

The plane's engines roared as our jumbo jet's nose lifted upward away from the runway and was soon swallowed by the black-ink sky. Our aircraft's formerly imposing presence at the terminal diminished to a mere speck as it faded in significance and became hidden by the vastness of celestial space.

Settling into my interior self, I recognized that just as the midnight sky had consumed our plane as it left one destination for the next, I too was suspended in limbo for the next five hours—having left my motorcycle adventure behind and pausing before meeting my former life face-to-face again.

I felt a bit sad and lost, having just said good-bye to the daily companionship of my dear riding friends—Eva, Ron, and Alberto. I was also leaving behind my rented motorcycle, northwest scenery, and daily adventures, but I had recently come to understand that everything is impermanent. These endings provided space for new beginnings. Just as Mount Mazama's volcanic destruction made possible the metamorphosis of its flattened and collapsed mountain peak into the new breathtaking Crater Lake, my present life was ready for its own personal rejuvenation using lessons learned during this motorcycle adventure.

As I turned and refluffed my pillow I thought, *Yes, partnering with life sure beats trying to control it.* For the past eighteen months I had tried to continue driving straight when the road beneath me had clearly turned in a new direction.

Looking backwards at this nearly completed blind curve, I wondered: *How is this "new" Linda, curled up inside this plane, different from the "old" one who had felt trapped in a life that no longer made sense?*

My friends and family would point to the sensational aspects of the motorcycle part of this vacation. After riding for only four weeks, I had flown across North America and safely covered 2,500 miles, riding my own full-sized motorcycle in two countries, one province, and three states. This was the story everyone was eagerly awaiting. I agree that this was a significant accomplishment for anyone, yet alone a fifty-seven-year-old woman, and especially one with no former motorcycle experience. However, this was not the story that excited me the most.

I was surprised and amazed by the shadow road trip I had ridden. On this internal journey, I had tested my full range of the "old" Linda repertoire—life experiences, business principles, beliefs, routines, behaviors, and spiritual wisdom—in trying to survive the challenges presented by such a formidable goal. Some elements of my former self had served me well, but others weighed me down and needed to be shed.

During the year prior to this trip, I had tried to glue the broken shards of the "old" Linda back into one congruent whole. My attempts were as futile as those undertaken by the king's men who (in the familiar children's nursery rhyme) ". . . couldn't put Humpty Dumpty together again."

I now knew that it's impossible to reconstruct life by simply piecing together fragments of the past. To reinvent a "new" Linda, I first needed to expand my former notions of who I was. By erasing old boundaries I could try out new ideas and behaviors—keeping some and discarding others.

Although there were many lessons I'd learned on this trip, there was one I had jotted down in my travel log so that I'd remember it. I'd written: *When the unknown, unwanted, or undeserved occurs our answers often are found around blind curves where expanded horizons reveal increased possibilities and new ways of being.*

Blind curve living was now going to become a routine way of experiencing life for me.

Even though the difficult curves on this road trip held possibilities of failure, each also offered the potential for something new and hopefully better. It's impossible to know what's around any corner, but with the right perspective, limitations transform into wealth.

With my recent discoveries I had launched the new journey of defining myself as a single woman.

The question—What now?—that had precipitated this motorcycle adventure vibrated inside me. Unlike in Mendocino when I fled from this inquiry, now I repeated it and smiled. I didn't have to know the complete answer all at once to move forward. Reinvention, I had learned, is a continual task. All I had to do was pursue the trial-and-error I had begun and savor the ride. Discoveries were waiting to be found around each corner.

The open space created by clearing outdated repertoires was exciting. I was ready to fill my snow globe with whiteouts, snowdrifts, and even swirling chaos so that I could play with the many possibilities that might answer my "What now?"

Playfulness was one of many souvenirs I had acquired on this trip. If I had to give up lots of nuggets in my penny jar to spend a few, playfulness was one I'd continue holding because it's a necessary fuel for all explorations.

I wondered what new directions I'd choose now that I had this newfound energy to embrace life again. In college I had a tennis instructor who had emphasized the importance of keeping our weight forward and feet dancing as we prepared to receive a serve, explaining that it's easier to react quickly from movement than from a resting, anchored body. With the current momentum I had created on this road trip, and a body and mind agile from constant moment-to-moment participation, I was ready to channel this reclaimed zest in navigating the opportunities exposed by my widened playing field.

My sleep was interrupted by the flight attendant's announcement to prepare for landing. Looking out my window, I viewed the first familiar scenery I had seen in the last ten days. From the air I could name Virginia highways, towns, and familiar landmarks. This had been a great vacation, but it was good to be returning home.

Just as I couldn't fathom the twists in the road that had disrupted my life and later spurred my rebellious threat—"I'm going to learn to ride a motorcycle!"—I knew that ahead of me other seemingly innocuous events would present blind curves filled with new challenges, adventures, and discoveries.

Although life often appears to be filled with a myriad of unrelated events, it's amazing how they eventually collect and flow seamlessly together, forming a beautiful whole, just as trickles of melting snow at the top of Washington mountains form raging rivers in the valleys below. With the passage of time, life wasn't a series of separate adventures, but rather one continuous road trip. Incidents that seemed like "dark nights of the soul" could fade in significance after a good night's sleep. Things labeled "good" or "bad" often changed value when viewed later as part of the collective whole. Each moment, every moment, was precious, holding rich value and connection to the oneness with all life.

With the fuel created on this trip, I was ready for whatever new blind curves life presented. I had painfully experienced the futility of avoiding and resisting the many twists that accompany life, but I could learn to ride through them, re-discovering a rhythm and an ability to trust myself as I leaned into the curves, knowing that my solid internal grounding would anchor me as I slowed before the turns and accelerated out of them. Whatever fears, setbacks, or roadblocks I discovered in the middle of each blind curve could be handled with moment-to-moment focus. And each successive curve expanded my world by widening the boundaries of what was known and available to use in navigating life's ventures.

I laughed thinking about how I had briefly traded my business suits for motorcycle leathers, high heels for steel-toed boots, and designer scarves for a faded railroad bandana. The bicyclist, greenie, businesswoman, corporate executive, mother, and now motorcyclist was ready to embrace all of these roles, and probably continue adding new ones. But regardless of any outward image, I would always be Linda.

Walking out of the Dulles-Washington International Airport terminal, I smiled as I spotted Lindsey pulling over to the curb, driving our dark plum PT Cruiser. It was exciting to be home.

Walking toward the car I thought, *You've done it! We rode all of those miles without getting hurt. We've all made it successfully to the end of the trip, still friends. We're all safe and happy.* And now I was ready to charge forward. I was no longer bored with me. Most of all I trusted myself to live life fully again.

"Well, how was it?" Lindsey shouted as she got out of the Cruiser and walked toward me.

Standing in the road behind our car, I paused, then slowly took a wide-seated stance as if I were riding my motorcycle. I reached my arms out wide in front of me, grabbing imaginary handlebars, flicked my wrists, rolling my hands back toward me: "Vroom, Vro-oom, VRRR-oooom!" I roared.

We laughed, then hugged and headed for home.

In the car Lindsey turned to me. "That should be your new catch phrase, Mom—VROOM!"

Epilogue

What Now?

You don't sing to get to the end of a song.
You don't dance to get to the end of the piece.
You don't eat pie to clean the plate.
You don't ride to get to the end of the road.
Life happens in THIS moment.
All else is an illusion.
Honor this breath. This place. This being.
This now is your destination.
Vroom, Vroom!

My story about motorcycling and this road trip didn't really start with my suddenly getting fed up and pushing aside traditional advice, by choosing the *blind curve* alternative of learning to ride a motorcycle so I could escape my life. All of my life is a continual road trip filled with both minor and significant construction zones, resulting in necessary detours, getting lost, asking directions, and trying different routes before finally getting life back on track—but never on the same route as before.

Bill's diagnosis of cancer was a stupendous detour on which I discovered the strength of love as Bill and I were drawn closer together by our joint struggle. We danced beautifully together as we had throughout our marriage, each one enhancing the other, taking turns leading and following, adding counterweights for swings, providing grounding for extra balance when the other needed it, and constantly teaching ourselves additional steps that went with the new rhythms of life.

In our last eleven months together, we grew closer, bonded by our deeply shared mission of his survival and finding ways to enjoy each day. I finally even learned through love to release him to move on without me physically by his side as his spirit departed from this life to whatever comes next.

After his passing, I grieved multiple endings. First my grief was about his death. It focused on his leaving too soon and all that he had been through and would miss in the future. Throughout those final months, he said he wasn't afraid to die—he just didn't want to hurt anyone who loved him. He wanted to be there for our three daughters, his eight siblings, his nieces and nephews and friends. His words—"A lifetime isn't enough time to spend with you"—were his arms that held me after he left.

The second part of my grieving was about the ending of the "old" Linda. This grief was one I hadn't expected. I was suddenly single again and didn't want to be. I loved the partnership that comes from marriage, and the benefits of living with my best friend. I could no longer continue our life-story video business, *Fond Memories Studios*, which had so perfectly combined our unique talents. How hard we had worked to build this new venture, how much fun we had doing it, and now, I was closing it down forever, crating up and sealing away all of our joint creative efforts in dull, brown boxes. Without him there was no enjoyment in continuing this business. There was too much Bill in it to hire someone else. He was a one-of-a-kind man.

I looked at my shattered life and was surprised by what I discovered. We had always wanted to remain two separate individuals with some different activities and interests. When either of us traveled alone, the other functioned fully and well. But after he was gone, I realized how everything in our lives truly had been interconnected, reflecting each other's strong influence and abilities.

Without him, little in my life made sense anymore. My food, my home, my interests, my friends, my business, my fun, all had aspects tied to Bill. Without him they were incomplete and no longer quite right. I slowly learned to cook differently—spicier and with fewer starches. I redecorated parts of my home—more modern, playful, and colorful—reflecting an expression I had modified when we married. Slowly, I developed new interests—knitting scarves, soul-stirring music, and adventure travel.

On the one-year anniversary of being alone, I was surprised to find myself more miserable than ever. The grief hadn't subsided. Instead it had grown and was raw and unending. I had expected that in this first year I would have resolved the estate issues, completed major home repairs, and closed our life-story video business. I had expected to have my former corporate consulting business open again, operating in full swing.

Although most of these efforts were in various stages of happening, none had been adequately resolved. Every time I worked on any project, the problems became muddled and the tasks escalated. I could check nothing off on my endless, ever-growing to-do lists. My former self who felt she could climb any mountain was now sliding backwards downhill.

So on the first anniversary of his death, I asked myself the same questions I would have asked my clients: *What can you do now that you couldn't do before? What will make your heart sing?* I knew that until I was happier again no clients would want to work with me, I wouldn't be able to find healthy single friends, and most importantly, I wouldn't enjoy my life.

Go learn to ballroom dance and downhill ski, I answered these questions.

So I did Internet searches, compared possibilities, and began lessons. I did enjoy these new activities while doing them, but my feelings of happiness were confined primarily to the moments when I was engaged in dancing or skiing. They rarely carried over into the in-between times.

Eighteen months after his death, my frustration built to the point where I rebelled and threatened to add a jumbo bag of potato chips and motorcycling to my life.

The motorcycle road trip was the first time since Bill had died that I had been continuously happy for ten consecutive days. It changed something inside me as I processed my fears about surviving with the excitement of riding. A resilient "new" Linda was reinvented by riding through the blind curves of this journey.

For me there was great value in choosing a difficult, almost impossible-to-reach goal, immersing myself fully in it, and discovering the triumphant joy that resulted from overcoming setbacks and surmounting obstacles. It wasn't the people, places, or things that made me happy on the trip. It was reconnecting with myself and discovering a nearly forgotten inner strength and passion for living.

My rebellious desire to expand the boundaries of my life and create new ways of being did not end with the completion of the Northwest trip. Finally, I had the faith, energy, and momentum to do something more visionary.

I began to look at rebuilding my career. *Should I follow my former traditional path or break away and try something new?* I was ready to create a whiteout in my snow globe, explore possibilities, and take action. I asked my now familiar question: *What now? What work will excite and feed my soul?*

My earlier statement—*Every time I say I'm not going to do something, it's presented as the next path*—proved itself true one more time. I'd also said I'd never write for a living, yet the only pursuit I could get excited about was just that. And so another side trip heading into a different, but equally challenging, *blind curve* was started.

Erasing old boundaries, exploring the unfamiliar, and frolicking in newly expanded horizons is now an integral part of my life's routine. I've found that answering "What now?" and creating something new rarely happens all at once.

It starts with sitting on a motorcycle, walking it across the parking lot, and making lots of mistakes by letting the clutch out too fast or giving it too much gas.

Then it's learning to ride in first and second gears and to apply the brakes—a lot like learning ballroom dancing and skiing. Step-by-step, each successive skill builds with every new action—successes as well as failures.

And as with the motorcycle trip, soon the new space becomes something that is not just visited occasionally for a few moments but can be sustained for ten days and finally integrated into the ever-widening territory that's become a part of my life.

Now that I have experienced the power of exploring blind curves with all of their magical revelations, I find myself choosing and welcoming them as I navigate life.

There are still plenty of moments of not knowing what to do next when the road I'm riding bends in directions I never expected. But now I trust that—if I look inside myself for guidance; try new things daily; get up when I fall down; harness anger, fear, and frustration to keep moving forward and remember to enjoy the moment-to-moment ride—life becomes precious and the narrow blade of my knife widens into a broad highway surface as I open up my throttle and savor the ride.

Life comes together; it falls apart. Ahead there will be more break-downs when the unwanted, unexpected, and undeserved happens, and I ask: What now?

But now I know how to handle these detours as I continue on this beautiful journey of life, learning to *be* and not just *do*.

I went on a road trip to discover who I should become.

Instead, I simply learned, *I am.*

ACKNOWLEDGMENTS

Writing this book has been a blind curve much larger than the ones described on these pages. My book road trip began when the idea for *Blind Curves* was birthed during a workshop lead by Sam Horn. Sam has continued to be an invaluable mentor and navigator who provided many maps to support this journey. Her initial words of encouragement were quickly joined by my writer friend Nancy Eskridge and my youngest daughter, Lindsey Boyle, who agreed that this story was worthy of a larger audience. Thanks to all three for reading and critiquing numerous drafts.

An invaluable riding partner on this journey has been Kevin L. Miller—my dear friend, cousin, artist, and illustrator extraordinaire—who skillfully brought concepts, stories, and scenery to life with his drawings that can be found on my website. His illustrations and candid insights motivated me to make the writing worthy of his expressive art.

This trip's itinerary included several annual expeditions to the Maui Writers Conference where I was fortunate to participate in three separate weeklong writer's workshops taught in successive years by Ron Powers, James Rollins, and Anne D. LeClaire. There I also met agent Susan Crawford who encouraged me to continue my writing studies. Thanks to each of you for showing me ways to become a stronger writer and removing many roadblocks.

A major hill to be climbed in writing *Blind Curves* was finding my own voice. For this, I thank the many writers and contributors to the *Washington Post*. I've spent numerous days studying how their sports writers captured readers with their catchy opening paragraphs, travel writers described scenic places and tourist experiences in new ways with rich descriptions, and bloggers—such as Petula Dvorak and Carolyn Hax—demonstrated how to take a position on local daily occurrences that make us reflect on how we live. Thanks to these many influencers and role models.

During times of covering endless miles, oft-needed rest stops were provided by friends and family. Heartfelt thanks to my mother, Helene Snider, my sisters—Carol Russell and Anita Wooley—and my three daughters—Kim Ray, Heather Strickland, and Lindsey Boyle—for the thousands of ways you provided me with opportunities to renew myself. My sincere gratitude also goes to my many friends—Yvonne Hoffman, Jim Sercu, Zulay Torres, Sue Wellman, Louise Mallory, Karin Gwin, and so many others—who requested updates and cheered me on around endless corners.

Special help also came from my early readers—Jan Kahl, Hanna Standau, Jim Parker, Jasmine Schultz, Elizabeth Miller, Jim Solo, Martina and Lars Droege, Joy Stoney, and John Choumeau. Your feedback influenced some necessary route changes. Thanks also to Kathryn Johnson and Judith Webster for your special edits; Kristina Bouweiri, Cynthia deLorenzi, and Grace Keenan for great intermissions; and The Croquet Society, WOW-Capitol Cruisers, and Capital Speakers for your endless rallies of support.

As the trip came to a close and the book was written, my new guide, Amy Collins, arrived to show me many detours. Many thanks to Amy for introducing me to my agent, Anna Termine, who navigated me expertly around potholes and secured the ideal publisher for this book.

A major detour happened two years ago when I was diagnosed with breast cancer and the publication of the first version of this book was delayed. But it was a time of discovering a world of new support from fellow survivors and those who care deeply about them. I was fortunate to have medical professionals from Johns Hopkins Hospital in Baltimore who made this surprising new route smooth and safe. Endless thanks to them and all who make future cancer journeys unnecessary.

Lastly, without the generosity of my riding companions (renamed Ron, Alberto, and Eva in this book) this adventure never would have happened. I will always be grateful for your unending patience, praise, protection, coaching, and encouragement on the trip and during this writing journey. It was a trip of a lifetime, and I am forever changed by your generosity. You showed me how to face my fears, expand my horizons, and live fully again. Beep, beep!